WomanSpirit

WomanSpirit

The Rise of Feminism and the
Empowerment of Women in
Liberal Religion

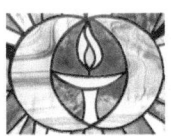

Denise D. Tracy
and
Emmy Lou Belcher

Flaming Chalice Press™
San Diego, California

10 9 8 7 6 5 4 3 2 1
First Edition 2024

ISBN 13: 979-8-218-40332-4
Library of Congress Control Number: 2024911157

The profits from this volume will be contributed to the vision, mission and advocacy work of the International Convocation of Unitarian Universalist Women. The ICUUW supports equality and advancement of women and girls across the globe. Their dream: "Imagine a world where girls and women are treated equally."

Front Cover Photo Caption
Top Row: Bev Bumbaugh, Joyce Smith, Leslie Westbrook, Marni Harmony, Frederica Leigh, Vi Kochendoerfer

Middle Row: Dense Tracy, Carolyn Owen-Towle, Eileen Karpeles

Bottom Row: Maryell Cleary, Ellen Dohner Livingston, Joy Atkinson

We dedicate this book to those who worked
tirelessly to open our liberal religion to the power
and experience of women and other people who
have been marginalized. The Unitarian Universalist
Association of congregations has been changed
by this struggle, witness, and work.

IN PARTICULAR, WE LIFT UP TWO LIVES
The Rev. Carolyn Owen-Towle and
The Rev. Liz Strong, who began this book
with us and died before it was finished.

Acknowledgments to

*Kyle Liam Tracy Decker for endless technical and computer assistance.

*Elena Castillo for her typing skills

*Nellie Sabin and Annette Marquis for information about publishing

*Kay Montgomery for pushing us to include the context for the events of the growth of feminism in the UUA

*Charlotte Cowtan for being our first reader and for both her honesty and encouragement

*Emily Mitchell for her extraordinary cover design

*Carolyn Owen-Towle for joining and supporting this project

*Tom Owen-Towle for his wisdom and unflagging energy

*Bill Decker who is a stalwart in any storm

*Thank you to Matthew Greenblatt of Centerpointe Media for his competence, kindness and gentle style of shepherding us through this publishing process.

*All the Unitarian Universalists who supported the entry of women into ministry and leadership in our Association of Congregations.

Foreword

Kay Montgomery

IN THE LATE 1960s, A FRIEND CONTACTED ME to say she had just read a terrific book that had changed her life. She wanted me to read it too. It was The Feminist Mystique by Betty Friedan. Of course. So, Marge came over. We sat in my backyard, drinking tea, reading. I found the book interesting, even important, but I just didn't have space for it. I was newly pregnant with my second child and that was important enough for me just then. However, the book did get my attention.

Over time, Friedan's message took root. It matched my own middle-of-the-night musings. And soon I was obsessed with her ideas. I obsessed, talked endlessly, found other women equally obsessed. Bored my friends, I'm sure! Shortly after that a friend was getting divorced. She and her husband had a "final" talk. He advised her to spend less time with me, adding that she probably didn't realize how ruthless I was. Oh my! I puzzled over that adjective and finally settled with it as a compliment. Such a nice, masculine insult!

Time passed. I and many of my friends changed. One friend went to law school and eventually became a judge. Another friend opened a high-end shop of arts and crafts, the kind of shop you'd cruise every few months and eventually, after looking for the perfect gift for someone, you'd remember seeing it there. And there was more: Another friend attended Harvard at age 50! Starting medical school after being turned down decades before. The culture changed. I divorced. Found a job I loved. Moved across the country (Atlanta to Boston). Traveled a lot. Became "myself." Finally. My sons became who they are now, terrific men. I found work with great people who cared about the things I did.

Every now and then I think of Marge and Friedan's book and wonder if the culture and I might have turned out differently at another time. We'll never know. But what I DO know is that I'm glad it all happened as it did. I don't have the life I imagined when I was a kid but what I do have is a life that suits me, makes me happy and satisfied.

It's now more than a half a century since Friedan's book was published and my friend, Marge, and I drank tea in my backyard. Thank God I came around at the right time!

Four years ago, when Denise Tracy called me to describe the book she wanted to edit, together, we crafted the initial question we would want every woman (and a few men) to answer. This is the question: "How did becoming a Feminist change both you and Unitarian Universalism?

The essays gathered here capture the transformative feel of that era. The successes. The road blocks. The insults. The decisions. The possibilities!

WomanSpirit

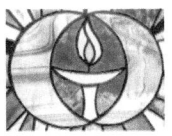

Table of Contents

Part One: **The Beginning**

Part Two: **Our Stories**

Part Three: **Appendix/Resources**

Part One
The Beginning

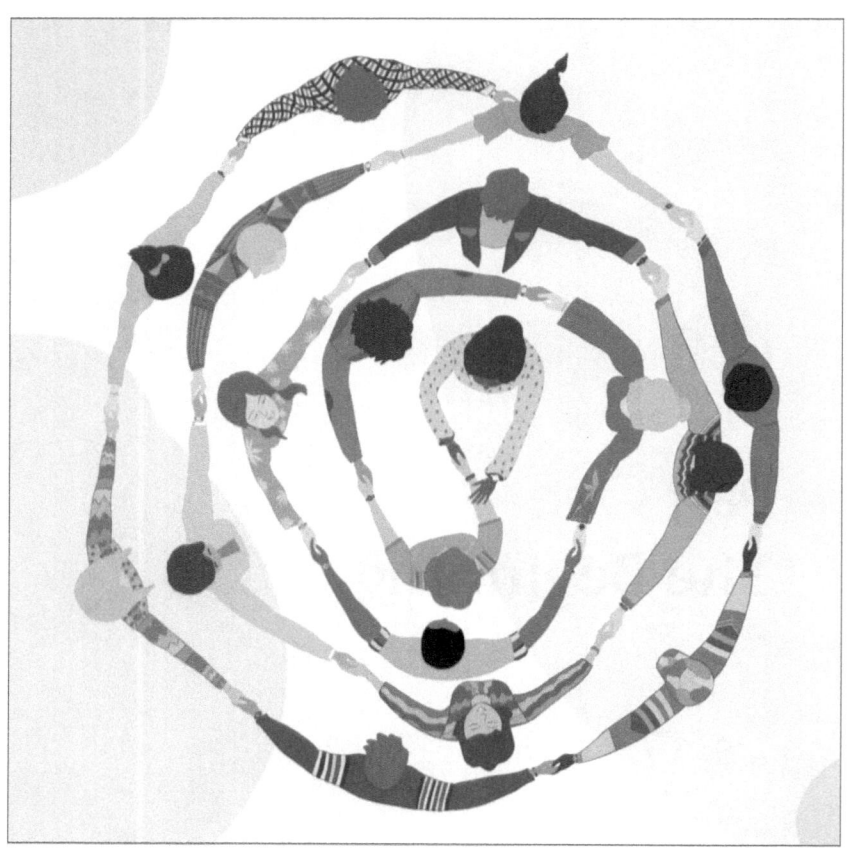

"*We found that we could agree that feminism need not be solely focused on women, that it can be and should be inclusive, meaning working for the liberation of all people; as someone said, 'pro-human.'*"
—FROM WOMEN IN MINISTRY
BY MARYELL CLEARY

Introduction

Denise D. Tracy

I HAD AN IDEA. To collect stories of women in the second wave of feminism, those who stepped forward and into the vision that our beloved Unitarian Universalism needed to be more inclusive of women—old, young, gay, straight, theist, pagan, brown—diverse and faithful, all.

I wrote women that I knew were still alive. I asked them if they would be willing to tell the story of their becoming feminist and how they changed and, as a result of their feminism, how their involvement in liberal religion changed. Some were eager and wrote papers quickly. Several said," I am not capable any longer." Several said, "If I wrote my story, and told the truth, I would be at risk professionally. I thank you for asking and no thank you." Along the way there have been changes. Two men were added. Tom Owen-Towle, who with his partner and spouse Carolyn, became models of shared ministry. Gordon Gibson, witness for social justice in Selma and beyond, joined our crew.

Liz Strong, early advocate for the Minister of Religious Education program, wrote her paper, received editorial suggestions, revised her submission, resubmitted it and then died. We are fortunate to have her last words. Alice Blair Wesley's beloved husband, Joe, supporter, and advocate of her ministry also died. Carolyn Owen-Towle, who early on worked with me as co-editor on this volume, also has died.

Time moves on. I thought the volume was complete with 19 voices writing about the change that began as a few drops of water and grew into a river and then a waterfall with changes as powerful as Niagara Falls. Emmy Lou Belcher joined as co-editor when Carolyn stepped away. We sent the collection of essays to two readers. The stories were fine both said, and they also agreed, "There needs to be more context."

So, Emmy Lou and I went back to the drawing board. We have gathered background materials that set the stage for the transformation of the Unitarian Universalism from a white male club to a more diverse endeavor of our liberal faith.

We include the 1977 Women and Religion Resolution, an election promise of UUA President Paul Carnes. This resolution set in motion a new appreciation and awareness of the roles women could have in our Association of Congregations.

The original Women and Religion Committee in 1978, articulated a need for a new faith statement. Two Grailville Conferences, one for 29 of the then 40 UU women ministers in 1978, (all 40 were invited). Maryell Cleary wrote an article for Kairos about this conference. For the ministers who attended, this gathering was both life changing and life affirming. The second Grailville conference in 1979 was gathered for the members of the 21 District Women and Religion committees. Here work began on what became The Seven Principles. Over the years there was much Feminist Theology being written. The 1980 Women and Religion Convocation in East Lansing, Mich. included Dianne Arakawa's splendid paper called *An Assessment of the New Theology Being Written by Women*. The Vancouver General Assembly had a UUWF workshop where Linnea Pearson presented a paper for consideration. The UUWF created The Feminist Theology Award. The UUWF FTA funded books and resources on Feminist Liberal Religious Thought. The Chair of this committee, Anne Olson, has written about the story of this literary and theological advancement.

The resource/appendix section includes materials on the original Women and Religion flyer, UUA Affirmative Action for Women in Ministry flyer (AAWIM) and the AAWIM final results brochure.

These resources trace the background and show the support provided for the very radical change we were imagining, advocating, leading, and experiencing. The provisional unanimous adoption of the Seven Principles in 1984 and their final adoption in 1985 showed first, how slow change occurs in our congregational polity. Secondly, two different and separate years of congregational study moved congregations from opposition to understanding and unanimous acceptance, by 2,000 delegates, in both 1984 and 1985. I learned that change takes hard work and support of incremental movement. All is possible with patience and listening.

If anyone believes that transforming the white male club that was Unitarian Universalism of the 1970s into an inclusive and diverse Association of Congregations was simple or easy, do not be fooled. The blood, sweat, and tears of those advocating change to supposedly liberal people was rugged, difficult work. Liberal folk believe that we are open, and some of us are. Yet, many of us come predisposed with fixed beliefs because we have had to fight to maintain our liberal stance against the status quo. Sexism is ingrained in each person and manifests itself in surprising ways. Every feminist has had to argue, convince, cajole, or move forward without support or agreement or in defiance. Inch by inch we helped change occur. The LGBTQ folks in Liberal Religion and the members of the BIPOC, following in women's footsteps, have similar stories to tell. Feminism began the slow steady revolution in our faith toward inclusion and diversity. It is a wheel that keeps turning and hopefully will always push us toward new paths of openness.

After a 20-year absence from attending UUA General Assemblies, in June of 2023, I attended the GA in Pittsburgh. There, the change that we had begun and advocated for in the 1970s was evident before my eyes. A rainbow of human skin colors, people gay, straight, trans, old, young, religious diversity too—it was a dream come true for those of us who dared to envision that our Association of Congregations could embrace all who wanted to dream with and for us.

Women and Religion Resolution

WHEREAS, a principle of the Unitarian Universalist Association is to "affirm, defend and promote the supreme worth and dignity of every human personality and the use of the democratic method in human relationships;" and

WHEREAS, great strides have been taken to affirm this principle within our denomination; and

WHEREAS, some models of human relationships arising from religious myths, historical materials, and other teachings still create and perpetuate attitudes that cause women everywhere to be overlooked and undervalued; and

WHEREAS, children, youth and adults internalize and act on these cultural models, thereby tending to limit their sense of self-worth and dignity;

THEREFORE, BE IT RESOLVED: That the 1977 General Assembly of the Unitarian Universalist Association calls upon all Unitarian Universalists to examine carefully their own religious beliefs and the extent to which these beliefs influence sex role stereotypes within their own families; and

BE IT FURTHER RESOLVED: That the General Assembly urges the Board of Trustees of the Unitarian Universalist Association administrative officers and staff, the religious leaders within societies, the Unitarian Universalist theological schools, the directors of related organizations, and the planners of seminars and conferences. to make every effort to (a) put traditional assumptions and language in perspective and (b) avoid sexist assumptions and language in the future.

BE IT FURTHER RESOLVED: That the General Assembly urges the President of the Unitarian Universalist Association to send copies of this resolution to other denominations examining sexism inherent in religious literature and institutions and to the International Association of Liberal Religious Women and the IARF (International Association for Religious Freedom); and

BE IT FURTHER RESOLVED: That the General Assembly requests the Unitarian Universalist Association (a) to join with those who are encouraging others in society to examine the relationship between religious and cultural attitudes toward women, and (b) to send a representative and resource materials to associations appropriate to furthering the above goals; and

BE IT FURTHER RESOLVED: That the General Assembly requests the President of the UUA to report annually on progress in implementing this resolution.

The above was passed unanimously.
Ithaca, NY 1977

To Make a Significant Difference

Kairos #14 Spring 1979

Lucile Schuck Longview

THE RESOLUTION, *WOMEN AND RELIGION*, adopted unan-imously by the General Assembly in 1977, calls on the Unitarian Universalist Association to make a significant difference in the religious perceptions of our time. It calls on religious professionals and laity to bring into focus the basic assumptions that undergird our world view and to see their sexist nature. It calls on us to name that which is so obvious we are blinded to its presence, to anime the fact that all religions with a Judeo-Christian heritage have as their mythic basis the assumptions that man is the human being, that male perception is total, that he rightly speaks for all and that he is the keeper of the gate.

For centuries women have waited outside the gate, our being and our experience ignored, socialized to believe that we are somehow among the counted. But a new consciousness is arising. Feminist theologians and women in congregations are beginning to recognize that the patriarchal religious message is not inclusive of women, and we are choosing various ways of responding to that understanding. Some are theologizing from a feminist perspective and attempting to broaden the concept of God and to emphasize the liberating message in the teachings of Jesus. Others are reaching into pre-patriarchal times seeking the roots of female identity among the cultures that worshipped God as a woman. Still others are moving away from patriarchal religion claiming there is no place for women in the conceptual systems of traditional theologies.

There are those of us in UU congregations who are alienated by worship services that ignore our presence while confirming the existence of males sitting beside us and we have chosen to take yet another path. We have faith that UUA professionals and members will work with us to expand our denominational religious thought and practices to make them inclusive of our spirituality. Acting on this faith we initiated and promoted the resolution *Women and Religion* which might have been more descriptively titled "the religious roots of sexism" or "the religious basis for women's oppression."

The resolution speaks to the nature of relationships between women and men and to the power of myth, whether recognized or not, in our individual acculturation process. Which of the religious myths commonly assumed among us as church people contributes to undemocratic human relationships in which males are dominant and females are submissive? Can we re-myth the infrastructure of our system of belief or must we start anew to develop a faith that will be equally inclusive of women and of men? These are some of the questions which confront us as we undertake the implementation of this resolution.

At its heart is a concern for female-male relationships in the family and for the extent to which all of us, especially children, internalize and act on cultural and religious role model stereotypes. It asks all UUs to examine religious myths that sanction the undemocratic male-female relationships that all too often are played out daily in our homes. We look to our church and to our denomination to reach for domestic justice by promoting attitudes and behavior that will contribute toward a sense of equality in self-worth and in dignity for girls and boys and for women and men.

The resolution is unique not only in that it was initiated and promoted by women in congregations but also in calling on the institution, the UUA, with its affiliates and members to question and broaden the basic assumptions on which our system of values rests. We do this in the belief that the quality of all our lives will be enriched by the incorporation of women's values and experiences into our religious tradition. It is a call from women in congregations for worship services, whether designed by women or by men, that recognize our presence and build our dignity and self-worth. We are asking that the gate be opened.

Seeking out and putting into historic perspective the sexism that pervades the mythic basis of our religion and exploring to what extent religiously authenticated sexist attitudes influence sex-role stereotypes within our families is no easy task. The undertaking will remain with us to the end of our lives and the lives of our descendants as will the job of avoiding sexist language and assumptions in our day and theirs.

The tasks are there and the UUA, through adopting this resolution, agreed to take them up as its own. The responsibility for careful interpretation and for implementation of the resolution rests with each of us but particularly with our ministers, our theologians, and our theological schools for it is they who determine and deliver the religious message. We are building the way toward spiritual equality for men and for women, a path which other religious organizations must ultimately follow. We are doing the courageous work in religion today.

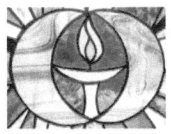

Women in Ministry:
A Report from Grailville
Kairos #14 Spring 1979

Maryell Cleary

I WAS EXCITED WHEN I HEARD that there might be a conference for all the Unitarian Universalist women parish ministers. I was skeptical, too, that it would ever happen. Then the pieces of paper began to arrive. Did I want to attend? What questions would I like us to address? Then many questions to be answered to help the planners. At last, the good word that it was really going to take place. We were to gather at Grailville, a women's center near Cincinnati, October 10-13. My last communication beforehand was a call from Denise Tracy, since I was driving, would I bring a supply of drinks and snacks? I would.

We came to Grailville with a mixed bag of emotions: excitement, anticipation, reluctance, trepidation, curiosity, joy, concern. I know that I spent some of the five and one-half hour drive from Cleveland speculating about what the conference would be like, and thinking, "Well, at least there'll be a few people there that I know. I liked the look of the Grailville setting: lots of trees and an interesting mix of old and new buildings on both sides of a road outside Loveland, Ohio. And I knew that my immediate welcome was assured because of what was in the trunk of my car. But I admit to some nervousness as I walked up the path to the Caravansary, the building where we would hold our meetings.

We sat in a big circle that afternoon and looked around at faces, known and unknown. We were 29 separate women, old, young, married, single, divorced, in ministries with husbands, in ministries of education, in associate ministries, one retired, one from "25," most solo ministers in churches, all with experience in the parish ministry save one who was about to begin, and, as she said, "scared stiff."

A Determination to Share

This conference grew out of a discussion at Meadville Winter, 1977. Denise Tracy and Marni Politte called together all the women with parish experience who were there, and out of that came the determination to have a gathering where all UU women ministers in the parish could share common concerns. In that preliminary discussion ten areas of concern were pinpointed, which stayed very much the same after many others had had the opportunity to put their concerns into the pot. With a grant from the Council on Education for Professional Religious Leadership to make it financially feasible, the conference dream became a reality. All who came are grateful now to Denise and Marni for taking the initiative and carrying through.

Marjorie Leaming wrote in her newsletter after the conference:

"Because we came from such a common background of experience, we could communicate in a unique way that would not have been possible otherwise. Diversity may be a wonderful ideal. It is in fact what keeps us going as a denomination. But the bond to be found in the unity of our common female parish experience made it possible for something fantastic to happen. It was exhilarating, joyful, inspiring, refreshing, stimulating, and energizing to experience it. I've never spent four days with male colleagues (really never even four hours) that I didn't get a lot of painful put-downs always so subtle of course that I could never be sure that it wasn't just my paranoia. The experience of spending four days with colleagues and not having that dreadful thing happen even once has left my whole self, whirling. Instead of coming away bleeding and feeling empty, I came away full of health and joy."

What made the Grailville experience so good for all of us? In our closing session all of us spoke about it with the enthusiasm that's in Marjorie's written words. Even those who came reluctantly went away converted. Was it just that we were all women, and so we were kind to one another? No, we were not there to bolster one another's egos and tell each other how wonderful we are! It came about because we faced most issues honestly, because we did not avoid pain or conflict.

Our First and Only Crisis

The best illustration of what I mean is that of our first, and only, major crisis. Besides the 29 of us in the circle that first day there was a toddler, Gayle Lehman-Becker's daughter, Lee. Gayle had been encouraged to come and bring Lee, though she had made it clear that she was nursing Lee and therefore the little girl would be with us much of the time. That sounded fine to start with; we women want it to be possible for mothers to be active ministers. Certainly, we didn't want to exclude one from our gathering just because she was nursing her child.

But the actuality of the situation came down hard on our ideals. We were in an immense room with a very high ceiling. Words were swallowed up in the empty space across the circle. It was hard to hear one another at best; when Lee was making the happy sounds of a child, or when she was crying, we could not hear each other at all. Gayle did her best to take Lee out when she was disturbing us, but that meant that Gayle was missing much of our meeting. So, that first evening, when Lee had made some noise and Gayle had taken her out, someone voiced what many of us were feeling: irritation at the child and at Gayle for bringing her. Others chimed in with a blend of sympathy for Gayle and concern because they were missing so much of the discussion. Two volunteered to talk with Gayle about finding an alternative arrangement. When a daytime sitter, a member of the La Leche League, was found, we were all relieved. But then we had to face a hurt and angry Gayle. We could not turn the issue aside or ignore it; we had to talk it out, allowing Gayle her anger and her hurt, and ourselves our uncomfortable mix of feelings. The solution was a good one; Gayle could be fully involved in our sessions, and Lee thoroughly enjoyed her stay at the sitter's home. When she came back to us at dinnertime, we could all enjoy her.

The Knotty Issue of Feminism

Besides that immediate issue, we tackled issues in our ministries. Feminism, pain, lifestyles, settlement, power, support, UU religious goals, personal goals in ministry. Sometimes it was hard to be open about our personal experiences and feelings, sometimes we just crashed through and did it, no matter how hard. The only time we avoided an issue was early on, before we had felt our closeness. It was the knotty issue of feminism. Probably we should have left it until later in the week, when we had learned to trust one another. As we talked of what feminism meant to us, we were aware of differences, but we emphasized the agreements. Most of us consider ourselves to be feminists in some sense, though one preferred to say that she "rejoiced in her femininity." Some of us were excited about being part of something new and very important, a struggle going on all over the world. We found that we could agree that feminism need not be solely focused on women, that it can be and should be inclusive, meaning working for the liberation of all people; as someone said, "pro-human." We noted that feminism brings anger with it, our own and that of others. We get angry at sexist language and at the chauvinists in our congregations. We experience the anger of those who see us as too committed to women's rights, or not committed enough.

I came to Grailville hurting from some things going on at home. I didn't become fully engaged in the conference, emotionally, until our session on our pain. Barbara Merritt had been awake late on the first night, and the next morning she told us of hearing several of us moaning and crying in our sleep. She suggested that some of us must be experiencing pain right now, and that all of us experience it at times in our lives and our ministries. So why not deal with it here? With some reluctance, we agreed.

That session was one of the highlights of the conference for me. We divided into threesomes, randomly; I was with Mary Moore and Carolyn Owen-Towle. Each of us had something urgent to talk about, something hurting at that very moment. I didn't know why it was so easy to share, but it took us no time at all to plunge into the causes of our distress; in just a few minutes we were sitting knee to knee, holding hands awash with tears. I have a special feeling for Carolyn and Mary, for it was with them that I let my shell crack and my vulnerability show. There was no judging, no advising, in our sharing. I learned later that ours had been a fortunate grouping, for not everyone had a pain to share, or was willing to share it, and some who shared felt that they had not been understood. We didn't simply wallow in pain and tears, though; there was another part, in which each of us wrote a "myth" about ourselves and our pain. In language like "Once there was a beautiful princess" and "Once there was a land divided by a wide river," we began to write down our ideas for creative solutions. Spelling of pain reminds me of our sessions on support. Some of the pain, certainly, is eased by having a human being to share it with.

"We were not there to bolster one another's egos and tell each other how wonderful we are!"

For some of us such a person is close at hand. The married women almost unanimously spoke of their husbands as their best friends, the persons they went to for encouragement and support. For those of us who are single or divorced, the problem is more difficult. Some pile up long-distance telephone bills talking to good friends, sometimes seminary friends. Others found friendship and support from colleagues in ministerial associations, UU ministers' groups, women ministers' groups, groups of ministers undertaking some special project together.

It's hard to find time to make friends in the community, so many of us have our friendship groups within our congregations, and that can be very good. Those who serve on staff teams in large churches find that there is collegial support in those relationships. We had had little experience with UUMA Good Offices Persons, and some of that experience had been quite negative. We suggest that Good Offices Persons call the ministers in their districts twice a year just to ask them how things are going, and then really *listen*. GOPs, we think, could be more useful in supportive ways than they presently are.

The Sources of Strength

Ultimately, we recognize that we must be our own sources of support, that our inner strength and ability to stand on our own feet are essential to being good ministers. A number of us spoke of the great value of a spiritual life, a time of meditation or prayer daily, time to get in touch with our sources of strength, however we may name them.

In one session, we wrote endings to sentences beginning "I feel filled with power when …" "It robs me of my power when …" and "I like to feel powerless when …" As we shared what we had written, it became clear that we were not talking about having power over other people, but rather of our feelings of competence and self-confidence. We realized that no one else can take those feelings away from us unless we let them, though when we're feeling low it's easier to let what others say or do move us even further down. At first it was hard to own a liking for a feeling of powerlessness, but a little reflection brought realization that it's good at times to stop our busy competence and let the universe take over in our awareness. Looking up at the stars, floating in water, lying on grass, walking in the rain—at such times and many others we feel at one with the universe, and are conscious of its power. Somehow in that experience we are empowered again.

In questionnaires sent to us beforehand we'd been asked to characterize our settlement experiences. Stressful, vague, frustrating, slow, long, consuming, exhausting, demanding, anxiety-producing, angering, difficult, intense: all these words appeared in our responses more than once. So did: challenging, affirming, fun, exciting, ego-boosting, and interesting. Negative words appeared much more often than positive words, so when Deborah Pope-Lance and I led a session on the subject, we started it off with a group yell! We stood up and let out some of our anger and frustration LOUDLY. Then we gathered in small groups to discuss what helped the settlement process go well, what hindered it, and how it might be changed for the better.

The Settlement Process

Lack of information came off in first place in what hindered the process. We need to know more about the churches our names go out to, more than the Search Committees put into their packets. We ended knowing more about "how to do it" and how to do it well, more about how to put together a good packet, more about the interview process. Our colleagues who've been through the process a couple of times could pass this kind of information on. Some of us have had good experiences with the Settlement Office, others not so good. Unanimously we felt that David Pohl is over-burdened and needs help. We also agreed that another person's judgment on whose name should be sent to which church would be useful, and that it would be best to have that second person be a woman.

Going into interviews with good questions to ask the Search Committees was one thing that helped the process go well. Another which had been helpful to some was a videotape of preaching. Cordial Ministerial Settlement Representatives who gave good sound information about churches helped a great deal. Best of all was a positive attitude on our part that "I'm going to enjoy this interview!"

Those who had experience as assistant or associate ministers suggested that there be clear ground rules for hiring in multiple-staff churches, and that there should be a candidating week for associate staff just as for senior ministers. Another practical suggestion which we intend to find ways to implement is that there be workshops to fill the gaps in our education on how to go about getting a job. These might be sponsored by the Department of Ministry, the UUMA, or by the women ministers themselves.

Women do not have easy entry into the political world of the denomination—yet. Men have theological school buddies who can say a good word for them. Women so far are outside the power structure. We were not entirely sure that we wanted to be inside the power structure, but we realized that, if we are to get the kind of jobs in the ministry that we want and are capable of doing well, we need to know the people in power positions and let them know our abilities. For that reason, another practical suggestion was a workshop for settlement representatives and Interdistrict Representatives, sponsored and carried out by women ministers. A number of us volunteered to work on this.

> **"I have a special feeling for Carolyn and Mary,
> for it was with them that I let my shell crack
> and my vulnerability show."**

What Are Our Religious Goals?

By the afternoon of the third day, we were tired and perhaps still wound up in the intensity of our discussion of settlement with its personal ramifications. Marjorie Leaming and Vi Kochendorfer, leading us in a session on UU religious goals, found it hard to build any enthusiasm about the topic. Still, we made a long list of religious goals of our denomination. I can't list them all, for there were too many. But I am choosing a representative sample; I think they could well serve as the basis for discussion in our churches and fellowships. Are these the directions in which UUism should move? And if so, how do we get that movement started? Here they are:

- To understand power in a liberal way;
- To recognize the need for growth as a denomination or we won't be here!
- To understand the power in the real meaning of congregational polity and liberal thought;
- To lead in ethical imperatives;
- To have a less top-heavy, power-dominated church;
- To find ways to deepen our sense of the religiousness of all life;
- To articulate a positive liberal religious (not just UU) faith;
- To express that positive faith so that it is widely known;
- To encourage the opening of closed minds;
- To leave our suburban captivity;
- To develop value/symbol communication;
- To strengthen the affirmative movement of faith.

There was so much more! I'd like to include everything, but that's impossible. So, I'll jump here and there over some of the rest of my memories. We talked about our lifestyles, and that brought forth much emotion.

We'd like our congregations to trust us, to accept that we are adults and responsible people with a great deal at stake in our ministries. We'd like them to recognize that there are many different and equally OK lifestyles in existence today, and that we represent a number of them. Some of us live miles from our churches, but we're available. Some of us have overnight guests at the parsonage and would appreciate our parishioners refraining from curious comment. Some of us have difficulty getting time and space away from church members; "the minister is always available in time of need" doesn't mean she's available for social conversation at home at nine o'clock on Sunday morning! We need privacy in our personal lives.

A Time for Grace

In one hilarious session we answered several questions from the pre-conference questionnaires in the roles of male ministers. There were some good mimics among us! In lots of laughter, we vented some of our anger about the stereotypes we see male ministers putting on us. Then we heard what some male ministers had actually answered to those questions, and found out that our stereotypes were partly right, partly wrong.

Most satisfying for me was our easy and natural movement into and out of moments not designated worship yet which felt like worship. We had two morning worship services with preaching, and they were good. Beyond them were brief times when worship seemed to happen. Our sessions opened and closed with an individual presenting a favorite something. They ranged from a glorious time of rubbing each other's backs in a circle to the sharing of poems and quotations and the lighting of a candle. Betty Baker read a poem on aging from Nancy Wood's collection of Indian poems, *Many Winters*, which spoke to my condition. More than the content, the feeling of those moments comes back to me. We were experiencing our time together as religious time, a time for giving and receiving special grace.

On our last evening this was especially true. We had talked

of our primary values in ministry, of such values as integrity, spirituality, and concern for society, and then sat in the darkened room, rain pouring down outside, a candle flame in the center of our circle, and were silent. No one said, "Let's be silent." We came to silence as if by common agreement. At last, one by one, some of us dropped a sentence or two into that silence, something deeply felt and good to think upon. I recall that I asked the group to remember and celebrate the mothers of us all, Olympia Brown and Antoinette Brown Blackwell. I'm sorry that I don't remember what others said. Their words were good. The feeling was best. We were there, separate persons, yet close to one another and part of a great many things greater than ourselves. In those moments of silence, I was aware of those connections which link me with all that is, the connections which make life and the world sacred.

A Closing Communication

I am not accustomed to using the word "spirituality." It was used quite a bit during the conference. I had to ask someone to tell me just what was meant. When it was explained I realized that I meant the same sort of thing though I used other words. "Spirituality" was very important to many of the women present; to them it meant being in touch with the element of the sacred in daily life. They felt that bringing this into the awareness of their congregations was one of the major purposes of their ministries. They felt that women had a concern about this dimension of our religious commitment to which many men are less attentive.

"We can trivialize our existence if we choose, or we can treat ourselves and our world as if they were of ultimate concern, truly sacred."

Using my own terms, I would say that the only distinction between the sacred and the secular is the one humans make. We can trivialize our existence if we choose, or we can treat ourselves and our world as if they were of ultimate concern, truly sacred. To treat each part of our daily lives with respect, care, and love—to behold all with wonder and awe as wholly holy universe—this is to live religiously. This requires our attention and our personal discipline. Living this way, if all humans even began to try to do so, could change and renew human lives and the natural world we live in.

And so, we came to the close of what someone called "the first really *religious* conference" she'd ever attended. We signed up to do some practical things to carry on the ideas that had come out of the conference. We made plans for a General Assembly get-together at the Unitarian Universalist Church of East Lansing, Mich., where Denise Tracy is minister. We enjoyed having Lee Lehman-Becker with us for our last session, and commented on how relaxed we all were about that now, including Lee. We had a closing communion of mother's milk, which celebrated our uniqueness as women. We hugged one another, in happiness and some tears, and said our good-byes.

And then we parted. There will be other conferences for UU women in parish ministry, I'm sure; there will never be another with quite the same quality of feeling as this. For this was our first, a landmark, something to go into the books of UU history. For the first time there were enough of us, and we felt strongly enough about our unique problems and our unique strengths to come together to talk, to share, to laugh, to cry, and most of all, to celebrate. We went back to our churches more able to share ourselves, and with more to give.

Photo from the Grailville Women in Ministry

Bottom Row: (l to r) Lisa Wiggins, Polly Laughland Guild, Maryell Cleary, Ellen Dohner Livingston, Joy Atkinson

Second Row: Marjorie Leaming, Gayle Lehman-Becker, Vilma Szantho Harrington, Denise Tracy, Carolyn Owen Towle, Eileen Karpeles

Top Row: Deborah Pope Lance, Mary Moore, Diane Miller, Gertrude Lindener, Marge Keip, Betty Baker, Barbara Merritt, Holly Bell, Agnes Zuniga, Bev Bumbaugh, Joyce Smith, Cynthia Edson, Leslie Westbrook, Marni Politte Harmony, Frederica Leigh, Vi Kochendoerfer

The Story of the UU Principles
Unitarian Universalist Congregation of
Grand Traverse and Its Benzie Group

Misty Sheehan

IN THE 1970s I LIVED IN JACKSON, MICH., which had no
Unitarian Universalist church. When I decided to look at Unitarian Universalism, I chose the nearest UU church, the East Liberty
Universalist Church, which was the only building in a nearby
farming community. I looked at my Order of Service and was
dismayed: oh, no, the minister was a woman. I had never had a
woman minister leading the service. The minister in the Methodist Church I grew up in was an old gentleman with white hair who
never spoke to young people like me.

Reverend Ruth Smith from the East Liberty Universalist
church was different. It was autumn and she spoke of the apples
and the squash and the pumpkin coming in as the grasses from
summer dried out and made ready for the winter snow. She had
a college degree but no religious training and was a farmer's wife.
She was ordained but had never been fellowshipped, serving the

church from 1963-1983. She followed the seasons through the year just as she did on her farm, finding the joys of each season and teaching us of our relationship with the growing plants that changed each season. I liked her immediately and soon found myself the Religious Education Director, and she soon became a good friend.

Chapin-Crane Woman and Religion Team

In l975 Lucille (Shuck) Longview attended the UU World Conference on women and returned to spearhead writing the Women and Religion Resolution, which was passed unanimously at General Assembly1977. The Resolution stated that the Unitarian Universalist Association would examine and put aside sexist assumptions, attitudes, and language to explore and eliminate religious roots of sexism in myths, traditions, and beliefs. At the same time Reverend Denise Tracy had completed divinity school at Andover Newton and became the minister of the Greater Lansing Unitarian Universalist Church. She put out a call for four women to join a woman and religion team. I was ready to look at what women in religion would bring to us. I was one of the four chosen along with Billie McCants from Greater Lansing, and Janet Gabrion of Ann Arbor. Denise named us The Chapin Crane Women and Religion Team, after two 19th century UU ministers. I was on the team from 1977 to 1985. I was newsletter editor, and, later, Chair of the Chapin Crane Woman and Religion team.

The late nineteenth century when Crane and Chapin lived was a time of religious change with a focus on human virtue and progress. The Christian Science church was founded; the Spiritualist Church was founded, and these changes were precipitated by women. Augusta Chapin (1836-1905) was denied admission to The University of Michigan because she was a woman, so she attended Oberlin College in Ohio, which did admit women. She was the second woman ordained in the Universalist Church and the first to receive a Doctor of Divinity Degree. She became an important itinerant preacher. Caroline Bartlett Crane (1858-1935) was appointed minister of the First Unitarian Church of Kalamazoo in 1889 which later became the People's Church in Kalamazoo. Social Action was most important to her, and she was active in the suffrage movement. She ran manual training schools similar to those of Jane Addams in Chicago, was a civic sanitarian promoting pure food laws and advocated prison reform. She started an African-American literary club; she was against capital punishment; she advocated prison reform and women's property rights. She was a leader in her community.

These ideal women whom we had never heard of before opened a world that we know about. They didn't just preach but were active in their communities making the world a better place. And we were "just housewives," the world said, intelligent housewives, but what were we doing to make the world a better place?

In the 1970s, the women's movement was growing; it penetrated more and more women's minds throughout the country leading to feminine dissatisfaction and questioning. We, on the Chapin-Crane team, were educated women in an era when women were returning to college to enable them to begin a professional occupation. Rev. Tracy had just graduated from Theological School. I was attending the University of Michigan studying History; Janet

Gabrian had her teaching degree from the University of Michigan, and Billie McCants had gone to college in the 1930s when it was exceptional for women to attend college.

We worked according to consensus. Our group collaborated on what we wanted to accomplish; that is, we listened to each other, and the agenda and decisions were made by the group. This was not a democratic process as set forth in the current 1950 UU Principles. Dissidents were listened to in the discussion of major points; and a growth came out of that listening.

We identified several concerns that we wanted to address. First, was the obvious lack of reference to women in hymnals and published materials. Second, the lack of women in leadership positions in the church. One could count the number of women ministers in the denomination on one hand. Women were the major congregants who welcomed people at the door, though men served as ushers. Women staffed the kitchen and served as Religious Education teachers. We were allowed on the membership committees. But we usually were not found on the Board of Directors or finance committees. We observed that women were vulnerable to strong male (and female leaders) who pushed a private agenda forward, and often pursued an agenda for exclusion of women as church professionals and in community leadership.

First Women and Religion Convention

The first Woman and Religion Convention was held in Grailville Ohio in 1979, and we, the Chapin-Crane Team, attended. UU musician, Carolyn McDade, who wrote "Spirit of Life," was the musician for the conference and she introduced us to her religious songs which spoke to us. "Precious Memories," "Hark for the Sun is Returning," "Awakening." Workshops addressed women's issues —Why was the hymnal only using sexist language when women were to be singing the verses? What about women ministers? I came to see that Rev. Ruth Smith wasn't an aberration in her clarion call to her people. She was leading in a new direction that gave women a spiritual and intellectual space that allowed us to feel a part of the church and fostered a connection with the cycles of the earth and the cycles of life from the land that we lived on.

But then, what about the Principles? Did they reflect the older style of ministry, or could they lead us into the future? We set up a separate committee that met late at night. Lucile (Schuck) Longview from Boston, in her proper Bostonian navy blue suit and black laced shoes, and the original advocate for women within the church, even though she was sixty-eight years old, joined us, spread out on the floor discussing the Principles. Several problems existed:

(1) women's issues and naming were not included ("the dignity of man");

(2) the emphasis on democratic methodology reflected thought from the '50s and was no longer current nor necessary to a new religious organization; and

(3) they mentioned (a Male) God.

The old Principles totally refused to confirm women. Now some Unitarian Universalists accepted the idea of God, but many considered themselves agnostics, Buddhists, or had no faith in a Supreme Being, but were focused on changing the world. Building by negotiation, the new Principles that we came up with did not include the word God, which was only one of many religious traditions within the denomination. We rewrote the Principles following the contemporary needs of women and put them forth at the Women and Religion Convention for everyone to vote on. They were accepted amongst cheering and acclamation from the women present.

At the General Assembly in 1980, we decided to attend and put on a workshop. I attended and hosted the workshop. The women who were present were very excited about women's needs being addressed by Women and Religion thoughts and ideas. Nothing came forth from the workshop, but word got out, and women liked the revised Principles that had been written in 1979, went back to their churches, and spread the word. Women and Religion held workshops at General Assembly 1981, and 1982 as well and the word was getting out to many churches of the proposed change in the Principles.

In 1983 the revised Principles were placed for a vote in the General Assembly. The revised Principles caused stress particularly in UU Christian churches. Four Unitarian Universalist ministers invited some of us to lunch one day. They were Christian and told us that their Christian churches would leave the denomination if the new Principles were passed. Their reasoning was that we were eliminating God from the Principles. We replied that wasn't our intent; eliminating God from the Principles didn't eliminate God from individuals or their churches, but across the nation, most UUs considered themselves to reflect other than solely a Judeo-Christian heritage. The newly written Principles reflected that a broadening of spirituality amongst UUs. The newspapers got word of the elimination of God from the Principles which were to be voted on. Reporters started calling up the Women and Religion team asking if it were true that we were taking God out of our religion. We didn't reply to the reporters, feeling that we did now want them to intrude on internal church business.

High Unitarian Universalist Association officials called Women and Religion representatives to a midnight meeting, wanting to postpone the vote on the resolution until more study had been done. (This was a significant recognition that Women and Religion were the important players in the new resolution.) They wanted more of the denomination to reflect on the changes and agree. I felt they had been brought before the General Assembly now for three years and the result had been positive. This was ignored by these UUA officials. Women and Religion did not agree. It was a long night, but finally the denominational officials, with support from UUWF President Denny Davidoff, won this argument. I did see that it would be more constructive if the wider denomination was more aware of and educated about these changes. On the floor the next day, the vote on the Principles was tabled. A committee was established to work on the study process of the new Principles. People, who supported the new Principles as they were written, not just members of Women and Religion, were very much upset by this; they liked what we had written, but the General Assembly passed the UUA's study recommendations. The committee was then announced— and not one of us who had originally rewritten the Principles was on this new committee. We were devastated. Only white male ministers were on the committee. It seemed to us that an invisible line had been drawn by the denomination between white male degreed ministers who were a part of the administration, and lay women, 'who were members of UU congregations. We felt that the individual and collective voices of women did not count in the administrative center of our denominational organization.

Looking back on that General Assembly I can see several points which I would do differently. First the newspaper reporters pushed the UUA representatives to the wall. They wanted a sensational story over something that recognized a change in our UU religious belief. I'm sure they talked to UUA representatives, too, who also stonewalled the reporters. Second, a midnight meeting between high UUA administrators and several Women and Religion Team members is not an ethical way to solve a problem. That meeting should have been held in the daylight, not in the dark of the night, and should have been open to other concerned members as well. The old Principles speak of democratic action, but this process was not democratic. This was an elite meeting designed to cut the Women and Religion Team out of the voting process on the floor the next day. The vote for a year of study passed.

The Principles and Purposes were finally adopted provisionally at the next General Assembly in 1984. There would be one more year of discussion before final approval. At the 1985 General Assembly there was discussion about the phrasing of the seventh principle. Rev Paul L'Herrou stepped to the microphone and suggested the phrase, "Respect for the interdependent web of all existence of which we are a part." Immediately there was a collective sigh of relief from the Assembly. It was adopted with only one negative vote. More than eight years of work and our Association of Congregations had a new faith statement, begun by women in 1977. These new Principles are good and have held up these eighteen years. People in churches across the country use them and refer to them as they develop their own spirituality and their own social justice principles. They are positive, but the process by which they were revised and developed, reflected an older era and its administrative process.

District Women and Religion Groups

Appointed in 1978, the Rev. Leslie Westbrook was charged with accomplishing the equality of women in the UUA. I was confused about what her function really was. She was not a roadblock, but she just didn't seem that interested in what we, women, as representatives of congregations, were doing and what our needs were.

We held a Convention on Feminist Theology in East Lansing in 1980. Women and Religion groups were established in each District across the continent. These District organizations followed in the blueprint of the Chapin-Crane District. Women applied to be on the committee. We worked by consensus, were egalitarian, and, most importantly, derived our thinking from the greater women's movement across the United States. Our group was held together by a newsletter called Old Wives' Tales. This newsletter was sent to people who had registered for our Chapin-Crane conferences. This newsletter served to educate people on issues the Chapin-Crane group was focusing on bringing forth new ideas that others felt were important.

In 1984 a greater percentage of women attended theological

school, and women became 15% of the ministry in the denomination. In 1986 "Cakes for the Queen of Heaven" was created by Reverend Shirley Ranck which provided materials for individual churches or individuals to study following the history of women and religion in the European tradition. In 1994 *Rise Up and Call Her Name* was published by Elizabeth Fisher. The first lesbian was called to a congregation, Barbara Pescan, at Beacon Unitarian Church in Oak Park.

In 1985 the UU Women's History Project was set in motion by Dorothy Emerson including UUWF, Women and Religion, LREDA, CUUPS, and MSUU. That same year, the UUA Board funded two joint meetings for the Unitarian Universalist Women's Federation (UUWF) and Women and Religion. A women's room was set up at the General Assembly shared by both groups. Despite the strong changes occurring throughout the country due to Women and Religion principles, in 1996 UUA sunsetted the Women and Religion Resolution. No longer worth supporting? To me, once again, an administrative decision by leaders who didn't understand the power and the passion that individual women were feeling. After that, academics took me away from the country. I had a fellowship to study in India, then I was invited by the Chinese government to teach in China for four and a half years. Upon my return to the United States, I became a Professor at College of DuPage in Chicago in 1991. I visited the Oak Park church and the Naperville church, but they just didn't interest me. I'm from a small country church, East Liberty, where everyone knew each other and churches with 200 and 300 members were uncomfortable to my shy self.

In 1991, I heard Central Midwest Women and Religion was having a retreat in Michigan and decided to attend, though I knew none of the people. As I was driving around the bottom of Lake Michigan, as Chicago people know, the traffic was bumper to bumper, it was a hundred degrees, the air conditioning in my car decided it had had enough and revolted. I decided to stop at a rest stop and was standing in line waiting for my meal and a COLD drink, when the person behind me said, "Aren't you Misty?" I turned and it was Carol Hosmer, an old friend from my years at East Liberty Church in Jackson County. We sat for an hour in the air-conditioning and caught up. She was on the Central Midwest Women and Religion team and was going to the same weekend retreat where I was going.

The retreat was just what I had remembered: intelligent, white, middle-aged women, of all sizes, shapes, and hairstyles. I enjoyed the active minds of the women over the weekend and, when I returned home, I sent a note to the Central Midwest Women and Religion Team that I would like to be a member and was accepted onto the Team.

We, the Central Midwest District, held conferences around the Chicagoland area headlined by major writers on topics of interest to Midwest women which usually included two hundred to three hundred participants. These types of egalitarian, nurturing conferences were held in many other districts. Writers like Starhawk, Margo Adler, and Vicki Noble were some of the speakers.

To me, these conferences, and the women I met from around the United States and Canada, represented the new strength of women. Unitarianism Universalism was founded under the principle that the trinity is not written into the New Testament, instead the authors wrote it with an understanding of One God. Despite this major change in theology, Unitarian Universalist services were very similar to other protestant denominations, centered around a male minister, who preached his ideas of spirituality to the congregation. I had faith in myself, not a deity, that I used to create a situation where I could live out my spirituality, not the ideas of a male minister.

I looked to myself and the new feminist writers that represented a forward way of thinking, focusing on the individual, rather than a male minister. The Women Religion conferences across the country were organized by and illustrated a new way of thinking for Unitarian Universalists causing a rebirth of the feminist faith in the UUA. They were planned by a committee that represented the women in the district and fostered different types of affinity. The central organization served as a network for women and religion groups from churches, and single women within the district, sharing resources, programs, and advocacy of issues. These committees were focused on leadership training for all participants, a feminist process, and a circle of equals, creating a "symbolic clan" of women with the same goals of mutual support. Setting aside sexist assumptions, attitudes and language did more than anticipated: it created a new dimension in our denomination.

Gretchen Ohmann, a computer and design expert, was the center of the Central Midwest Women and Religion Committee, creating connections within the group and across the country digitally. As well, she was critical in the work of the Core Women and Religion Group that formed in 2002 and is still the informational center of Women and Religion. I was a member of the Core Women and Religion Committee from 2004 and Co-Chair from 2005-2006. Reverend Ranck's Cakes for the Queen of Heaven was rewritten by Reverend Ranck and a committee that included me, Gretchen Ohmann, and Dorothy Emerson. It was republished in 2008 in two volumes: On The Threshold, and In Ancient Times. Under Gretchen's expertise Women and Religion continues to have a presence, a bookstore, and visibility at General Assemblies.

The Future

To me, the Women and Religion experience is still an important movement within the Unitarian Universalism though fewer women and religion organizations exist. A Conference was held through Zoom by the Pacific Central District in March of this year "Hanging in, Hanging on" with the question: Where do we go from here?

We have, from my experience, two women who epitomize the importance of the local church in people's lives. Caroline Bartlett Crane in the 19th century had to listen to the people in her church to find out what their needs were. Many of them were new immigrants, like those women Jane Addams ministered to in Chicago. Reverend Crane listened to the immigrants. Then she searched for people from the broader community to provide the knowledge these immigrants needed. Reverend Ruth Smith knew all the congregants in her church intimately and was oriented to their needs, not oriented to power. The needs were more spiritual than practical, and she addressed them in her sermons and relationships. Gretchen Ohman elaborates on the style of leadership elucidated by both these ministers in their respective congregations. A process of shared leadership was used by both to hone participatory group process skills. This process was utilized by Women and Religion committees in their meetings to establish which direction(s) the committees wished to pursue. They actively used consensus decision-making, a style developed in district Women and Religion Committees and developed in regional lines. Reverend Ruth Smith brought out another important concern that wasn't much discussed in the UU denomination at the time: concern for the environment. Women and Religion hasn't addressed the environment much, but another women's organization has—under the leadership of UU songster, Carolyn McDade, now 86 years old. Carolyn has written three types of songs: songs praising women and women's rights, which came from her work with Women and Religion; civil rights songs; and songs for the environment. When she turned to the environment, groups sprung up in the U.S. and Canada who had developed a new concern for their land and its inhabitants and its vegetation which also addressed my concerns for the environment. At one point Carolyn worked with 18 Unitarian groups across mainly Canada and the US. I am in a group "Singing Sisters" of about 20 women from the Traverse City MI area. Another group, "Gaia Singers," of about 30 women from the Detroit area, and Toronto, Ontario (before the border was closed by the government due to the pandemic) has been strong and growing in Detroit and eastern Ontario. Both groups together have put on concerts in support of the people of Flint, MI using songs Carolyn McDade has written on the importance of trees, rivers, lakes, and the ocean, donating their proceeds to Flint MI where the Mott (applesauce) Foundation doubled our donations for the children forever scarred by lead poisoning in their water. Our leadership style is very similar to women and religion groups. Everyone gets a chance at some time to put forth her ideas and songs for the groups to share and sing along with. Our group has now stayed together for fifteen or twenty years, caretaking, nurturing and providing mutual support, gathering at least once a month to share womanhood and our concern for nature.

Carolyn McDade's groups are focused on one issue, the environment, but are formed much like the Women and Religion groups were formed eclectically, and work by consensus. Today, they are the center of UU women's activity in Michigan, sprung from the model created by Women and Religion, and, like Women and Religion, addressing contemporary women's desires for a better world.

Permutations from the Women and Religion experience, I hope will continue to address contemporary issues. The UU Principles, represent to me, the process of personal change that has been a major landmark and for contemporary UU women who care about issues, specifically women's rights and the environment.

I know that, for me, women and religion gave me a place in the church organization where I felt most comfortable. Women and Religion provided space for women's (and men's) spiritual experience to develop placing the emphasis on acknowledging one's personal values, one's shifting values, one's concern for a better world as the center to one's spiritual enlightenment.

An Assessment of the New Theology Written by Women

A Position Paper Presented at "UU Women and Religion" Convocation 1980 in E. Lansing, MI. Nov 15, 1980

Dianne Arakawa

(Then Minister of the Community Church of New York)

The Five R's of Feminist Theology

THE WOMEN'S LIBERATION MOVEMENT, which gained momentum on the late 1960s and which continues to exert pressure upon sexist society, was born when women perceived themselves as a minority group within a male-dominated world and when they began to bond together for solidarity. This was no small feat.

Neither was it anything new, for any women of history—for example, Elizabeth Cady Stanton, Susan B Anthony, and Margaret Sanger—had also struggled for women's rights and liberation from oppression.

However, the Women's Movement that was born over a decade ago was distinctly different. It witnessed a uniting of women on a more massive scale. Women across the country gathered into what became known as "consciousness-raising groups" to discuss each other's experiences, women's history/her story, religious issues, political rights, and art and more. Mothers and daughters even began sharing with one another more candidly.

This weekend we gather to consider some of the major facets of the Women's Movement, which continue to call for our attention. We come because we are curious, because we earnestly want to learn, because we need to for our own very survival. We come because it is our religious responsibility to open our ears and listen—really listen—to one another and perhaps change our behavior.

My task this evening is to share with you some of the things that I have learned about feminist theology over the course of my ministry and studies in religion. I have discovered that like the Women's Movement itself my task it not an easy one, for, it involves the assessment of reams of women; writings and its concise presentation to you.

Your task, I believe, will be to bring your experience and open minds to this address. In this way, you are commended to dialogue with me and—if you have not already read the books or periodicals which I mention—to look at them for yourselves and form your own opinions about them.

So let us begin.

Valerie Salving, Professor of Theology at Hobart and William Smith College, wrote an article in 1960 entitled "The Human Situation: A Feminine View," which set off the present wave of feminist theology. [1] She argued that the theologies of Reinhold

---

[1] Valerie Salving, "The Human Situation: A Feminine View," *The Journal of Religion*, April 1960, University of Chicago, Chicago, IL.

Neibuhr and Anders Nygren speak to the experiences of *men*, but not women. In doing so she asserted that theology is rooted in the particularities of human experience, including the theologians experience as male or female. She asserted that theology has traditionally been rooted in the male experience to the detriment of women.

Keeping in mind Salving's assertion, let us look at what seems to me to be five main categories of feminist theology. I name them reactionary, reformist, radical, revolutionary, and recalcitrant. Needless to say, all of the typologies overlap a great deal. My address this evening will briefly describe the first and fifth categories but concentrate on the three middle ones as they appear to be more valuable to us religious liberals.

The first category of feminist theology—which I call *reactionary*—is not really feminist theology or feminist. It includes women theologians who believe that nothing needs to change very much. Phyllis Schafley, head of the anti E.R.A. movement, Anita Bryant and Marabel Morgan, author of the book, *The Total Woman*, are among this group. They perceive that the system is already redeemed by the goodness of God—I should add—a male God. We women need just properly align ourselves with the patriarchal structure and everything will turn out for the best.

The fifth category of feminist theology—which I call *recalcitrant*—is not really feminist theology or theology. It includes women thinkers who do not believe that religion, particularly organized religion, is of much value to human life. Some Marxists and existentialists belong to this group as they purport to go beyond religion and institutional religion.

This group raises several questions for me. What is its definition of religion? Is it merely organized religion—the outward structures of faith—or does it involve individual conscience and ethics? Has society really evolved past a spiritual or religious culture? It seems to me that this category, like the first one, has somewhat removed itself from dialogue. We cannot carry on a fruitful discussion with its proponents.

So let us turn to the three middle categories for the remainder of our time.

The second category—which may be called *reformist*—includes those whose foundation for theology is the Judeo-Christian tradition. They believe, as did Elizabeth Cady Stanton with her *Woman's Bible* of 1895, that scripture and tradition can be revised and rewritten, for, the tradition contains within itself the seeds of its own liberation. God is both Father and Mother, and more than either. Sexist language has the capacity to be edited to be more sexually inclusive. Reformist theologians, I believe, include Phyllis Trible, Elizabeth Shussler Fiorenza, Rosemary Ruether and the early Mary Daly.

Phyllis Trible, professor of Old Testament at Union Theological Seminary in New York and author of *God and the Rhetoric of Sexuality* asserts that the Old Testament, particularly the account of creation and the fall in Genesis 2-3, does not necessarily legitimate the supremacy of men over women.[2] Trible says that ambiguity occurs in the use of the Hebrew word *'adham*, which some scholars have translated as "man" while she translates it

---

2 Phyllis Trible, *God and the Rhetoric of Sexuality*, Fortress Press, Philadelphia, PA, 1978.

as "humankind." That it is not until the end of the passage. She asserts that, 'adham or humankind, is differentiated into male and female. This differentiation at the end suggests woman's equality with man.

There are other examples of woman equality. Unlike the animals the woman is the fit helper of God. She is created by God not man. While dust is used to create man, so a rib is used to create woman. Any superiority attributed to man, according to Trible, is not from the text itself but from outside sources.

Trible, furthermore, refutes the notion that because man named woman, he had superiority over her. Trible says that man never named woman; rather, woman was named by God. The word "woman" is a common noun and not a generic noun designating person.

Why does the snake tempt woman and not man? Trible refutes many male theologians on this count. She says that since man and woman are co-equals man is as responsible as woman for what happens. Perhaps Eve is the more assertive and independent of the two while Adam is more silent and passive. Trible says, "I stress (this) contrast not to promote female chauvinism, but to undercut patriarchal interpretation alien to the text." [3]

Trible asserts that after the Fall man and woman are one in their sense of guilt and alienation. When woman says that her husband shall rule over her, she does not mean that he shall have supremacy over her, but rather that he shall condemn this pattern of behavior. It is at this point that Adam calls his wife "Eve," and

---

[3] Trible, *GRS*.

that the couple is banished from the Garden.

Trible concludes: "Visiting the Garden of Eden in the days of the Woman's Movement, we need no longer accept the traditional exegesis of Genesis 2-3. Rather than legitimating the patriarchal culture from which it comes, the myth places that culture under judgment. And, thus, it functions to liberate, not enslave." [4]

Another theologian who expresses ideas of the reformist typology is Elizabeth Schussler Fiorenza. She is a professor at Notre Dame University and author of the book, *The Apocalypse.* In an article entitled "Women in the New Testament" she like Trible, posits that scripture is an adequate foundation for theologizing. [5] She says that while modern theologians could not hope to find all the early Christian passages and sources that have been lost, what we do have is a remarkable lot.

Fiorenza points out that the Jesus movement was, unlike other groups such as the Pharisees and the Essenes, radically inclusive. It consisted of men and women, who were social outcasts or ostracized from their own religious communities. For Jesus' message called everyone, particularly the oppressed, to join him in service to God.

For Fiorenza Jesus' inclusiveness and equality are exemplified in the baptismal confession of Galatians 3:28 which reads, "There is neither Jew nor Greek, there is neither slave nor free, there is neither male nor female; for you are all one in Christ Jesus." As a

---

[4] Trible, *GRS.*

[5] Elizabeth Schussler Fiorenza, *Women in the New Testament, New Catholic World,* December 1976, Paulist Press, N.Y., N.Y.

result of this, says Fiorenza, women in the early Christian church were able to assume not marginal, but leadership roles within the church.

One leadership position was that of apostle. The requirement for this position was that one have witnessed the resurrection of Jesus from the tomb. Fiorenza observes that women, such as Mary Magdalene, followed Jesus from Galilee to Jerusalem and were the first witnesses of the resurrection.

Another leadership role was that of prophet. While no women prophets are named, the Book of Acts, Corinthians, and Revelation bear witness to their authority within their religious community.

Finally, another leadership position was that of missionary. Herein there were many women who were particularly prominent and wealthy. Lydia, Nympha, Prisca, for example, led house churches. Phoebe was probably a diakonos and prostatis, that is a deaconess and leading officer. Fiorenza, thus, extracts from the scripture significant images of women leaders.

Another reformist theologian is Rosemary Ruether. She is Georgian Harkness Professor of Theology at Garrett Seminary of Northwestern University and author of many works including *Religion and Sexism, Liberation Theology* and *New Woman/New Earth.*

Perhaps one of Ruether's most well-known articles which expresses her prophetic theology is called "Mother Earth and the Mega Machine: A Theology of Liberation in a Feminine, Somatic and Ecological Perspective." [6] In it she uncovers the dualism, that

---

[6] Rosemary Radford Ruether, *Mother Earth and the Mega Machine: A Theology of Liberation in a Feminine, Somatic and Ecological Perspective.*

Christianity has inherited from other traditions, such as apocalyptic Judaism and Neo-Platonism. She says that it is this dualism involving mind/body, society/nature and masculine/feminism that has led to the subjugation of woman and minorities.

During the first two millennia, suggests Ruether, society was generally holistic. There were few dualisms. Then sometime during the first millennium B.C. a fragmentation in the communal worldview began to emerge. The former religions of the world became appropriated as private cults, and humankind became alienated from nature. Christianity, according to Ruether, appropriated these dualisms. Men became identified with the mind and spirit while women were associated with the body and passions.

Ruether, furthermore, indicates how the dualism has infiltrated much of modern theology, particularly in the works of Karl Barth, Rudolf Bultmann and Gogarten. She criticizes the escalation in competition, armaments, and pollution because of the dualism.

In another article, "The Cult of True Womanhood," Ruether says that this dualism is even expressed in some city plans in which cities are isolated from suburbs, from which men commute to their places of business and where women are left to take care of their households and children. [7] She points to the problem of how many women who want to work must either hire domestic help or remain childless.

Ruether invites women to be reconcilers between this dualism and the spokespersons of what she calls "integral communal personhood." She summarizes "… we must create a living pattern

---

[7] Ruether, *The Cult of Womanhood.*

of mutuality between men and women, between parents and children, among people in their social, economic, and political relationships and. Finally, between (humankind) and the organic harmonies of nature." "To seek the liberation of women without losing this sense of communal personhood is the great challenge and secret power of the women's revolution."

In sum the works of Trible, Fiorenza and Ruether posit reformist theologies that receive their primary authority from tradition and scripture. Trible and Fiorenza, in particular, advance that non-sexist criticism of scripture reveals the vision of a liberated world. While Ruether may disagree that the message of scripture is fundamentally egalitarian, she calls for the collapse of sexist dualism and liberation of the oppressed.

The final reformist theologian whom we shall consider is the *early* Mary Daly, who is Professor of Theology at Boston College. She advanced reformist typology in her 1968 book, *The Church and the Second Sex.* [8] In it she described herself as a "radical Catholic." In looking back to this she comments, "I perceived clearly that (I) had hoped to_*reform* Christianity." Now of course, she calls herself a "post-Christian feminist." I shall say more about this later.

In her early book which was a response to the Second Vatican Council that she attended, Daly pointed out some of the inequities that women experienced within the church and called for equality between men and women. She revealed how the French feminist philosopher, Simone de Beauvoir, had profoundly influenced

---

[8] Mary Daly, *The Church and the Second Sex*, Preface, Harper and Row, N.Y., N.Y., 1976, p. 6.

her and provided her with a viable critique of the church. At the same time, however, she refuted de Beauvoir's atheism in favor of Christianity.

Daly explored the conflict between Christian teachings on the worth of every human being and the actual misogynistic practices. She defended the goodness of the basic doctrine of the church, protected scripture, praised Pope John, spoke to the problems of Catholic married women, sister, and nuns and all in advanced "equality with patriarchy."

Let us now turn to the third category, which may be called *radical*, incidentally, the word "radical" derives from the Latin word meaning "root."

This category includes feminist theologians whose works are informed not by traditional or scriptural roots, but by pre-scriptural and apocryphal myths, legends, and rituals. Proponents of the typology include Merlin Stone, Elaine Pagles, Judith Plaskow and in the middle Mary Daly.

Merlin Stone, author of *When God Was a Woman*, is an artist and art historian. In her book she explores the legends, temple sites, sculpture and ancient rituals of the female deities. [9] She identifies Ashtoreth as the Great Goddess, who in other cultures is known as Asharta, Nanna, Nan, Nut, Anat, Ishtar, Isis, Ishara, Ahseran, Ashtrat, and Hathor.

Stone says that archeologists have traced the worship of the Goddess back to the Paleolithic period about 25,000 B.C. The Goddess was worshipped until about 500 A.D. when the Christian

---

[9] Merlin Stone, *When God Was a Woman*, Dial Press, N.Y., N.Y., 1976.

emperors of Rome and Byzantium closed the last goddess temple.

Theories of the Goddess are as follows: The Goddess was revered as the Giver of Life. For, only women could produce their own kind and men's role was not yet identified, Goddess worship included worship of female ancestors and the matrilineal social structure. Venus figures that were found where there were small communities give possible evidence of the great Mother cult.

Instead of Goddess worship, Elaine Pagels, Chair of the Religion Department at Barnard College and author of the *Johannine Gospel in the Gnostic Exegesis. The Gnostic Paul,* and the *Gnostic Gospels* look to another source. It is Gnosticism, that is, the religious or philosophical movement of the first three centuries A.D. which shared the conviction that while humankind exists in ignorance one can through knowledge or gnosis attain spiritual liberation.

In her most recent book, *Gnostic Gospels*, which was reviewed in *The New York Times Book Review* (1/20/80), Pagels says that gnostic circles about 200 A.D. were well known for affording women positions of authority that were denied in more orthodox communities. [10]

Pagels highlights the gnostic Gospel of Mary and suggests that is may have been co-authored by a man or a woman as it strongly defends the right of women to preach in public. In the Gospel of Thomas, which was condemned as heretical between 100-150 A.D., Pagels shows that God is described in feminine terms, as divine Mother, and eternal Silence. The Secret Book of John char-

---

[10] Elaine Pagels, *Gnostic Gospels*, Random House, N.Y., N.Y., 1979.

acterizes the divine Mother as Holy Spirit. The gnostic Gospel of Phillip declares that whoever becomes a Christian, gains both a father and a mother. The Great Announcement characterizes the divine Mother as Wisdom.

Pagels asserts, All the texts secret "gospels" revelations, mystical teachings—are among those rejected from the select list of twenty-six that comprise the "New Testament" collection. As these and other writings were sorted and judged by various Christian communities, every one of these texts which gnostic groups revered and shared was rejected from the canonical collection as "heterodox" by those who called themselves "orthodox" Christians ... By the time this process was concluded, probably as late as the year 200 A.D., virtually all the feminine imagery of God had disappeared from 'orthodox' Christian tradition. [11]

The question remains for Pagels as to what the reasons for the rejection of the gnostic texts from the canon were and for the suppression of feminist imagery.

Another theologian who expresses a radical typology is Judith Plaskow. Professor at Wichita State University and co-author of *Woman and Religion* and *Womanspirit Rising*. Plaskow uses the Judeo-Christian legend about Lilith as the basis for her theology in an article called, "The Coming of Lilith: Toward a Feminist Theology." [12]

The Lilith legend describes not Eve, but Lilith as the first

---

[11] Pagels, G.G.

[12] Judtith Plaskow, *The Coming of Lilith: Toward a Feminist Theology, Womanspirit Rising: A Feminist Reader in Religion*, ed. Carol P. Christ and Judith Plaskow, Harper and Row, San Francisco, CA, 1979, pp. 198-207.

woman and wife of Adam. However, because she was assertive and uppity God banished her from the Garden and created Eve. Adam told Eve all sorts of stories about Lilith as a demon, who threatened women in childbirth and stole children from their cradles in the middle of the night. Later, Eve caught a glimpse of Lilith and saw that she was not a demon, but a woman like herself. She stole over the garden wall to meet her, and eventually they became the closest of sisters. The legend ends with God and Adam fearing the return of the two women.

Plaskow uses this legend to convey that sisterhood is "an individual process of coming—to wholeness within community." [13] She, like Stone and Pagels, are radical in basing their theologies on sources other than tradition and scripture. By so doing, they are left with the haunting questions as to why their feminist sources never became popular. In any case they seek to find a place for them in their own works.

The *later* Mary Daly, author of *Beyond God the Father: Toward a Philosophy of Women's Liberation*, advanced the feminist theology must go farther than did her first book. [14] She asserted that the entire conceptual system of theology and ethics, developed under the conditions of patriarchy, must be destroyed, and transformed. The idea of God the Father and God the Noun must be superseded by the process notion of God as Being-Becoming and God as a Verb.

---

[13] Plaskow, WSR, p. 202.

[14] Mary Daly, *Beyond God the Father: Toward a Philosophy of Women's Liberation*, Beacon Press, Boston, MA, 1973.

The method that Daly employed had not previously been used by male theologians. It included what she called liberation, castration, and exorcism. She interpreted abortion, rape, genocide and war, and ecological devastation to be manifestations of sexist society. She advocated androgyny—the state of being both male and female, going beyond Jesus and the Church to Sisterhood and the Anti-Church.

Let us turn to the fourth category, which may be called the *revolutionary*. This group includes those feminist theologians who have gone beyond the reformist and radical and describe themselves as "post-Christian feminists" even witches. The base their theology on different sources of women's experience. They call for the immediate collapse of sexist society and the creation of a totally new structure. Carol P. Christ, Naomi R Goldenberg, Zsusanna E Budapest, and the contemporary Mary Daly are a part of this group.

Carol Christ, Professor of Religion at San Jose State University in California and co-editor of *Womanspirit Rising* and *Diving Deep and Surfacing: Women Writer's on Spiritual Quest* has taken up literary criticism as the primary means of affecting the theology. [15] For, she believes that women's literature—prose and poetry—best expresses women's life experience. She says that stories give shape to lives, providing orientation, meaning and sacrality. She adds: "In a very real sense there is No experience without stories." [16]

Christ maintains that women's literature possesses both a

---

[15] Carol P Christ, *Diving Deep and Surfacing: Women Writer's on Spiritual Quest.* Beacon Press, Boston, MA, 1980.

[16] Christ, *DDS*, p. 4.

spiritual and a social dimension. She says, I believe that women's spiritual and social quests are two dimensions of a single struggle and it is important for women to become aware of the ways in which spirituality can support and undergird women's quest for social equality ... Women's *social* quest concerns women's struggle to gain respect, equality and freedom in society—in work, in politics, and in relationships with women, men and children ... Women's *spiritual* quest concerns a woman's awakening to the depths of her soul and her position in the universe. [17]

In her book Christ discusses five different writers. The first is Kate Chopin, author of the novel *Awakening*; the second is Margaret Atwood, writer of *Surfacing*; another is Doris Lessing author of the five-volume set called *The Children of Violence*; Adrienne Rich, poet of *Diving into the Wreck* and *The Dream of a Common Language* is the fourth; and Ntozake Shange, playwright of *for colored girls who have considered suicide /when the rainbow is enuf*. It is Shange who writes, "I found god in myself/and I loved her/I loved her fiercely." [18]

Another revolutionary theologian is Naomi Goldenberg. She is professor at the University of Ottawa in Canada and author of *The Changing of the Gods: Feminism and the End of Traditional Religions*. Unlike Christ who uses women's literature as the basis of her work, Goldenberg utilizes dreams and fantasies. [19]

Goldenberg traces the death of God the father, but with a psy-

---

[17] Christ, *DDS*, p. 4.

[18] Ntozake Shange in *DDS*, p. 118.

[19] Naomi R. Goldenberg, *The Changing of the Gods: Feminism and the End of Traditional Religions*, Beacon Press, Boston, MA, 1978.

chological metaphor. She finds in the Goddess of witchcraft the fullest expression of feminist theology, which she spells with an "a." To Goldenberg witchcraft represents liberation, for in it there are female deities, no body/soul dualism, the evaluation of nature a cyclic notion of growth and decay, a spiraling notion of time, and the absence of a sacred text.

Another theologian who exemplifies the revolutionary typology is Zsusanna Budapest, founder of the Sisterhood of the Wicca (wise Woman) and High Priestess of *The* Susan B Anthony Coven Number 1, as well as author of the *Feminist Book of Lights and Shadows.*

Zsusanna Budapest is said to have chosen to name her coven after Anthony because of an anecdote she found. It relates how Anthony, when asked whether she planned to go to heaven or hell after she died, declared that she would go to neither place. Rather, she would keep militating right on earth until the women's movement succeeded!

Budapest's main contribution does not seem to be her scholarship about witches, goddesses or Amazons, but a ritual that she calls "A Self-Blessing Ritual." [20] She encourages all women to practice it. The ritual includes the following elements: an altar, some salt, wine and water, and a flower, white cloth, two white candles. According to the High Priestess it basically affirms the divine within the woman.

Finally, the contemporary Mary Daly, author of *Gyn/Ecology: The Metaethics of Radical Feminism* is a representative of the

---

[20] Zsusanna E. Budapest, *Self-Blessing Ritual: in WSR*, p. 269.

fourth category of revolutionary theologians. While her first book, *The Church and The Second Sex*, exemplifies a reformist theology and her second book, *Beyond God the Father*, expresses a radical theology her most recent work exceeds her previous positions.

She has left the Church for a feminist community, rejected God because she believes God can never be rid of masculine allusions, given up any serious consideration of androgyny because it is just too vague, and stopped using the term, homosexual, because it overpowers the possibility of lesbianism.

Daly summarizes, The Journey of this book, therefore, is ... for the Lesbian imagination in all Women. It is for the Hag/Crone/Spinster in every living woman. It is for each individual journey to decide/expand the scope of this imagination within her. It is she, and she alone, who can determine how far, and in what way, she will/can travel. She, and she alone, can discover the mystery of her own history, and find how it is interwoven with the lives of other women. [21]

Her book is cast in three passages, which she characterizes as exuberance when breaking through barriers, soberness when encountering enemies and earnestness when moving into new regions. She describes and cries out against: Indian suttee, the Hindu custom in which women throw themselves on the funeral pyres of their spouses and rulers; Chinese foot binding; African genital mutilation; European witch burning; and American gynecology including radical mastectomies and hysterectomies.

The form of Daly's theology—its language—is expressive of

[21] Mary Daly, *Gyn/Ecology: The Metaethics of Radical Feminism.* Beacon Press, Boston, MA, 1978, p. xiii.

her creativity. She makes up words, mixes pronouns, uses irregular capitalizations and breaks into incantations. She uses the word, spinster, which comes from the root for spinning; ecology which describes the complex interrelationships between organisms and their environments; hag which derives from the Greek word, "hagios," meaning holy; and crone when she discusses chronology.

Daly's theology has turned inwards, but she never gives up hope in the future.

In summary we have viewed a wide spectrum of feminist theologians. First, the reactionary and fundamentalist theologians who maintain that the church and society do not need to change very much; rather, we must learn to align ourselves with the patriarchal structure. Second, the reformist theologians such as Trible, Fiorenza and Ruether and the early Daly. They assert that we can work within the system by reforming traditions and scripture. Third, the radical theologians including Stone. Pagels, Plaskow and the later Daly. They advocate that we should look beyond what has been institutionalized to pre-scriptural and apocryphal sources. Fourth, the revolutionary theologians such as Christ, Goldenberg, Budapest, and the contemporary Daly, who have embraced women's literature, dreams, rituals, and experience. Fifth, the recalcitrant philosophers including some Marxists and existentialists who do not believe in a life of the spirit.

The three categories on which we have focused present us religious liberals with several options from which we can choose and appropriate in our lives. The diversity of the three categories provokes the fundamental question as to whether there actually is such a phenomenon as women's experience, that is, one body of common experience. It raises the question of what are the implications of women's experience for ethics and politics?

Another question which arises is, what about God? Gordon B Kaufman, Edward Mallinckrodt, Jr Professor of Divinity at Harvard stated in a recent issue *of The Harvard Divinity Bulletin* (January, 1980) that "the central task of theology is to analyze, criticize and interpret what is meant by "God," all other work being derivative from and logically secondary to "God talk." [22] What does this mean for radical and revolutionary feminist theologians for whom there is no place for God?

This leads us to the question, what is theology? Kauffman suggests that "theology must inevitably be radically constructive in character rather than descriptive or expository because all talk about God or the world or ultimate reality is grounded essentially in the mind's imaginative and constructive powers ... [23] Again what does this mean for feminist theology, which is both constructive and descriptive?

At last, what is the role of feminist theology in our liberal tradition? In the *Kairos* newspaper (Spring, 1979) Mary Daly speaks to the question of why she is *not* a Unitarian Universalist. [24] She says that she is not lured by the "seductiveness of liberalism." For, while it operates under the delusion of being liberated it is still haunted by patriarchal Images. She strongly admonishes against

---

[22] Gordon D Kauffman, *The Harvard Divinity Bulletin*, January 1980, Cambridge, MA, p. 7.

[23] Kauffman, *HDB*, p. 8.

[24] Mary Daly, *Why I Am Not a Unitarian Universalist*, Kairos, Spring, 1979, Brewster, MA, p. 7.

any form of tokenism, involving women. She proposes, "In the case of the Unitarian Universalist church ... it is conceivable that some women who have been in it for many years might want in some way to function on the boundary of that institution, without making it the primary source of their spiritual sustenance. [25]

The question remains, what about our families, churches, and society, including both women and men? Is feminist theology genuinely liberating? I believe that he diversity within feminist theology is its very strength. As Rosemary Radford Ruether asserted in her recent address, "Feminism and the Future of Religion," which she delivered at the Arlington Street Church in Boston:

I would regard all the feminist theological positions as having elements of truth. All respond to real needs of different constituencies of women (and men). It is unlikely that any of these views is likely to predominate but all will work as parallel trends in the ensuing decades to reshape the face of religion. [26]

This, too, I believe. Only the future will
answer the questions which linger.

---

[25] Daly, *Kairos*, p. 7.

[26] Rosemary Radford Ruether. *Feminism and the Future of Religion, Unitarian Universalist World,* March 1, 1980, Boston, MA, p. 4 .

Feminism, Religion, and Unitarian Universalism
An Immodest Proposal

E. Linnea Pearson

THIS IS A PAPER *IN EMBRYO* PRESENTED to a UUWF (Unitarian Universalist Women's Federation) workshop, Vancouver 1983. It is reproduced here at the request of the women who attended that workshop under the aegis of the UUA Women and Religion Committee. It is meant to be provocative, not definitive; the dictionary promoting a scholarly pronouncement; just another step in the process.

Our words both imprison and empower us; we are limited and liberated by our conceptualizations. We define ourselves with words, but often our vocabularies fail to enlarge at a rate commiserate with our experience and our personal and collective realities.

I have never liked the label "Feminism." On the one and, it connotes images of weakness; the dictionary tells us "feminine" means docile, meek, passive—and other qualities supposedly characteristic of females. On the other hand, in contemporary parlance, Feminist connotes images of wild-eyed bra-burners (although as far as I know, there were never more than two bras burned in both the U.S. and Canada.)

I don't like the term; yet it is, presently, all we have in in a language system controlled by images of male dominance—in which the male is the form.

So, as the Friends took upon themselves the title "Quaker," derisively given and decided to accept the label of shame, as a badge of honor. It seems women feminists and their male supporters have decided to accept and affirm he term Feminism—perhaps somewhat in the same manner that our forebear Margaret Fuller, decided to accept the universe! There are many branches on the tree of Feminist ideology. What I hope to present here is a working definition with which I think many Unitarian Universalist Feminists would agree.

Feminism is an approach to and means of experiencing religion available to men as well as women. Like Theism, Christianity, and Humanism, Feminism is both an ancient and modern form of religious experience. Because it affirms the so-called feminine values and modes as highly as the masculine in a culture that has negated, devalued, and denied them, because it questions the established power structures and mechanisms of dominance, because it is on the side of the poor, the oppressed, and the excluded. Feminism is iconoclastic, and thus well within our established UU tradition of iconoclasm.

Feminism is both an alternative to modes of religious thought and experience and an added dimension to the experience and expression of traditional religious modes. In many ways, Feminist theology is akin to process theology. In other ways, it is linked to liberation theology, black theology, and the theology of hope. At times it is reformist, at times radical, at times revolutionary.

Feminism may or may not be part of the theist, Christian, and Humanistic traditions. If it is part of the theistic tradition, it challenges the dogma of an omnipotent male *theos*. If it is within the Christian tradition, it is likely to question the theological implications of a gospel in which a male savior is surrounded by male disciples. If it is within the Humanist tradition, it questions the Humanist emphasis on Man as the measure of all things and reason as the process.

In many ways, Feminism acts as a corrective to the nineteenth-century religious emphasis on ever-expanding progress and control, social Darwinism, and spiritual rationalism. Like the Transcendentalism of Margaret Fuller, Ralph Waldo Emerson, and James Martineau, Feminism asserts the primacy of intuitional spiritual experience. The personal is the origin of the political.

Feminism questions the established modern hierarchies of persons and usage of high technology, the rape of nature, and massive overkill capacities and reasserts the value of the natural and the organic. After centuries of affirmation of the superiority of the male, it reaffirms the value and worth of children and women.

In a world beset by rapid technological innovations, unprecedented attacks in relation to all the earth's people suffocating from many forms of deadly fallout, nature's integrity, and increasing threats on the survival of all species, life comes as a gift of the Spirit, offering hope for the renewal and rebirth of valuing of the earth's irreplaceable regenerative powers. It reaffirms the nature of the human body, mind, and spirit in relation to the earth and even the cosmos from which the earth emerged. Feminism breathes new life into people suffering from the many forms of deadly fallout.

Whereas the ancient tribal circles of the fathers were exclusive, tribal circles of the mothers were inclusive. Feminism emphasizes the human family, encompassing all within the circle of love and protection.

Surely, if all those brave souls in our Unitarian and Universalist tradition who gave their lives for the integrity of their religious faith were alive and functioning creatively today, they would apprehend and applaud the Feminist religious vision.

Parallel Lines

Denise D. Tracy

IN 1957 BETTY FRIEDAN CONDUCTED A SURVEY of her Smith College alumnae asking about their life satisfaction. She found out that the roles of wife, mother and helpmate were unfulfilling and frustrating for many of her sister graduates. She wanted to write an article on what she discovered, but finding no interested publisher, she expanded her research into the ground-breaking book *The Feminine Mystique*. When it was published on Feb 19 in 1963 Friedan's book sent shock waves through women's lives. The idea that women might find marriage, raising children and keeping house less than ideal as life's most important purpose resonated throughout American women's lives. One million books sold immediately.

Questions of happiness and fulfillment were raised in homes, schools, and relationships—marital, filial and parental. One of the places where questions were raised was the church. In Unitarian

Universalism many churches had governing boards and congregational Presidents that were solely male. The women's sphere in many churches was filled by participation in the UU Women's Federation. Raising money through teas, rummage sales, educational endeavors etc. Women were highly valued for the sphere they did fill, but that sphere was lesser and unequal.

As women began entering theological schools for the purpose of ministry, women in the local congregations began rethinking their role in the church. Women began serving on congregational boards, as Church Presidents and filling roles in ever expanding leadership. As women entered the workplace, often the church women's group moved meetings to evenings or there were two groups, one in the daytime and one at nighttime. As the 21 District Women and Religion Committees were established and educational materials were developed, District conferences, congregational classes were held. Curriculum materials such as *Cakes for the Queen of Heaven* by Rev. Shirley Ranck and book discussion materials by Rev. Denise Tracy's Delphi Resources made expanding women's groups much easier.

In 1977, the same year that the Women and Religion Resolution was unanimously passed at the UUA General Assembly, the first woman was also elected to the position of Moderator of the UUA. From 1961 to 1977 two men had previously held this role. The Moderator of the UUA serves as the Chief Governance Officer of the UUA, presiding over the General Assembly, the Board of Trustees Meetings as well as Committee meetings. When Sandra Caron ran for and was elected Moderator of the UUA in 1977, she had served on the Metro New York District Board and the

UUA Board of Trustees. Her election signaled that Caron had become the highest woman in leadership in UUA history. Caron was a member of All Soul's Church in New York City, was a lawyer by profession. When elected she was the Assistant Transportation Commissioner for the State of New York Transportation Department. Her vision for UUA Moderator was not to just chair various continental meetings but to be Moderator full time and year-round. She requested a travel allowance—a first for the position.

Caron's vision was captured by the Pittsburgh Post Gazette. "Unitarian Universalists can talk freely about race, sex, and politics, but the spiritual and transcendental embarrasses them. We find people much more willing to be contemplative. There is more of a wedding of the rational and the aesthetic. It is a process of moving toward a wholistic religion." Caron brought intelligence and focus to the role of Moderator.

When Caron announced her intention to run for the Presidency of the UUA, she became the first woman to aim to be the head of any religion in America. The role of Moderator, which she had held, had always been filled by a lay person and a volunteer. The UUA Presidency was a paid position, which up until this time had been filled by an ordained Caucasian male minister—perhaps she stepped too far. The then UUA President, The Rev Eugene Pickett had been appointed by the UUA Board of Trustees after the death of elected President Rev Paul Carnes. Pickett publicly opposed Caron's candidacy. Caron lost the Presidency to Rev Bill Shultz by a 2 to 1 margin.

Many people say that Shultz was successful in his Presidential bid partly because he promised to promote Kay Montgomery to the position of Executive Vice President of the UUA. The VP is the second highest staff (paid) position in the UUA. Montgomery had moved from Atlanta, where she had been the Administrator of the Atlanta Church (UUCA) where Rev Gene Pickett had served. Picket invited Montgomery to join the Development and Fundraising Department of the UUA. When Shultz won the election, as promised, he promoted Montgomery to be the Executive Vice President. As both a female and a lay person, Montgomery expanded the influence of a feminist in a key leadership position. Kay had a warm and comfortable interpersonal style and tackled day to day administration with a calming presence enacting liberal religious values. She served as Executive VP for 30 years.

Overall, the UUA seemed comfortable with a lay woman as the elected Moderator of the UUA rather than as elected for the paid position of President. In 1985 Natalie Gulbranson was elected UUA Moderator to follow Moderator Sandy Caron. Gulbranson had a wide volunteer portfolio. For 23 years she had served as a member of the town meeting of Wellesley, MA. She was on the Wellesley School Committee and the Wellesley Human Relations Committee. She had worked with both the Girl Scouts and the League of Women Voters. She had served as President of both the UUWF and the International Association of Religious Freedom Boards. She was a member of the Partner Church Council which linked Transylvanian Unitarian churches to congregations in North America. She was a mother to five children and married to her husband who was a dentist. She was also a member of her church council in Wellesley, MA. She was smart and determined to follow in Caron's footsteps by leading every day of her term, not just on meeting days. She traveled across the country and across the globe representing liberal religion.

A favorite story about her travels: Bill and Linda Lu Shultz and Natalie and her husband, Melvin Gulbranson, were traveling to represent the UUA and to work to save Unitarian churches from being destroyed by the despotic leaders of Communism in Eastern Europe. Staying in a hotel, Natalie commented to her husband about how harsh the toilet paper was. In the Gulbranson's rooms from that point on in the tour, there was soft American toilet paper. (This confirmed that the rooms had been under audio surveillance.) Other travelers, when they heard of the change in toilet paper for the Gulbranson's, tried to vocally complain in their rooms at night. Alas only the Gulbranson's received such luxury.

Natalie Gulbranson served as Moderator until 1993, for two four-year terms. At the completion of these 8 years, she received an honorary Doctorate from Meadville Lombard and the UUA's distinguished service award.

Denise T. Davidoff was elected as Moderator in 1993. Denny was an advertising Executive who had served on the GA Planning Committee, the Ministerial Fellowship Committee, and on the Board of the Church of the Larger Fellowship. She preached at over 100 congregations and advocated for gender equity and anti-racism. Like Gulbranson before her, Davidoff had served as President of the Women's Federation. Like the two female UU Moderators before her, Davidoff broadened the position of Moderator to one of increased influence, including working for pay and benefits equity for both ministers and staff of congregations. She also mentored many future UU candidates for ministry. Her office also produced charts for pay based on local communities and church size, as she won the support of congregations. A ruling was passed that if staff did not have health benefits based on hours worked, then the minister would not be able to access that benefit from the UUA. When asked what she would like to see for the future of the UUA, Davidoff said, "I wish for a year in which the First Principle, affirming the inherent worth and dignity of every person, switches places with the last, affirming the interdependent web of existence of which we are a part."

As women expanded their roles as Moderator of the UUA and as Executive Vice President, it would still be 2017 before a woman, The Rev Susan Frederick-Grey, would be duly elected as President of the UUA. As women were increasing in numbers in ministry, the sphere they filled throughout the denomination was also expanding. The two lines of women leaders, lay and ordained, were moving forward, side by side and together.

Part Two
Our Stories

"This historic gathering would eventually help us settle down and feel greater rightfulness within our roles, greater competence, and authority than we had heretofore granted ourselves, and most importantly, increasing hope and joy in our work."
—FROM WOMEN OF THE CLOTH
BY CAROLYN OWEN-TOWLE

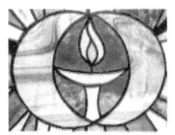

A UU Sisterhood/
WomanSpirit Rising

Denise D. Tracy

WHEN I ENTERED UNITARIAN UNIVERSALISM IN 1972, I felt I had discovered heaven on earth. In our denomination, I had found a faith where all religions were affirmed, a faith that was inclusive and non-creedal and a faith that married social justice with personal conscience. I felt that the world would be a better place if Unitarian Universalism was better known and was more predominant in the world at large. I was 22. I was naïve and innocent of the difficulties of moving and changing a group of people with an abundance of graduate degrees, upper middle-class status and an individualistic and independent streak that marked our faith from its very beginnings. Little did I know that pledging my allegiance to this denomination would be the most exciting and most frustrating journey of my lifetime.

When I started attending District and Denominational Minister's meetings, there were usually a few white-haired older women sitting together off to the side or to the back of whatever sanctuary or ballroom the meeting was being held in. It took me a few meetings before I realized that these women came to these meetings as much to see each other as to attend the meetings. They seldom spoke to the gathered group. After a few meetings, I asked who these women were. I was told they were women ministers from the pre-World War II era. I had read UU History. I knew of the early women of the late 19th century. I had never known of their heirs, this next group of women. I saw them for years and I never engaged them in conversation or asked them to tell me their stories.

It was not until Cynthia Tucker's book, *Prophetic Sisterhood* (Beacon Press, 1990) was published on the Iowa Sisterhood that I realized that I had missed an opportunity to discover the stories of women from an era in our ministry that must have been both challenging and profound. Why had I not cared enough to speak to them? Why had I not asked them to tell me what entering the ministry in the early 20th century was like? I think now that I am 73 and sit in the back of meeting rooms with my colleagues and friends, that when I was young, I was arrogant and thought I knew much more than I really did. My bravado covered up my insecurity. What if I had gotten off my high horse and walked across the room and asked these women to share the stories of their lives and how they chose to enter ministry? What if I had asked what it was like to raise children while carrying out the duties of professional ministry? What if I had asked what were their most difficult struggles and how did they deal with opposition to their chosen career? What if I had asked what were the sweetest gifts of your ministries?

What kept you working in these fields of liberal religion? What story would you like to tell me, that I have not asked you about?

Every month when the retired Minister's newsletter reaches me, I read the names of those who have died, and I know the women's names universally. I began to ask myself whose stories are we losing this time? What are the newer and younger ministers missing as the colleagues from my era pass from this world? I woke up one night and felt compelled not to miss another era of women in ministry stories. I wrote feminist ministers and lay leaders from the '70s and '80s. Would you write your story? I'd like to preserve both your learnings and struggles. Some were interested, some were not. A few said, I am no longer able. One person, wrote her story, revised it and two weeks after submission, died.

I do not think this volume is complete. Ideally every story could, perhaps even should, be told and preserved. These gathered stories are from a slice of time. These writings tell the stories of women Unitarian Universalists in the '70s and '80s. Not all were or are ordained. Feminism was the central issue in our faith during this time. The power of male dominated language and theology, a white male dominated denomination and congregations whose liberalism was tested by the growing presence of an increasing number of women's names on search committee lists and the prevalence of empowered women in our congregations.

There are many people who felt that once we had a hymnal with inclusive language, we had done enough on the issue of the empowerment of women in liberal religion. The reality is that empowerment is an unending human struggle. There are younger leaders now, who like me, are arrogant enough to think they know all they need to know about truth and change. They change traditions and exclude the voice of wisdom from the forbears living in their midst. It is my hope that these pages will present some of the gathered knowledge from those of us still present but sitting to the side of the meetings. Sojourner Truth once said, "I am sitting among you, waiting to tell you what time of night it is." Many who have gone before are still present. It is now that time of night.

Women of the Cloth

Carolyn Owen-Towle

IT ISN'T AS IF WOMEN HAVE NOT ALWAYS BEEN part of the story of our Association. Women are the ones who in the local parish have kept the fires burning, the meals coming, the halls dusted, the children taught and tended since time immemorial. Women married and took care of ministers. Women's role was to see that communities of faith survived and flourished. Historically, this has been women's place in virtually every religious tradition.

Women have been central to the history of our denomination and its precursors, Unitarians, and Universalists, for many years, but the 20th century saw UU women's ministry finally and rightfully come into its own.

As you know, the Universalists were the first denomination to accept women as fully ordained. Initially it was Olympia Brown, in 1863. One day, it is said, Olympia heard Antoinette Brown Blackwell, the first female mainstream Protestant minister, preach, and an inspiring sense of possibility swelled up within her. Blackwell, in her talk, proclaimed that women were needed in the pulpit as imperatively and for the same reason they were needed in the world—because they were women. Women would, she believed, become indispensable to the religious evolution of the human race. Antoinette Brown Blackwell had come from a family that staunchly believed that education was as important for a woman as for a man. She was a determined abolitionist and suffragette.

Olympia Brown had long since converted from fundamentalism to Universalism, and seminary, then and there, became her central goal. It is sobering to note, "The Unitarian School of Meadville, Pennsylvania, replied to her request for admission saying that "the trustees thought it would be too great an experiment to admit a woman." Oberlin replied that she could be admitted but could not participate in public exercises. Finally, Ebenezer Fisher, President of the Universalist Divinity School at St. Lawrence University, offered Brown admission. However, he added that he "did not think women were called to the ministry." "But" he continued, "I leave that between you and the Great Head of the Church." "This," Olympia thought, "was exactly where it should be left." "But when I arrived," she said, "I was told I had not been expected and that Mr. Fisher had said I would not come as he had written so discouragingly to me. I had supposed his discouragement was my encouragement." Entering divinity school in 1861, she completed her course of study in 1863. She had to then convince those opposed to women in the ministry that they could complete the required course of study as commendably as she had. And beyond that, she had to convince the Universalists to ordain her and allow her to be called to the parish ministry. The Unitarian Universalist Church in Racine Wisconsin, where she once served, has been renamed the Olympia Brown UU Church.

In 1871 the Unitarians ordained Celia Burleigh. Celia was another lifelong activist and reformer for women's and children's rights. All three of these ordained women successfully served congregations.

Beginning around 1880, not coincidentally, there became increasing demands for a more virile and manly ministry; claims that there was a "crisis of effeminacy" resulting in a "pantywaist ministry." Believe it or not, we UUs heard this same criticism, blessedly, without the "panty waist" reference, again in 1984, when the "tipping point" of 15% of UU ministers had become women, and concerns were heard that the profession of ministry was being unduly feminized.

The Unitarian Yearbook of 1893 listed 19 women ministers; at the same time the Universalists had ordained 27 women and licensed an additional 9 women as preachers. Skipping ahead to 1914, of the 640 Universalist ministers, 75 were women. These women ministers, as Cynthia Tucker's historical research pointed out, were called only to the small or shakier congregations that men refused to take. In 1900, Samuel Eliot, was elected the first President of the American Unitarian Association to be given executive power. He served in that capacity for 27 years. They say, "he defined his unprecedented ecclesiastical office with vision and engaged it with vigor." Eliot, incorporating many aspects of institutional authority, devised a plan for keeping women out of the pulpit by instead "helping" them to become "parish assistants." The Depression made finding a pulpit for a woman even more difficult. In the three decades of the 1930s, '40s, and '50s, only one Unitarian woman and nine female Universalists were ordained,

The merger in 1961 did little to raise the issue of women in the ministry, but soon, in 1963, there was, amidst other startling literature, the publication of Betty Friedan's *The Feminine Mystique*. Liberation was given a new radical meaning and women were finding the language that had been missing. They found that their religious traditions had not set them free. Many, although certainly not all of us reading this and other books, discovered that we were indeed feminists.

The '70s and '80s saw the Women's Movement light a flame of hope and aspiration heretofore unknown. Partly due to the Second Wave of feminism, an increasingly educated female population began envisioning new possibilities for our lives. Instinctively concerned with matters of the spirit and ultimate meaning, and eager to set a more inclusive place in religious life for women, growing numbers of us felt a call to the ministry. But theological education beyond college was not only impractical it was a familial and financial stretch. Nevertheless, in the 1970s and 1980s, Unitarian Universalist women began preparing for ministry and coming into our Association in growing numbers.

In May 1974, the UUWF published an overview of the problems that still blocked women's progress within our movement. There were 858 male ministers in Fellowship with the UUA, and 44 female ministers; 760 of those male ministers were serving congregations while just 5 of those women were parish ministers.

That same year at General Assembly in New York, female clergy took the radical step of gathering in the UU Women's Federation suite in the American Hotel at 5 p.m. on Friday, June 28th. This decision to meet and caucus separately from their male colleagues was radical. It fueled a kind of raw psychic energy that would not have abided in a co-ed environment. It foretold the beginning of the Ministerial Sisterhood, UU.

By consensus the gathered women agreed to organize as a group to give support, concern and encouragement to their ministerial sisters, limiting their members to women ordained in UU ministry, accredited women directors of religious education, and women theological students headed for professional work. The Rev. Marjorie Leaming, settled minister in Santa Paula, California, (and former graduate of Meadville), was the leading light in addressing her colleagues' needs.

Still a student preparing for ministry, I shall never forget that 1974 G.A. Gloria Steinem, leader of the feminist movement, journalist, and political activist, was present stirring everyone up. Mary Daly, radical lesbian feminist, philosopher, and author of *Beyond God the Father*, was there also creating an uproar. During the question period I squirmed, as did many others, I'm sure, when Daly allowed only women to speak. I heard several male harrumphs around the room. Daly's behavior was utterly foreign to both women and men. It raised quite a commotion and left me with feelings of uncertainty (I wasn't about to raise my hand), yet at the same time I felt a growing sense of my own evolving permission to authority as a woman ... as a minister to be.

Something was changing for professional women. No longer

willing to accept the *status quo* of sexist assumptions by male colleagues and lay leaders, to accept the stinging unconscious prejudice, and to accept our sense of marginalization, we sought full gender equality within Unitarian Universalist ministry. How this would be achieved was the elephant on the table. At first the Ministerial Sisterhood, MsUU, stumbled along often in confusion, ambivalence, and angst. The "sisterhood" carried with it envy and criticism as well as support and solidarity, both among women as well as men. The younger ministers, keenly aware of feminist theory, believed that political means were necessary to change the status quo within our movement. Yet the means to communicate and organize were incredibly limited. Initially, a simple newsletter served as the one and only means of recording herstory and connecting the new, loosely formed MsUU.

> Rev. Leaming wrote:
> "If we do nothing else as an organization, just by existing we give credibility to the idea of community as opposed to individualism. By being a member of MsUU, we declare our vulnerability, acknowledge our dependency needs, avail ourselves of an opportunity to be cared for and to care, grant that we are not omnipotent, and acknowledge that there is a greater good than ourselves."

From MsUU's inception, Leaming's hope, as well as that of all of its members, was that changes for the better would eventually signal no need for our separate organization to exist.

I, along with my colleague and mate Tom, was called to First Unitarian Church of San Diego in 1978, the year after the Women and Religion Resolution was passed at GA. I was ordained, and we were formally installed there at the end of that year. Rev. Leslie Westbrook, who had been newly appointed by President Paul Carnes as Minister to Women, took part in this service.

Co-ministry was a new and fairly untried form of ministry then. There were two co ministries on the east coast, each ½ time. Our Church was taking a leap of faith when they called this married couple. Both of us were called to full time ministries, and I was the first woman to serve in this 105-year-old congregation. In that year, 1978, The UUA Dept. of Ministry reported 63 women in Fellowship, only 32 settled in parish ministry, 26 full time with an average compensation of $14,593, and 6 part-time for an average of $6,773.

What I didn't know then was at what a propitious time I had begun this ministry. Our youngest child was 10. I was in my early forties. First Unitarian Church of San Diego was a large church, the first to which a woman had been, or would be called for nine more years. Tom and I shared our familial and ministerial responsibilities equally. Several of my contemporary colleagues were still at child-bearing ages and were thus limited in their mobility. I recall Diane Miller telling me how she stepped up to her pulpit one morning saying, "When you called me to fill this pulpit you did not fully know to what extent I would fill this pulpit. I am with child!" To make my point, I had more freedom to say yes to requests beyond our Church than did many of my younger ministerial sisters.

These circumstances eventuated in my growing leadership in the larger Movement, with UUSC, the UUMA, the Presidential run and more.

I recall a sermon I delivered, probably within the first year. It being painfully clear that the UUA's Principles of 1961, had failed to affirm women, with phrases such as "the dignity of man" I spoke about the meaning and significance of the use of inclusive language. How well I recall several parishioners approaching me in the line afterwards attempting to reassure me that this, of course, was a bogus issue. After all, we certainly knew that 'mankind' meant both women and men.

Instantly, I realized that speaking about inclusive language caused resistance. The way to go about it, I decided, was simply to use inclusive language and see that every printed word, every service, including lay involved services, managed to use language that embraced both sexes. After a while, I thought, people would *hear* the difference when they were not included. The aged, LGBTQ, children, people of color and those with special needs gradually came to sense their genuine place in the Church community.

Over time the internal workings of the larger Movement also took notice of the power differentials in policies. Gradually, one by one these were addressed. An example is the revised "Singing the Living Tradition," 1993, which eliminated sections titled "Man" and "Love and Human Brotherhood." As Rosemary Matson, UU feminist leader repeated many times over the years, "It is still a patriarchal pie. We do not want a piece of the pie. We want to change the recipe."

In 1978, it was recognized that with 40 or more women now

serving congregations we had reached a critical mass—enough to plan for a gathering. Grailville, Ohio was the chosen site. Revs. Denise Tracy, Marni Harmony, and others put together an agenda that held untold importance, I would say, almost *urgency*, to all of us who attended. We women clergy eagerly arrived literally starved for role models, colleagues, and answers to a myriad of theological and other questions surrounding our ministries.

So much expectation rode on that particular gathering. Keenly, I remember both the eagerness and anxiety I felt as we convened. This historic gathering would eventually help us settle down and feel greater rightfulness within our roles, greater competence, and authority than we had heretofore granted ourselves, and most importantly, increasing hope and joy in our work.

But the meeting did not proceed without tensions. A clergy mother with a nursing baby attended. Several times the baby cried during meetings. Because we women were in such almost desperate need, it was difficult to bear the interruptions. The mother, offended, was about to pack up and leave, and probably abandon her own ministry as well, when with tender, thoughtful intercession, the crisis was stilled. The conference leaders found and paid for a sitter to assist mother, child, and attendees. Soothing understanding won the day and the conference ended with a communion of mother's milk.

During that time, from 1979 to 1981, I was the third President of MsUU. As noted earlier, the one connection that linked together our members was the newsletter that came out but twice a year. And GA was the only time we would gather in meeting; those clergywomen, that is, who could afford to attend. In the display area of the G.A., MsUU annually rented a table on which women clergy were invited to place photographs, copies of articles and sermons they'd written. I thought the effect was rather barren and lacking in imagination. And so it was during my tenure that the tablecloth project was born, literally out of whole cloth. Stitching together two pieces of fabric, I fashioned a tablecloth to cover the MsUU table at General Assembly.

This evolved into a piece of folk art not important simply for its loveliness or the significant fact that it was created by both female clergy and laity. The tablecloth became a tangible object that represents a period of stunning growth in the evolution of women's ministry in Unitarian Universalism during the years from roughly 1980 to 2005. The names represented are not exhaustive. Signed by those who came in contact with the cloth, primarily at General Assemblies (GAs), the signatures represent an estimated one quarter of those who served our Association during that epoch of time.

The fame and notoriety of Judy Chicago's magnificent artwork, the "Dinner Party," created in 1979, was reverberating throughout the country with its bold ceramic dinner plates glorifying 39 mythical and historically famous women and their sexuality. Set on magnificent hand-embroidered place settings, the work included over 1,000 names of women scattered on porcelain floor tiles in the center of the three-sided work. Part of the artwork's magic was the venerating of women's craft and domestic art as opposed to the more culturally valued, male-dominated fine arts. This stunning work is on permanent exhibition at the Brooklyn Museum in New York.

I hoped, less ambitiously than Chicago's work, to set marking pens out on the bare off-white cloth and invite ordained women to sign it, using "*Rev.*" before their name. The beginning of the tablecloth was modest yet significant, for as recently as 1973, there had been just four female ministers in pulpits. Seven years later we had grown substantially in numbers, and women comprised something approaching 50% of theological students in UU seminaries.

The first 15 or so names did not look as I had anticipated. The pens didn't write well on the textured fabric, and the result appeared rough and ragged. Disappointedly, I evaluated it as having been a good experiment and might have tucked it away in a drawer to be forgotten had Rev. Marjorie Leaming not said, "No, keep it and *embroider* the names."

What an idea! I returned to San Diego and invited those in our church, who might teach me, including men, to come to my home for an evening of embroidering. On that occasion a core of what would ultimately grow to 29 women embroiderers was born. The tales we told on that first and subsequent nights regarding nostalgically remembered sewing circles, and the delight we shared regaling one another with family stories made the enterprise evolve into an ongoing project of work and love.

Each year as ministers signed the tablecloth at GA, I brought it back to San Diego where women gathered and embroidered ministers' names. If an embroiderer pricked her finger, she simply devised a flower to cover the reddened spot. One minister, misunderstanding the cloth's intent wrote a message in ink before her name. Having no way to erase it, San Diegan women creatively devised a decorative flower garden to cover the errant words.

After several years it was decided that some kind of border de-sign would enhance the aesthetic dimension of the cloth. I invited my sister clergy to send me bits of lace from their grandmothers' and mothers' lace boxes. A Celtic border was designed, drawn, and damask was sewn in strips, and appliqued in place, incorporating the lace. This was all designed and effected by a very creative wom-an in First Church. Fondly, she nicknamed the work the "Hagrag." More years went by, and many more names were added.

The cloth took on a life and "herstory" of its own. It concerned me that while we were making visible and relatively immortal the names of female clergy, the women whose blood and time were being given to the project remained anonymous. In 1987, we gathered to find a way to add the embroiderers' names to the tablecloth. We decided that their autographs would be stitched in a floss color close to that of the cloth along the Celtic border. Across one end we embroidered:

"WROUGHT WITH LOVE BY THE WOMEN OF FIRST
UNITARIAN CHURCH FROM 1980 FORWARD."

At a 1988 MsUU conference in Santa Barbara, women created worship incorporating the tablecloth, which now included 136 names. A time was made during which ministers remembered and called out the names of their sisters who were not with us. It was both thrilling and revealing that the calling went on for minutes. At that point 20% of UU ministers were women. We sat around the cloth spread on a carpet in a lovely chapel and made sacred its meaning in our lives.

When we at First UU Church of San Diego ordained our women interns, a signing of the tablecloth became part of their ordination. In 2000, the tablecloth hung for several months in an exhibition of UU women's history, at the UUA headquarters in Boston, where more signatures were added. In 2005, at a Pacific Southwest District meeting some final signatures were penned and attending women, and at last, a man or two embroidered names. Rev. Byrd Tetzlaff generously took the tablecloth home, completed the embroidery, had it cleaned, and returned it to me.

A number of religious meanings are learned from this cloth. The most powerful lesson, perhaps, is the recognition of the love and respect that laywomen have shown their sisters in ministry. Countless hours of careful stitches have transformed this simple fabric into a sincere statement of prayerful regard. Each year the same women, as well as one or two newcomers, came forward, needles and floss in hand to participate. No more than a few embroiderers considered giving up on the project until the cloth was clearly filling up and, coincidentally, I was concluding my ministry.

I believe the tablecloth sends a message from sister to sister that we appreciate one another and that our leaders in faith are worthy of recognition. It is notable that this is not stone, but cloth—a typically women's creative tablet. A feminine art, as ancient as time, has been employed to create a supple monument. Its vivid, motley hues remind us that we need not be pretentious; we are precious in our most homespun ways. The traditional time-consuming act of embroidery contrasts with our ever more technological lives. I suspect that a laurel to herald women today would be in another medium.

Ministering to ministers' is represented in this work. As female clergy care for their parishioners, their own partners, and children, one can imagine their asking, from time to time, "Who ministers to ministers?" The cloth symbolizes the interdependence of ministry as in all life and reminds us that receiving is as blessed as giving. It bears witness to the steady, persevering progress of women within our Unitarian Universalist journey—women who have at bedrock understood that they had the will, the right, and the responsibility to give back to life through ministry. There are a total of 259 clergy and 29 lay women's names on the tablecloth. The tablecloth is per-

manently displayed at Meadville/Lombard Theological School, a Unitarian Universalist anchor in the middle of the country (Chicago) where many women have matriculated over the years and continue to prepare for ministry.

Carolyn Owen-Towle
with Denise Tracy

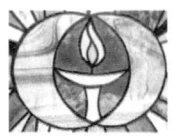

Carolyn McDade
in Her Own Words

Marian L. Shatto

Note: Ecofeminist singer-songwriter Carolyn McDade, best known among UUs for her beloved song "Spirit of Life," spent more than four decades writing music to accompany and support her work of organizing activist women (and some men) around justice issues. Realizing that the "movement songs" of the nineteen sixties and early seventies did not include a woman's experience, she set out to fill that gap. With expanding attention to social and international concerns, she grounded anti-war, anti-racist, and Central America solidarity activism in a clear feminist perspective. The sampling provided in this article begins with her story of how "Spirit of Life" came to be. It then moves through fifteen years of her "singing the soul of the liberation struggle" with four examples illustrating in prose and lyric her gifts of vivid image and fierce commitment to justice, equality, and community.

Spirit of Life

"a song, not written, but prayed into being."
©1981 Surtsey Publishing

I wanted to share with you just a bit about creativity in my life, especially around this prayer that we sing together sometimes. It was a time that was very tumultuous, very active, a great deal of social movement. The times are so thrilling when ordinary people get so activated about what is important. Then we take to the streets, go to the jails. We are in demonstrations, and it was a time of that nature—always writing letters, sitting-in on legislators' floors, doing this and that and the other. It was a rich, marvelous time in my life.

I was in the Boston area, very active in the movements of that time. I was leaving some late-night meeting, of which there were more than enough, with a friend. We went to my car and got in, and rode through the streets of Boston, driving along until we came to her community. Now this is an old friend and we shared much. In fact, she was the one that organized Gold Star Mothers for Amnesty; her name is Pat Simon.

I pulled over to the curb, and as she was getting out, I said, "Pat, I'm so dry. I just feel as if I'm like cardboard that sat in a dry attic for many, many years. And if someone came along and opened a window or door, and the air moved through, I'd turn to dust." And I sat there. She reached over, put her hand on mine, and we just sat. We had both been in that place before. You just come to a place that is dry. You don't know if you can go on. We sat until she squeezed my hand, opened the door, and got out.

So, I went right on through the wet streets of the night until I came to my neighborhood, which was completely dark. I parked my car. I went into the dark house, without turning a light on, and I made my way to the piano. If I don't know how I feel about something, I usually find out if I sing. I sat at the piano, my three daughters asleep upstairs, and I just let myself crumble inside. I sat there with my hands on the keys and waited. What I wanted more than anything in the world—and I was very clear about that—I wanted to remain faithful—faithful to all the movements of people who are willing to take the piece of clay of their lives and put it into forming something for the whole.

It takes a lot of love to give oneself to creating a world that is good for everyone. None of us quite makes it, but this movement of people—the long uprising of love—has been moving through us as humanity for a long time. We come in and take our place within it, do what we can, and then pass it on, let it be picked up by those who come after us. In that moment I was just crying out to something bigger and larger than myself. We don't always get ourselves through it totally alone; we know that. And somehow or another I began to sing, and this is the prayer that I sang, right there. It wasn't composed; it wasn't written; it was sung into being. The next day I wrote it down, and it made its way in the world. I do know that in telling this story I simply contribute my story to the many stories that are in this room and in other places where people sing together.

—excerpted from a talk by Carolyn McDade at
First Unitarian Church of Salt Lake City, March 1, 2015

Spirit of Life, come unto me.

Sing in my heart all the stirrings of compassion.

Blow in the wind, rise in the sea;

Move in the hand, giving life the shape of justice.

Roots hold me close; wings set me free;

Spirit of Life, come to me, come to me.

Reflection on Feminist Culture

As feminists we are creating new culture. I doubt that we come to culture at this time to tell us who we are, so much as to participate in our becoming. This is the deeper meaning of our cultural and spiritual work, where tradition and integrity, heritage and accountability, the formed and the innovative, converse. Here our skills of analysis insist that we see without delusion what is working and what is not; who and what benefit, who and what hurt, where life is called forth and where it is denied or closed down. An understanding of oppression is a part of envisioning beyond it. As one committed to creating new culture, I offer what I trust. Beyond that I hope a song goes into the world with these powers:

~ that it be useful to discernment

~ that it be open and strong, inviting a depth of diverse reflection

~ that it travel well through different shades of light

~ that it not be pretentious, but that it be willing to risk into usefulness

~ that it be willing to fail

~ that it not deny another her or his voice

~ that it serve what matters
~ that it be worthy of life
—written for the newsletter "Leaven Notes"

We Might Come in a-Fighting
©1973 Hyannis Music

Well, they say if you're livin' in a man's world, there's got to be
    a boss.
Someone a-giving orders, or it'll end in a total loss;
Yet we know just from living that all folks got stuff for giving,
And those hard lines of authority we are bound to step across.

There somehow is this feeling we've got to work from nine to
    five,
'Cause that's what makes a person worthy to be alive;
Yet most of what they're doin' is bringing the world to ruin,
Let's speed up on the living and slow down on the drive.

    Chorus: Well, we might come in a-fighting
    'cause there's lots that needs a-righting,
    we've learned a lot from living
    never taught to us in schools.
    If they say come in like a man,
    well they must not understand,
    when we enter in the game
    we're gonna change the god-damned rules.

Well, I want it on the record that I think that something's
　　wrong,
When some folks live in mansions, yet the poor work just as
　　long;
Well, we're here a-realizing that there's lots of equalizing
Due in this world and we will help to move it on.

Well, they say there's nothing more worthy than caring for our
　　young,
Yet after we bear and raise them they will tell us one by one;
Well, you can't come in expecting all the things a man is getting
'Cause a-looking at your record, there's nothing you have done.

Now what is more important in the life of anyone,
Talking with some friends or all the memos you have run
That are knee-deep you know where the forest used to grow—
Now the making of more garbage just ain't worth a-being done.

Now we're here for to tell you—gonna say it out so strong—
We want work worthy of doing and some time to call our own.
They may think we'll sweetly smile and be glad to wait awhile,
Won't be no feminine bargaining—that day has come and
　　gone.

Reflection on Community

Singing requires authentic community. To be a group of people
is not enough. We need to know why we come together, how far

down we must dig to come upon a common bedrock from which our lives are raised. We need to know how we differ, and value this difference. This will mean understanding conflict as well as consensus. This will mean leaning into the meaning of honest exchange, being willing to look at the ways we cause suffering and oppression in others' lives and to let this change our own. If our singing is true, it will lead us into confrontation with entrenched and unjust power.

—from the "Sister, Carry On" songbook introduction
©1992 Carolyn McDade

Call to Women
©1980 Surtsey Publishing

Our fury will melt all the weapons down
Our hands will bend ev'ry gun
We answer no bound'ry, no proud waving flag.
We stand o'er the earth as one.
Our tears are like healing rains on the land;
Love's fury is in our cry.
No more will we let them profane our earth
or send our young to die.

Chorus: Women of the earth
Arise in ev'ry land
and end their cruel and deadly wars.
'Tis with the tree of life we stand.

We stand as sisters unto the earth
her forests of living green,
The cypress and ginkgo, the oak and the pine,
the millions unnamed, unseen.
Our blood's in the seas pulsing on ev'ry shore.
The wind bears our word and our song,
So tender our step on this green growing earth
that carries life on and on.

We're firm as the mountains, as free as the wind,
as wild as the forest of old.
The rights of each generation to come
unite us with spirits bold.
So fierce is our love of this life that we share
these wars then must wither and cease.
Replaced by a justice for one and for all,
created by living peace.

Reflection on Creation

Our essence is to create—not as mindless vessels of another's energy, but out of our capacities to see what is around us, how all are affected, the interplay of personalities and participations. We discern clearly what hurts and what engenders health, what is diminished and what is brought to flourishing, what gives life and what deforms the ingenuity of our creativity, what affirms life and what is an affront to it. Each and every woman has her way to do this. Finding and enabling these capacities together is recognition that to keep creating social forms that have no genesis in the deeper meaning and energies of Life is to continue the possibility/probability of violence, delusion, oppression, annihilation. It is in deepening the resourcefulness within the integrity of our existence that we can create a human community committed to the well-being of the whole.

—from the "Sister, Carry On" songbook introduction
©1992 Carolyn McDade

Song of Woman
©1982 Surtsey Publishing

I come rising out of the sea
bare in a white moon shining.
I come down from far ancient hills
on the breath of a mustang foaling.
I come like fire when mountains are born,
my roots in earth still throbbing.
I come now and I'll never return
to the living death of silence.

I come now reclaiming my home
a panther among my people,
Dark from night in a rising sun
born from the depths of freedom.
A spark of light spit from the fire,
shivering at my power,

I come now and I'll never return
to the prison of denial.

I am born of women who've died,
daughter of their struggle.
I come now, my mother's child
like a serpent born of water.
I come reclaiming my womb,
tearing flags from my body.
I come now and I'll never return
to the bonds of intimate slav'ry.

I come with a thousand eyes
that see beyond forever.
I am born of raging skies
and today can never hold me.
O'er this earth with arm held high
I call my name Resistance.
I come now and I'll never return
to the great and cruel delusion.

I come a mother of wild,
my wings around my daughters,
Filling my lungs to blow from our lives
the words that do betray us.
I come now to gather the guns
and melt them deep in the mountain.

I am born of woman's pure rage
and I'll never return to collusion.

I come now releasing the wind
back to the winged bird flying.
I come now returning the fields
to the proud hands of the hungry.
I come now giving the seas
to the fish who live in the water.
I come now bearing the green
for I am earth's proud standing daughter.
I come now opening halls
to the voices of the silenced.
I come now revising the laws
to heave the breath of justice.
I come now like fire on the hills.
I come to birth a new vision.
I come now and I'll never return
for I come to stay forever.

Compassion Piece
©1987 Surtsey Publishing

A song of love and compassion, calling us to **leave the master's house** (all places of domination). Be we ones who benefit from the imbalance, or those oppressed by it, we are called to come together to prepare the field for **a harvest sown in justice, fresh with wonder;** to liberate love between and among us.

Within this vision, someone asks a woman about compassion. She ponders, responding, **ask me tomorrow**. Rather than answer too quickly, she prefers to wait and watch how she and others live. Her answer will come from this observation. She names four attributes of compassionate living for which she will look. It becomes clear, for her the personal will be within a collective act. When she has completed naming the four, she questions the one who has queried her. What is the staying power, the courage and vision of compassion as lived, its capacity to defy that which demeans, and its capacity to nurture hope? The song ends with the unexpected slant of her question: **Oh, will you come and let me go with you?**

The images within the song can be traced to a month lived with a revolutionary family on the outskirts of Estelí, Nicaragua. The year 1986 was a time of intense US supported contra activity. A truckload of us spent a weekend clearing stones from a field to be planted for food by people displaced by the war. We realized that to clear stones for a harvest by those long denied just access to their land was subversive of our government's policies. This song owes its beginnings to the widespread revolutionary energy, imagination, and resilience within a people fervent with plans and hopes for their country.

—introduction of song from "My Heart Is Moved"

©2007 Carolyn McDade

Love's firmest ground lies beneath the fragile
Within the vuln'rable She shouts her deepest prayer.
Love's firmest ground lies beneath the fragile
Within the vuln'rable God shouts Her deepest prayer

that we walk naked, naked with open arms
among the people who leave the master's house.
Our love to grow strong clearing away the stones
for a harvest sown in justice, fresh with wonder.
The powerful shall bend to the furrows.
The humble shall lift their own grain,
and we, earth's people, embrace without shame
desiring the golden field for all earth's people.

You ask me of compassion, ask me tomorrow.
Did we rise up unready and leave the master's house
with people robbed of the fields?
You ask me of compassion, ask me tomorrow.
Did we take but one loaf among us and seeds for planting more,
wrapped so loosely in coats of equal thread?
You ask me of compassion, ask me tomorrow.
Did we clear away stones when to clear away stones
was an act of subversion,
when to refuse not to love was to break some law?
You ask me of compassion, ask me tomorrow.
Did we answer God's prayer for rain,
passing buckets from the river hand to hand to hand to hand?
Did we answer Her prayer for rain,
passing buckets from the river hand to hand to hand to hand?
I ask you—will compassion
walk past shadows, deep and many miles long
shouting defiance and hope?
walk past shadows, deep and many miles long

shouting defiance and hope?
Oh, walk past shadows, deep and many miles long
shouting defiance and hope,
defiance and hope,
defiance and hope.
Oh, will you come and let me go with you?

Reflection on Singing

May we be fully present in our singing, and through song experience a deeper communion with ourselves, one another, and the wondrous creation of which we are intimately a part—that we may see, name, analyze, and transform the unjust structures—social, political, economic, ecclesiastic—which mount such massive human and planetary suffering in our time—that we may create a web of human relationships—compassionate, limber, mutual, just, and unadorned—that, after us, our children and our children's children and the young of all life's generations shall flourish together to sing their songs of faith, joy, and praise.

—from "Songs for Congregational Singing"
©1991 Carolyn McDade

What's a Fellow to Say?
One Man Recalls Women Gradually
Populating Our Ministry

Gordon Gibson

WHEN I ENTERED SEMINARY IN 1961 at Tufts University's Crane Theological School there was one woman in our class of ten. She left after one year. Another woman entered when her husband became a faculty member. She too did not finish and graduate. There were a few male dropouts, but almost all of the male students stayed and graduated in three years.

From 1964 to 1969 I served the small Theodore Parker Unitarian Church in the West Roxbury neighborhood of Boston. With that location I was, of course, in close proximity to the "heart" of Unitarian Universalism. Did I have female colleagues? I don't recall any female colleagues at meetings of GBAUUM (Greater Boston Area Unitarian Universalist Ministers). Looking at old UUA Directories from that era women I now think of as pioneers—Janet Bowering and Edna Bruner, for example—were not yet in settled ministries or were in UUA RE positions.

During this era, I was part of the Greenfield Group, a venerable ministerial study group, which met twice a year at the Senexet House retreat center. Membership standards had loosened a bit and a couple of laymen in UUA staff positions, Royal Cloyd, and Ed Darling, were members of the group. A few of us in a category probably thought of as "promising young men" had also been admitted to membership. Along about 1967 someone suggested the Rev. Dorothy Tilden Spoerl as someone to be invited to the next meeting as a prospective member. There was much harrumphing by a few of the older members with voiced concerns about whether she would be "comfortable" and whether the facilities would provide appropriate privacy. She was invited, a membership invitation was extended, and she accepted. Thus, was added to the Greenfield Group a member with an earned doctorate.

I have a vague memory from about this same time of a continental UUMA gathering at which there was a woman listed on the program as a speaker—possibly once again Dorothy Spoerl. There were some overheard mutterings about whether she was even qualified to be there, especially in a speaking role. I think someone said something like, "She's just a religious educator," thus denigrating the religious educators, who were indeed mostly women, and who were a significant source of innovative thoughts and practices in the UUA and our congregations. The mutterings were quieted with the assurance that the speaker was indeed a fellowshipped and ordained minister with some years of experience. But the mutterings probably reflected an assumption and strong feeling that she *shouldn't* be there because there must have been a more qualified and deserving man.

These early years after Universalist and Unitarian consolidation were years when it was hellishly difficult for women to gain admission to our ministry. And once admitted there was palpable bias that impinged their career path.

From 1969 through 1984 I was in Jackson, Mississippi in a variety of roles. These were interesting times in an area coping with rapid change, not all of it welcomed. Early in that time I can point to a female colleague serving as called parish minister. The Rev. Vi Kochendoerfer was serving the Unitarian Church of Tallahassee in Florida after settlements in Provincetown, Massachusetts, and Calgary, Canada. She and I were among those colleagues invited to an annual fall retreat hosted by the Rev. Charles McGehee at his summer home in Mentone, Alabama. Those retreats were opportunities for deep sharing with colleagues, and I recall neither unease nor special treatment for Vi or any other participant.

Later in my Jackson years the UUMA chapter became more energized, especially as The Mountain Camp and Conference Center became its regular meeting place. Christine Robinson and Kate Rohde were among the women active in those years, but they were a small minority in the chapter membership. And I have since heard that they had to fend off sexual advances from male colleagues.

I remember a particularly good chapter program presented by Joyce Smith, then overseeing the UUA Ministry office; Joyce referenced the work of Carol Gilligan and prompted us to think about the significant extent to which proclaimed "human" thought patterns were overwhelmingly "male" and often were based on studies of all-male study sample.

I remember with some delight that the local clergy group in Jackson evolved to include in its meetings some of the nuns in Jackson, women who were not treated within their own church tradition as ministers. There was also an informal local interfaith group meeting on an as-needed basis. We, women, and men, were all engaged in forms of social action and needed each other's mutual support.

The Jackson years also afforded me some personal growth opportunities. Early in our time there Judy Gibson, my wife, was asked to host a feminist consciousness-raising group, probably the first in Mississippi. (The rationale for the request was that of all the women in the group Judy had the largest family room and so could best provide a private meeting place.) I was not privy to the group's conversations of course, but I did hear from Judy about tactical concerns such as, "We've been invited to speak to a group that is wondering 'what you women want anyway' and are debating whether to wear dresses or pant suits." I have to believe that such "how do I dress to minimize pushback and griping" is still an issue for women much more than men.

Late in our Jackson years I had the opportunity to spend four and a half years as the primary house spouse. Judy had landed a decent-paying job and that made it possible for me to flee soul-deadening work with a federal agency and focus on two part-time ministries, tending the house, and looking after our daughters. This role-reversal provoked growth for both Judy and me. I commend it as a learning opportunity for any couple.

It was in our last months in Jackson that I made the discovery that will probably be my little footnote in history if I even have one. In an ante-bellum mansion in Natchez, Mississippi I discovered that the personal letter books of Judith Sargent Murray, long thought to have been lost, were still extant. Judith was the first American to publish an argument for the dignity and rights of women, a 1790 essay, "On the Equality of the Sexes." She was also, in her second marriage, the second wife of the Rev. John Murray.

When I moved to Elkhart, Indiana, in 1985, I was in official terms following the Rev. Bob Dick. The reality was that the Elkhart congregation had been served by a team that they referred to as "Bob-and-Helen." Helen Hersey Dick was the daughter of a Universalist minister and had taken some seminary courses along with Bob. She was never ordained but was an integral part of Bob's ministry. When Springfield, Vermont later named Bob as Minister Emeritus they also recognized Helen as Minister Emerita.

While serving in Elkhart I initially found a UUMA chapter in which there were long-serving male colleagues who created a distinct "good ole boy" vibe. Due to some strong female colleagues this vibe was notably diminished in the next few years. There were still some interesting events, such as when the Catholic retreat center at which the chapter was meeting jumped to the conclusion Ruth Gibson must be my wife, rather than a colleague, and assigned us to be roommates.

One of the felt and sometimes voiced worries of male colleagues as we began having to share professional space and status with female colleagues was whether the presence of women would force us to censor our language. Sexist verbiage indeed needed to disappear as it should have even with no women present. Salty language still was in use when appropriate. I remember a late-night conversation at a chapter meeting when there was a movement afoot to move UUA headquarters out of Boston, perhaps to Indianapolis. Someone wondered what university in that area could possibly have the Unitarian Universalist connections to take the place of Harvard in the neighborhood of Boston. I suggested that Ball State University in Muncie bore the name of the Ball family, good Universalists. Immediately a female colleague objected, "That's not a gender-inclusive name. It would have to be renamed 'Ball and Boob State University.'" And in the Ohio River Group, a midwestern ministerial study group, it was a female member who added to our study session on the topic of sex her well-written soft-core porn short story.

Over the years from my 1964 call to the West Roxbury ministry to my 2005 retirement from Elkhart I experienced a movement from a combative, hierarchical profession toward a more collaborative and egalitarian community of colleagues. We are stronger for including not just women but also those others who were effectively and sometimes actively excluded in 1964: gay, lesbian, trans, and BIPOC people. But I think it is the women who deserve pre-eminent recognition for their role in forcing the door open and introducing some fresh thinking.

But the arc is longer than that. Longer, and more frustrating

Judith Sargent Murray (at that point Judith Sargent Stevens) in her first letter to John Murray on November 14, 1774, posed a question in theology. Over the years of their correspondence, both before and after they were married, theology and issues of church organization were often subjects of Judith's letters to John. Judith published her catechism, an aid to parents in the religious and moral upbringing of children, in 1782, earlier than any publication by John. After his long illness and death, she completed John's *Autobiography* to firmly establish the idea of his role as THE founding figure of American Universalism.

Two centuries later we had the ministry of Bob-and-Helen Dick. Again, the man held the title and got the credit, but the labor was shared.

Yes, we now have one woman succeeding another as UUA President. One of our two underfunded seminaries has a woman as President. Yes, as a man I am now in the male minority in our ministry. We have, mostly in our lifetimes, nudged that arc farther from grotesque injustice and closer to equity. But doesn't it still wobble noticeably?

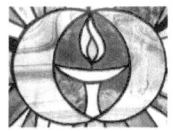

A Feminist Pagan View

Shirley Ranck

AS THE AUTHOR OF *CAKES FOR THE QUEEN OF HEAVEN*, I am delighted to contribute my story to this collection of Unitarian Universalist experiences with both ancient and present-day paganism. For me when I was a middle-aged woman a few decades ago, pagan traditions were closely connected to my growing feminism. Here is some of my personal story.

Today I am a feminist, humanist, pagan Unitarian Universalist. I enjoy our diversity and our increasing acceptance of a variety of theological positions.

I went to work at 17 as a typist at the New York Stock Exchange and obtained my first two years of college by attending a free junior college (Jersey City Junior College) at night. I got married at 19 and commuted to Montclair State Teachers College in New Jersey to complete my undergraduate degree. I worked summers and commuted to school part time for most of my higher education. One of the results of that path is that it enabled me to feel connected to people from all walks of life.

The four most important events in my life in those years were the births of my four children—two sons and two daughters. I always had at least a part time life outside the home (mostly as a student or a typist) but the children were my "necessary angel," the reality that grounded me even as I wrote and published my intellectual efforts.

I began to be fascinated with the subject matter of religion when in high school I read some of the works of Harry Emerson Fosdick. He made a deep impression on me. Religions and gods change, I learned, and they reflect the limited understandings of the people who generate them. These learnings were of enormous help to me later as I began to look with feminist eyes at the place of women in most religions.

The few women in seminary at Drew Theological Seminary with me in the nineteen-fifties were expected to go into religious education. I tried it but did not like it, so I became a psychologist instead. It did not occur to me to become a parish minister until I became a Unitarian Universalist in the nineteen seventies. What excited me most was the wide range of possibilities for creative worship, and the underlying commitment to growth and change.

The impact of feminism caused me to begin a process of growth and change within myself, and as a psychologist working with others one-on-one. I saw the Unitarian Universalist ministry as an opportunity to grow and to interact more creatively with many people. I brought with me a wealth of psychological training and experience. I found a continental community with which I could identify and within which I could grow into leadership.

I believe that the most exciting and central quality of the Unitarian Universalist movement is our freedom to grow and change, not only personally as individuals, but theologically as a religious community. This freedom is the power which informs and sustains our inclusiveness and our respect for all sorts and conditions of human beings. This freedom enlivens our worship by drawing upon the experience and wisdom of many traditions. This freedom calls us to respect each other's life journeys. For me as a woman such freedom means that my experience as a woman is respected, and that my community of faith is free to honor the insights of ancient goddess religion as well as those aspects of patriarchal traditions which we find inspiring. I decided to study further at Starr King School for the Ministry in Berkeley, CA.

As I was packing before leaving New Jersey to study at Starr King, I discovered an old notebook of mine from the nineteen-fifties, with pages I had written to discuss with my therapist—the pages I had never shown him. I considered them too crazy or confused to show to anyone, pages I had hidden away in the attic. I sat there in 1976 with tears streaming down my face, tears of astonishment at the feminist document I held in my hands; tears of grief that I had not been able to recognize and trust my insights when I first wrote them down.

While studying at Starr King School for the Ministry in the seventies I met Chris Bailey who also became a Unitarian Universalist minister. We had long discussions, at a nearby coffee shop, about the very ancient cultures which worshipped the divine as female. I took an archeology course at UC Berkeley to learn more. The scholars said it was believed in many cultures back then that a great goddess created everything and brought life into the world. Only later was a male god added and later still the goddess was often deleted from the godhead.

In 1980 when I was serving as minister at Northern Hills Fellowship in Cincinnati, I received a phone call from Rev. Leslie Westbrook who was working at the Unitarian Universalist office in Boston. She wanted to know if I would be interested in creating a new UU curriculum on pagan religion and its relationship to Unitarian Universalism. I was delighted to be asked. We started doing the research right away. The result ultimately was a colorful kit containing not only lesson plans but visual aids and three relevant books. We named it, *Cakes for the Queen of Heaven.*

A very special moment for me in the early *Cakes* years was the outdoor worship gathering led by pagan author Starhawk in the Midwest. I had been mostly an indoor urban person. Starhawk made me think back to my early teen years when I lived just a few blocks from the Atlantic Ocean in Ocean Grove, New Jersey. I rode the ocean waves into shore by day and in the evening stood on the boardwalk and watched the moon rise over the water. At Starhawk's gathering all those years later, I realized that the ocean and the moon were for me deep connections to the natural world. I also realized that the ancient pagan traditions were important to our relationship with nature as well as with feminism.

Cakes was finally published in 1986 after considerable controversy as to whether pagan traditions should even be included among our UU resources. The word "pagan" was still often meant to be very negative in those days. One instance of my personal experience with that negativity about paganism happened when I was invited to speak at First Unitarian Church in Cincinnati. I gave them a sermon title that contained the word "witchcraft."

The title appeared in very small print on the religion page of the local newspaper. About two-thirds of the way through the service a group of about a dozen people got up and left. An usher told me later that the group told him they had come to disrupt the service whenever we worshipped the devil. They got tired of waiting. The incident made me think more carefully about sermon titles, especially when they appear in the newspaper.

The big surprise for all of us who had worked on creating *Cakes for the Queen of Heaven* was the immense popularity of the course as more and more congregations and women's groups ordered the curriculum.

For me *Cakes* became the reason I was honored with awards from the UU Women's Federation (the Feminist Theology Award in 1994 and the Ministry to Women Award in 2006) as well as the Covenant of Unitarian Universalist Pagans Fuller-Thoreau Award in 1989. For a quiet little girl whose mother was always urging her to "Speak up!" these awards were amazing and deeply appreciated.

New Wave Feminism and the Parish Ministry

Joy Atkinson

I WAS 23 YEARS OLD, AND ALREADY A FEMINIST when I entered seminary, having had my eyes opened at Hunter College in New York City, where I studied English Literature, music, and teaching. I was bound, I believed, for teaching High School English. I completed my Masters in English and Teacher Education in 1970, picked up my teaching certification, and instead, made an about-face and headed off to California to attend Thomas Starr King School for the ministry. I had been attracted to the school and its individualized, progressive approach to education, and my friend Mitch Howard had gone to Starr King the year before, so I had a sense of what it was like to be a student there.

Mitch wrote letters to me in his first year at Starr King, conveying his excitement about the school. I was infected with his enthusiasm and decided to apply. I was not sure yet that I wanted to be a parish minister, but I did want to attend that innovative school. At the time I applied, there were no women students at the school, and there had only been three other students who were women since the school had begun in 1941 as Thomas Starr King School for the Ministry. (The school had an earlier incarnation as Pacific Unitarian School for Ministry. In those earlier days, a tiny trickle of women attended, and they were often encouraged to train as parish assistants, doing pastoral work, rather than as parish ministers. (Ref. Catherine F. Hitching, Unitarian, and Universalist Women Ministers, 1975.)

The entering class of 1970, a large one for those years, consisted of nineteen students—sixteen men and three women. The following year, we had a total of five women students at the school. In my third year, there were eight of us, and after that, women began coming in greater numbers. Years later, in the mid-1980s, when I was on the Starr King Board and a member of the Admissions Committee, I remember there being some concern that we were getting too few male applicants!

In the fall of 1970, at my first All School Meeting at Starr King—a regular gathering involving students, faculty, and staff—my friend Mitch, with his feminist ire up, stood up and introduced me as "Sister Atkinson." He emphatically told the gathered students, administrators, and faculty that we, Mitch and I, had some serious complaints. He passed the floor to me and I was a bit taken aback. I might have introduced the subject a bit less stridently, but I knew I had to broach it, so I talked about my experience applying to be a student. At the time, the school catalogue, impressive and innovative as it was in many respects, consistently referred to students as males. There was no acknowledgment that a woman might be a student. A feminist friend whom I had asked to write a reference for me reported that she was angered by the reference form, which also presumed that the applicant was male. One question on the reference form, for instance, said something like "Will his wife support him in his work at Starr King?" So, in 1970, seven years after Betty Friedan wrote the seminal book The Feminine Mystique, that helped launch the new wave of American feminism, Starr King, progressive as it was, had some cultural catching up to do!

After I aired my complaint about the catalogue and reference forms, Rosemary Matson, then an administrator at Starr King who was responsible for putting the catalogue together, recruited me to look over and edit the next catalogue and other documents, to clear out any sexist language and presumptions. Years later, she reported to me that this event was the start of her own feminist awakening. Rosemary went on to become a leading voice of feminism within Unitarian Universalism.

While I was a student, I felt generally accepted as a potential parish minister by students and faculty, although a couple of male students admitted to me years later that they were wary of my feminism and tended to avoid me. This surprised me, since after the All School Meeting where I mentioned the sexist language in the catalogue, I did not find it necessary to take frequent feminist stances within the school environment. I encountered more prejudice when I began to do some work in local churches. For instance, the senior minister in a church where I was interning told a couple that he couldn't perform their wedding, but he had an intern who he suggested could be authorized to do so. They were interested, but when he assured them that "she will do a good job," they backed away. They just could not envision a female officiant! The senior minister, who accepted me readily, was surprised by the couple's reaction.

I was graduated from Starr King in the spring of 1974 and attended the graduation ceremony in the fall of that year, which was customary in those days at Starr King. Each graduating student was given three minutes to address the attendees. I was the only woman in that graduating class and was the first woman to graduate from the School in six years. I mentioned that fact in my brief address, projecting a great change coming in our ministry as more women would emerge from seminaries. Later, friends told me that there was rumbling among some in the audience, with people audibly questioning why I would even mention such an irrelevant fact! "Why is she talking about that right now?" a friend overheard someone remark with annoyance.

My early years in ministry were full of events that brought home to me how unusual an undertaking it was for me to be in parish ministry. Some of the events were positive: People sometimes sought me out when looking for a minister to marry them, because, they said, they wanted the warmth they believed a woman could bring to their ceremony. I was also sought after by reporters and interviewers seeking to write articles and get me onto radio and TV programs featuring such a rare phenomenon as a women parish minister. I saw it as a way to promote the idea of women ministers, and a chance to garner some publicity for the congregation. Once, when I arrived in a new town to begin a ministry, I called the church page editor of the local paper and suggested that the paper might want an article about the new minister of the Unitarian Universalist congregation. The church page editor said that they didn't routinely do that when a new parish minister came to town, and asked "Is there something especially interesting or unusual about him?" I replied, "Well, you're talking to her." "Oh," she exclaimed, "that IS interesting! We will send out a reporter and a photographer."

Despite these positive experiences, I also faced prejudice because of my gender among parishioners, the public and even some colleagues. When I was the candidate for minister of the Duluth, Minnesota Unitarian Universalist Church in 1974, I was informed that one man rose up during the vote to call me and posed the question "What if she gets married and moves away?" Others, thankfully, pointed out that such a question would never be raised if I were a male candidate. When I candidated for the Unitarian Universalist Church of Davis, California in 1976, I was told that during the discussion on the vote to call, a woman rose and stated bluntly, "I don't want a woman as our minister! I want a father figure, not a mother figure!" When in 1987 I became the candidate for the San Mateo, California congregation, the one I served the longest, there was still some resistance to calling a woman, not much spoken out loud, by then, but voiced in written comments on the congregational questionnaire. One man did comment, I was told, that I shouldn't be pursuing ministry now but should stay home and take care of my children. I had one five-year-old at the time, and learned I was pregnant with another child on the very day I was asked to be the candidate! The Search Committee, when I told them of my condition, was very supportive. Sadly, between being asked to candidate and the beginning of Candidating Week, I miscarried, but I was grateful to the congregation members who were overwhelmingly supportive of the idea of taking on their first woman minister, and a pregnant one at that!

I served all these congregations happily, and many more as an interim parish minister, for a total of 41 years. I was aware, especially in my early days of ministry, that some parishioners were skeptical that a woman could serve them well and competently. When that prejudice was obvious or explicitly stated, I took it as a challenge, and worked to win them over. I only very occasionally talked in sermons about women's equality, sexism or ancient goddesses, but when I did, or even when I just carefully avoided sexist language like, for instance, saying "humankind" instead of "mankind," I would get feedback saying that I was "too feminist." I found that some people were quite touchy about the subject of feminism, and with it "all that stuff" about the Goddess, when that subject was popular among some feminist Unitarian Universalists. I was not part of the "Goddess movement" within Unitarian Universalism, but I did understand, and had also felt myself, that finding new symbols of the Divine to replace the pervasive, entrenched patriarchal images, was spiritually empowering for many women.

In 1980, I was part of an affirmative action project funded by the UUA and spearheaded by the Rev. Leslie Westbrook, Minister for Women and Religion at the UUA, to consult with ministerial search committees on behalf of women in our pulpits. Several of us women parish ministers were trained and then met with search committees around the country to raise awareness about women in ministry, and to urge them to consider seriously, and not automatically reject, women ministerial candidates on their recommended lists from the UUA. There were still few women ministers on those lists at the time, but I believe that our work helped to make members of search committees more open to seriously considering women as their candidates. Going in to talk with these search committees was eye-opening for us, as we encountered outright prejudice against women in parish ministry and, often, a lack of awareness that women were even interested in serving as parish ministers.

The number of women in Unitarian Universalist parish ministry changed rapidly in the years after I left Starr King and entered ministry myself. I used to say that I was looking forward to the day when I was not such a rarity, such a news item in every new church and community where I came to serve. I longed for the day when women parish ministers, finally, were commonplace. That day came to pass much sooner than I had imagined, as more and more women became parish ministers, and congregations began to accept them more fully. This was happening in other denominations as well, although a bit more slowly in most.

It was an interesting, challenging and ultimately rewarding journey for many of us who were beginning to enter and change the face of Unitarian Universalist parish ministry in the 1970s. By 1978, there were enough of us to hold a conference just for women parish ministers. The conference, organized by the Revs. Denise Tracy and Marni Harmony took place at Grailville Center in Loveland, Ohio, where twenty-nine women parish ministers gathered to share our stories, laugh and cry, and celebrate together. We enjoyed the special camaraderie of being with others who were treading this new ground. Like the "Iowa Sisterhood" of the late nineteenth century—a small, mutually-supportive group of Unitarian women ministers who founded and served congregations in the Midwest—we felt a special bond with one another that strengthened our resolve. It was reassuring to be with others who were also doing the sometimes exhausting, lonely and painful work of breaking down surprisingly persistent barriers against women in our pulpits. I feel blessed to have had the opportunity to be a part of this new wave, and deeply grateful to those few but determined pioneering women who went before us.

My Crazy Quilt Ministry

Nancy Doughty

IN 1962 FEMINISM WAS NOT ON THE TONGUES of women because Betty Friedan's book The Feminine Mystic was several months from being published.

I did not consider myself a trailblazer as I entered theological school at St. Lawrence University in 1958 where I studied under Dr. Angus MacLean. When I entered my intention was to study for one year for the Certification in Religious Education, but it was Dr. MacLean who recommended I enter the 3- year program for ministry which I did, my only concern being how was I going to pay for it.

Growing up in a small Universalist Church in Ohio I knew of or had met Universalist women ministers and heard stories from my mother of a woman being minister of the Eldorado Church in 1914 when it raised money and constructed the church I knew as my religious home. The Universalist Church was diagonally across the street from my home. From as early as I can remember I, along with my twin sister, regularly attended Sunday School classes (as they were named then) followed by church with our parents.

No woman served my Universalist Church during my childhood and youth. However, a woman Universalist minister had performed the marriage ceremony for my parents. My mother was active in the Ohio Universalist Convention, becoming the first woman president of the Board, and later member of the Universalist Church of American Board at the time of consolidation.

During my youth I attended Universalist week-long summer institutes meeting women and men leaders, many of whom were ministers. I remember meeting Dr. Dorothy Spoerl and Rev. Edna Brunner as well as Alice Harrison. It was Alice Harrison who invited me into Universalist youth leadership. During my college years I was on the Board as secretary of the national Liberal Religious Youth, where I experienced both women and men equally taking leadership. Attending continental LRY conventions for several years was where I was stretched in my religious searching by yes, mostly men, James Luther Adams, and John Hayworth, but women, too, in my growth. It was Frank Gentile, then minister at the Eldorado Church, who during my early collage years, encouraged me in religious work. In my consideration of ministry, I had been inspired, encouraged, and supported by men as well as women, so it did not occur to me that ministry was not an option for women. From early on I saw my ministry as educator, leading small groups in religious education, not behind the pulpit.

I began my ministry as Minister of Education at First Unitarian Universalist Church in August 1962 where Tracy M. Pullman served as Senior Minister. Although I was not fellowshipped at the time, he insisted I be ordained soon after I arrived. He always introduced me as his associate. I attended Board meetings along with him as well as occasionally preached.

UU minister's meetings, which included colleagues in the greater Detroit, occurred monthly. I attended these gatherings regularly and discovered most conversation to be centered around parish ministry topics. Since I was the only woman and engaged in religious education, not parish ministry, I listened more than contributed. On too many occasions there was teasing between some male colleagues that felt negative. There also was a sense of competitiveness as I listened to colleagues speak about (brag about) Sunday church attendance, a great sermon, or other programs. But there was comradery among colleagues too and social occasions during the year when partners were included.

It was the custom that area ministers "exchange pulpits" during the year. After about four years one colleague asked me to "exchange pulpits" with him which surprised me having no conventional pulpit to exchange. He said he would conduct the two worship services for children and youth I did each Sunday, so we agreed. Frank Gentile, my mentor, who was now minister in a Detroit suburban UU Church, commented to me that my colleague was doing penance by offering to exchange pulpits. I was puzzled by his remark. He explained that prior to my coming to First Unitarian Universalist Church of Detroit in 1962, there had been a discussion among "these male" colleagues about whether I should be invited to the minister's monthly meetings. It was he and Tracy Pullman who advocated for my being included. So, the invitation to exchange pulpits was evidence I had been accepted! Even though there were doubters, detractors, and critics of women early in my ministry I found support from men too. At some point I was even elected president of the MI UUMA chapter.

It was when I attended Ministry Days at General Assembly that I realized how much I was in the minority as a woman minister. There was only a springling of women in the assembled group. Mostly women, who were a generation older than I was. I usually sought out Alice Harrison, who had been an inspiration and supporter of me over decades, or classmates from theological school to sit with. I have no recollection of women being presenters or in leadership within the UU Ministers Association during these years.

During my years at 1st UU Church I discovered my continuing education was with the Liberal Religious Education Directors Association members and at the yearly conference they sponsored. It was with these talented women that I was inspired and with whom I shared success and disappointments. They were working in churches with programs similar to mine, many with years of experience and a variety of "formal" education courses. But they did not have certification as Minister of Education. It was in 1970 that the Scoville Report recommended to the UUA General Assembly a Minister of Religious Education category be established, but it was another nine years before the General Assembly voted to do so. Finally, women who had ministered to children, youth and families for years were recognized for our critical work within Unitarian Universalism.

I was not the only woman serving a UU congregation in Michigan in the early 1960s. Ruth Smith was serving the UU Church of East Liberty as minister at that time. She rarely attended monthly collegial meetings because of distance and the fact that she was not fellowshipped. Her colleagues, especially Tracy Pullman and Frank Gentile, insisted she be ordained by the UU Church of East Liberty. So, there were two of us women serving in Michigan UU congregations until Denise Tracy arrived at the Church of Greater Lansing in 1976. She was to be slowly followed by other women during the 1980s.

As women read The Feminine Mystic and Friedan's ideas spread among women about having a fulfilling life beyond house-wife and mother, I found myself moving against the tide. After being single and active as minister for several years, I married in late 1966, finding myself with an instant family of 4 daughters and a husband. The demands of ministry and marriage-mother were too overwhelming, so I resigned as Minister of Education in 1967. However, I did not give up attending monthly minister's meetings or the occasional wedding and memorial service when called upon.

Although I was not a regular attender of General Assembly meetings for the next several years, I was aware that change was taking place within Unitarian Universalism as I learned that res-olutions had been passed in 1970 urging congregations to recruit and call both women and men to ministry.

When I gave the UUMA 25 year in ministry sermon in 1987 I described my ministry as like a patch work quilt. Meaning I picked up pieces of ministry that were available in the Detroit area using them to create my unique pattern.

One "quilt" piece I picked up about 1975 was Extension Minister in Michigan. I traveled around the state weekends to small Fellowships, meeting with leadership on Saturday and conducting worship Sunday morning. The "religious" homes varied from a college chemistry lab to rented room, to a more permanent church building. I discovered I usually had to furnish the music, if there was to be any, with a tape deck, as well as bring a chalice. I had overnight home hospitality, which was the custom, as a way to conserve $$. Over these several years I began to appreciate what those "galloping ministers" of the 1850s were faced with. There were a few larger fellowships I visited regularly over 4-5 years who had religious education programs and solely depended upon lay leadership for Sunday programs and an occasional visiting UU minister.

My goal for these groups was to prepare them for employing professional leadership, i.e., a minister. I did not know it then, but it would be women who were called to be ministers in three of these fellowships. During the 1980s with the first wave of women in our ministry, it frequently was long time fellowships, now ready for professional leadership, who called women as their first minister. Not surprisingly, these women were taking their first professional positions with congregations that provided the most basic or usually volunteer religious education leadership and administrative support. Not only was it a challenge for women to have chosen ministry, become educated and credentialed, but once they were called by a congregation, the challenge continued with low pay and marginal support.

As I look back on my years of weekend ministry, I realize I

never thought about checking with Bob, my husband, how things were going at home with our 5+ year old daughter. I had completely shed my wife-mother role and was 100% minister!

I picked up another "quilt" piece again in 1980 when I took the part-time position of religious education at the Grosse Pointe Unitarian Church. I discovered there was no worship time for children and youth in the RE program, so I worked to establish a family service for children and parents prior to the usual Sunday Service and religious education classes. Support from church leaders for such a change was mixed, but there was encouragement from parents for the worship service. But my position ended after only 1½ years because I requested more compensation than the congregation would pay.

A new "quilt" piece was soon incorporated into my ministry. Through Dorothy Spoerl's influence, who was teaching a religious education seminar at Meadville Lombard, I was approached by M-L about 1980 to teach a religious education class for a Spring semester. For several weeks I flew to Midway Airport from Detroit, found my way to M-L on public transportation, taught a morning and afternoon class arriving back home for a late dinner. It was an exhilarating and exhausting time. Only because of cooperation and support from my husband and now our 10-year-old daughter, was this possible.

This was a stimulating, affirming and challenging time for me. With material from colleagues, I had to design the class as well as teach it. The class was for students studying for parish ministry who needed a basic understanding of RE philosophy as well as familiarity with RE curriculum. I think about 1/3 of the class were women intending to be parish ministers which was exciting! I took seriously the possibility of giving them any knowledge for their future ministry. I assigned students to examine and evaluate RE curriculum, to write a memorial service for a child who died, to develop a 3-year outline for their first ministry in a church with no RE director. Was there a difference of how women and men in the class handled the assignments? It was too small of a group of students to make a definitive conclusion. It seemed all the women did take the class seriously while some men in the class treated it as "fluff" compared to other classes there were taking. Unfortunately, M-L did not continue this one semester RE curriculum for their students, but condensed a RE component into a few sessions, which I taught one additional year. I did follow the careers of the M-L women over the decades, a few of which were called to significant churches.

An unexpected "quilt" piece arrived in 1982 when I was appointed by the Department of Settlement Office as the Settlement representative to the Michigan District. This quasi- volunteer position required three visits to churches seeking professional ministry, all to be arranged by me with church leaders. Yearly there was a gathering of all Settlement reps in Boston for update and sharing of concerns. The group of about 26 reps was overwhelming male when I began my eight years as Settlement Rep. I remember I was the only women clergy with one other laywoman in the group. By this time women were on lists for settlement although not in great numbers. The focus was on opening placement for gay men in our ministry. There was a Settlement Handbook provided to each congregation outlining the process for settlement. At this time the list of minister's names given to a Search Committee was controlled by the UUA Settlement Director. Settlement Reps were merely the conveyers of information and advisors to Search Committees about process, checking candidate references and answering questions. But I also urged Search Committees to request more candidate names if they were not happy with those provided.

In 1983 I was elected by the joint Ohio Valley and Michigan Districts to the UUA Board of Trustees. Sandra Caron was moderator, the first woman breaking into high elected leadership within the UUA in 1977. An active UU and lawyer from New York City, I had watched Sandy execute her Moderator role flawlessly at General Assembly. As I joined the Board for the first time I was intimated with the talent around the table. As I remember Judith Walker-Riggs and I were the only clergy women on the Board which was made up of several male colleagues and probably a balance of women-men laypeople. As a "newbie" I was mystified about the power dynamics within this group of at least 26. The longer serving trustees held the most influence, which in many cases was based on long-time working relationships or friendship.

At the first Board meeting I remember going into Executive session with newly employed Beacon Press editor, Wendy Jerome, to be informed about the precarious state of Beacon Press's financial situation. Only a few years earlier, the Board had seriously considered not continuing funding the Press. Over the next 8 years, it was Wendy's report to the Board, which was the most anticipated and celebrated as she shared future plans for the Press. Under her leadership Beacon Press was re-established as a viable small publishing operation, because of her selection of books to publish and her financial knowledge of the complicated book publishing world.

The Board and administration continued to wrestle with issues of discrimination of women for several years. When in 1984 Mary Andress-Overly was hired for the Department of Social Responsibility, but only part-time, it was women who protested loud enough for a change to full time employment. It was finally in 1987 that a Task Force was appointed to carry out a Sexism Audit. Once the report was issued, a Sexism Advisory Committee was established to implement the audit report because clearly there was work to be done!

In 1987 I was appointed as a Board member to the Ministerial Fellowship Committee. These were years when more and more women appeared before the MFC, some young, but most second career or experienced laywomen. Members of the MFC struggled to revise criteria for credentialing women. African-American colleague William Jones was a member of the MFC then. It was he who lead us (and the Board of Trustees too) in workshops about oppression, educating us how old assumptions had to change if more women, gays, lesbians, and black people were to feel comfortable and welcomed into leadership. Today I think of Bill as the wiseman of Biblical stature imploring us to change.

With more women entering our ministry, some women began to discover parish ministry was not for them and/or was difficult to be called. Of course, there were women, like me, who because of a spouse's employment were not free to move geographically. So, women created paths of our own of community ministry in a variety of ways and places. Some ways of serving were in conjunction with established churches. Others found working with non-profit organizations in the community avenues of carrying forth ministry.

When the first sexual abuse charge against a male colleague was lodged with the MFC by two women in his congregation, the MFC realized there was no established protocol for addressing this serious issue. Under the leadership of David Pohl, Director of the Department of Ministry, and the lay chairmanship of the MFC, Burton Johnson, a UU woman lawyer was employed to advise and guide the MFC on a path of action. After two MFC members interviewed the two women and the male colleague was charged, their report was conveyed to the MFC. The charged clergy, along with his support colleague, was interviewed by the MFC. Deliberation after the interview was thoughtful and difficult because MFC members realized the far-reaching effect their decision would carry. It was the decision to remove the charged colleague from UU fellowship.

The outpouring of reaction from colleagues about the MFC decision was intense. Women were relieved that finally a loud and clear statement had been made that sexual harassment and/or abuse was not acceptable behavior from UU clergy. Many long-time male ministers were outraged about the decision to remove a prominent colleague from fellowship. Some male ministers were angry with their female colleagues.

Members of the MFC and particularly Director Pohl received sharp and unexpected criticism for this decision which highlighted the power, the imbalance of power ministers have in relation to the laity, particularly women laity. But there was also support from men and women within the ranks for the decision.

As my term on the UUA Board ended in 1991, I remember then the journey for greater inclusion of women employed by the UUA and in other appointed leadership positions had begun, abet slowly. Natalie Gulbrandsen followed Sandy Caron as elected Moderator. The Hymn Book Commission included women and blacks, the Women and Religion Committee became more active, and more women entered UU ministry. However, there was a blemish and set-back when an African-American woman was dismissed as UUA Director of Social Responsibility in 1989.

The final "quilt" piece of my ministry was half-time ministry to a UU suburban congregation, now Beacon, then called Emerson Church, beginning in 1989. Although I did not preach each Sunday, I was responsible for conducting the worship service. The children were in the early part of the service for the chalice lighting, so I wrote a short unison affirmation for everyone to speak believing children should be included in rituals. I also changed the title of the "Children's Story" to "Message for All Ages" because religious values, expounded in story or message, appropriate for the young, I believe are applicable for adults. Since parents are the first religious educators of values to their children, I wanted to lift up this obvious, but unspoken role.

After all the years of "quilt" ministry, my years at Emerson Church were my first parish settlement. For the first time I began establishing files and collecting material for inspiration and sermons. I now understood what I had heard colleagues speak about years before, having many files in their offices crammed with paper resources, with stacks of paper clippings waiting to be filed. How different ministry was before technology was developed.

I retired from Emerson UU Church in December 1995, although I continued to serve a few more years in a second appointment as a Settlement Representative in the MI District.

Young, Female and Ordained

The Early 1970s, and Beyond, for One
Woman in the UU Ministry

Barbara Merritt

IN 1975, AS ONE OF THE FIRST YOUNG WOMEN to finish seminary at the age of 25, my survival and good fortune in the UU Ministry was made possible because I entered the profession fully identifying as a feminist. The Women's Movement at that time had already confirmed my identity as a whole person, worthy of dignity and respect. I never saw myself as a victim of prejudice or patriarchal institutions. To do so would have been to give my power over to others to diminish and dismiss me. That was not an option. I was too stubborn, too determined, and too convinced that women are fully capable of serving as clergy in our Association. Those of us in this first wave of 20th century women clergy were not to be defeated or deterred by the old guard.

Before sharing a few brief vignettes of the particular kind of challenges and opposition I encountered, it is important to put this journey in context. Then, women in the ministry were pioneers and trailblazers. Entering this traditionally male field meant we had to make our way through the wilderness. There were no roads, hardly any paths. Sometimes the wilderness was beautiful and welcoming. Other times it was tooth and claw, crossing a desert where "no woman had gone before."

My career of 35 years in the parish ministry would not have been achievable were it not for all the extraordinary support I received along the way. Mentors (both ordained and lay) took the trouble to befriend and counsel me. There were wonderful colleagues, and groups of women, like the Reverend Mothers, who cheered each other on. There were congregations (Hayward, CA., Shaker Heights, OH, Woodstock, IL. and Worcester, MA). Hayward took the risk to let me do an interim/internship. Shaker Heights gave me a scholarship. Woodstock and Worcester chose me to serve as their senior minister. The gracious welcome of parishioners, the constant support and encouragement from family and friends (especially my husband), gave me the foundation and the courage to get through the rough terrain. Add to the list of people who made this calling possible, all the spiritual teachers and poets and writers from every spiritual tradition, who assured me that even when things were occasionally difficult and discouraging, I could flourish and move forward.

The path into and through parish ministry was not smooth or easy for me. Here are a few brief incidents that insulted, horrified, and startled me along the way. (In retrospect, some of these stories are outrageous, laughable, and thankfully, unthinkable in today's more liberated era. Regrettably, some 50 years later, some of these memories are still surprisingly painful to recall.)

1970: At the UUA General Assembly in Seattle Washington (when I was still an undergraduate), I spoke with a seminary professor about the then, all male graduating class at Starr King. When I asked, "Can women enter our ministry?" he replied. "No. If you went into a bar and someone asked your profession, how could you explain that you were clergy?" (I decided on the spot that there were no significant barriers.)

1974: After receiving high marks from the Fellowship Committee, I was told afterwards, by three senior ministers on the committee, that I had only achieved such accolades because "I had the best legs."

1975: A young male colleague at the Minneapolis General Assembly (perhaps channeling Stokely Carmichael?) said, "The only place for women ministers in our movement, is on their backs."

1975: In the search process, a UU District Executive, told me that I had no right to refuse a congregation's interest in me as a candidate. If I didn't accept their call (no matter how inappropriate the church might be for me) then I was clearly not interested in becoming a minister.

1977: A member of my new parish, a grand-dame and extremely influential leader in the church, announced that having a woman minister didn't necessarily mean I was good at the job. "Like a dog on a bicycle," she said, "it is just surprising that she can do it at all."

1980: After only 5 years in the parish ministry, at the age of 30, I was asked if I would consider becoming President of the UU Minister's Association. Looking around me at the far more qualified and experienced ministers in my district, it was apparent to me that I was only be asked to be "window dressing" ... a token woman. I declined.

1983: When I was pre-candidating for the Worcester Church, I was called by one of the senior executives at the UUA in Boston, and in his office I was asked to withdraw my name because he thought I was "too emotional, too sensitive, and too young" to be an effective minister in a large and historic church. (read: too female)

1983: After being called to Worcester, a colleague I did not know in the Boston Chapter of the UUMA, stood up at a meeting and announced the "outrageous news" from Worcester, that I was pregnant, and that this automatically disqualified me from serving my parish.

1983: As part of an interfaith delegation to the Roman Catholic Bishop's installation, I was asked to process with other clergy. The starting point for our procession was on the other side of a large hall where 600 priests were robing, all dressed in white. I was dressed in black, and 8 months pregnant. While the image is one of stark contrast, at the time it was not funny at all. It was a terrifying and solitary walk across that hall.

2001: After 9/11, a group of interfaith clergy was invited to speak at Clark University as part of a panel. (As per usual, I was the only woman.) Afterwards, we were all lined up, and an Imam went down the line to shake everyone's hand. (At that moment I was flanked on either side by an Episcopalian priest and a Rabbi, both close friends.) The Imam withdrew his hand quickly when he approached me. In his Islamic tradition he couldn't touch a woman, because she was inherently unclean, i.e. she might be menstruating. Neither of my colleagues objected to my public, and embarrassing treatment. The Imam, at least, came up later to say that he "hoped that I wasn't offended." I explained to him that yes, I was quite offended. At the time I was in conversation with a black woman Clark professor, and I asked them both if they would have been offended if someone from another tradition would not shake any black or brown or Muslim hands. Both conceded that this would not be OK.

2005: In the receiving line after Sunday services, a stranger came through the line and said, "You are an abomination. Women should never be in the pulpit." He was an evangelical, fundamentalist Christian who was, in his mind, witnessing to the Biblical injunction that women should not be allowed to have any positions of authority in the church. His rage was visceral.

To repeat: What allows an individual woman to survive and flourish in a formally male dominated field is vast amounts of grace, wonderful colleagues, close friends and family and a persistent willingness to move through all the obstacles, challenges, and joys, in order to serve a calling. Parish ministry is an immense privilege, and I was glad to be able to do it for 35 years.

Nevertheless, after 13 years of retirement, some questions still haunt me and remain unanswered.

- What kind of wounds, insecurities and fears are in the hearts of certain men and women where they don't want women to be successful professionals?
- What is it exactly, that is so threatening about a woman in the pulpit?
- The Christian Century magazine reported that a man's sexual attractiveness is greatly enhanced by occupying the pulpit. But that a woman minister's sexual attractiveness is greatly reduced.
- Why is this?
- What motivates male colleagues to denigrate their female colleague's talents gifts and strengths?
- Why is it that financial compensations go down when women enter a previously all male field? (This is true for other work as well, such as lawyers and doctors.)
- How long will it take, for patriarchal institutions and structures, (which have been in place for thousands of years,) to finally release their grip on society? Will it ever happen?

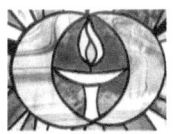

My UU Journey

Anne Olson

"The universe is made of stories, not of atoms."
—Muriel Rukeyser

"WARMING IN MUSIC—WORDS DEVOUT AND LARGE, that we are each other's harvest: we are each other's business: we are each other's magnitude and bond." Paul Robeson by Gwendolyn Brooks

My UU journey began in 1967 at the Unitarian Universalist Congregation of Atlanta (UUCA). I went there to hear Fritz Perls from The Esalen Institute: Center for Exploring and Realizing Human Potential. The talk was intriguing to me. I remember imagining new ways to think since I had been raised in a conservative and traditional home.

My father was a college dean and my mother a homemaker. My father was authoritarian, announcing on all matters "That's the way it is." My mother never pushed back so I had no model for that useful skill. We attended the Presbyterian Church as a family, and I was expected to attend, or I could not go on a date Saturday night. I lived at home during my four years of college. In the early fifties, my life felt like the girdle that we all had to wear.

My mother died in 1962. I was in graduate school in Kansas City, Kansas. It was also the year I got married, as I met my future husband there. My father's comment, "worse than marrying a Catholic is marrying a Democrat."

While at the talk at UUCA, I loved the intimacy of the circular sanctuary as I could see faces, not backs. I soon returned and joined within weeks, challenged to find a new religious home. The vision of acceptance and encouragement of each person's spiritual journey within the community felt capacious with possibilities for me. To find spiritual discernment and political awareness, so lacking when I grew up, all in one institution—what a new and incredible opportunity for me.

As a southern Unitarian-Universalist Congregation, there were few "born" Unitarian Universalists (UU)'s. Most of us were from another tradition: Methodist, Presbyterian, Southern Baptist, Jewish and families of mixed religious traditions. We met at newcomer orientation, small committee work, coffee after Sunday services, potluck, and spaghetti suppers, listening to and sharing our stories. We explored together our first steps as UUs. This was truly the beginning of my UU journey.

I was very fortunate to find a mentor at UUCA—the senior minister Gene Pickett. Gene seemed to me to be less patriarchal, very different from my father. We had occasional discussions in his small office as I raised my questions and concerns. He encouraged me to learn more about Unitarian Universalism by becoming the Chair of the Denominational Affairs Committee. I became a frequent delegate from UUCA to Unitarian Universalist Association (UUA) General Assemblies (GA). My first GA was at the Shoreham Hotel in Washington DC in 1971. Gene guided me through the many workshops, exhibits and events. I was hooked. Observing Joe Fisher and later Denny Davidoff serve as moderators to handle disagreements in a large audience of delegates in order to move the decision process forward for the denomination was impressive.

Gene shared with me the importance of civil rights and reproductive choice which for him was work he was doing as part of his UU commitment to justice. He served as a member of the Atlanta Pastoral Committee to assist women in finding abortion care prior to Roe v. Wade. He was an underground worker! My work for reproductive choice was supported at UUCA. After the 1973 (Roe v. Wade decision), I served as an escort for women who came for an abortion at The Feminist Women's Health Center. I remember one family that drove from Alabama in a pick-up truck, with several children in tow, asking where a bank was located so their last savings could be converted to cash for the procedure.

Gene's work in civil rights also supported my interest in voting rights. Prior to joining UUCA, I had become active in the League of Women Voters and chaired a chapter in Dekalb County that became the first integrated chapter when Bunny Jackson joined. Later I did more voter education and registration with her husband, Maynard Jackson (later the first Black Atlanta mayor), when he was a law student at Emory University. We worked in Kirkwood, Lithonia, and other areas with large populations of African Americans.

Some special moments I remember about Gene: a talk (not sermon) after he had been up all night at Grady Hospital with a young man from the congregation. He was shot in the back, paralyzed and not likely to survive (he did not). Gene told about listening to the young man as he began to struggle with and grieve about his future. Gene shared this story on that Sunday morning as he had not finished preparing his sermon. It was a moving experience for many of us. Another story about Gene—he was not good at remembering people's names, so he tried to find his wife, Helen, or me, to help him greet folks at receptions.

Soon I was on the UUCA Board of Trustees (1971-1974). The best part of board meetings (budget work was not my thing) was when we headed for a nearby pub to drink beer and informally get to know each other. After Gene left for a UUA position in Boston, it was difficult not to be angry as it seemed so much harder to be heard. I was often ignored when offering a suggestion, quickly followed up by a man saying the same or similar thing. The man's idea was always recognized. Patriarchy here, there, and everywhere. At another point, I volunteered to work as co-chair with my friend Alice for a new program committee. I was not chosen because male leaders decided that two women as co-chairs would result in a "cat fight."

During my more than 20 years at UUCA, I was very involved with various committees, expanding, and enlarging my UU understandings. Even though I did so much committee work, much of my spiritual work was done by reading and discussing books with small groups of women. This was a period when I no longer read any books by men. From an essay by Ursula K. LeGuin, from which this quote is taken: "We read books to find out who we are." One book I found helpful, among others, was Sara Paretsky's *Writing in the Age of Silence*. She grew up in a small Kansas town in the '50s, as I had. "The book deals with the dominant questions of my own life, the effort to find a voice ... the effort to understand and come to terms with the questions of power and powerlessness." She named my struggle.

Chairing the Program Committee meant there was a great deal to do. We organized Sunday summer services, the Sundays when the minister was not in the pulpit, as well as speakers in the evening. Later, chairing the Social Justice committee, our small committees jointly organized workshops about peace, anti-Vietnam War, the Mid-East conundrum, and women's rights. The workshops were well attended, likely because of our UU commitment to justice. Some UUCA members joined People of Faith for the ERA. Together we wrote letters to the Atlanta Journal Constitution editor, protested with others at the state capitol and generally tried to be disruptive. Unfortunately, Georgia did not agree to the ERA.

In the early seventies, I further developed my feminist conscience. Ms Magazine came out in 1971. I read *A Room of One's Own* by Virginia Woolf. That is probably the most meaningful book I had read to that point. It radically changed my thinking as books were the key that opened possibilities for me. Books gave me space to consider my spiritual path. I lived in a small house, with two small children and no assistance. When I had a few minutes, I was reading Adrienne Rich, Gloria Steinem, and Tillie Olsen, finding my voice in the safe space of reading poetry, stories, and essays.

My marriage ended in 1974. The children were now in school. A full-time job with travel responsibilities and little support from either my former husband or father made it difficult for me. Childcare, of course, was a real challenge but a neighbor's daughter worked out fairly well when I traveled.

At the GA In New York City, sitting next to the UU minister I was dating, we listened to Mary Daly as she refused to take questions from men. When she refused to take his question, he was furious. I was stunned. I dove into her books, one at a time as they were complicated, difficult and in a new language for me. I confess that I have found other feminist theologians easier to understand.

At the Philadelphia GA in 1981, The UUA Purposes and Principles were introduced by a working committee. The following year, congregations were asked to study and understand the new principles (under my hat as Denominational Affairs chair), and then were taken to the Vancouver, Canada GA for further review (more on my role later). Next came a perfecting meeting, leading to a bylaws draft. The Purposes and Principles were approved at the 1985 GA in Atlanta, Georgia. Though long and intense, it was an opportunity for me to appreciate as well as understand that participatory process.

At another GA, I found Voices of the New Feminism, edited by Mary Lou Thompson. I met her and had wonderful conversations with her, discussing the possibility of expanding roles of women in Unitarian Universalist circles and the administration. She also edited The 1974 Meditation Manual Stopping Places, the first UU manual devoted to women's voices. There were so many powerful pieces inspiring me on my spiritual journey. "A Communion of People" by Judy Deutsch spoke to my vision of inclusiveness.

As I had always been an avid reader, my exposure to many new authors from Beacon Press (at the GA exhibits), where I shopped too much, usually sending a box of books home, was perfect. I loved chatting with Sonia Sanchez about her newest poetry. By the middle '80s I was reading Audre Lorde and bell hooks as well as other women of color. Up to that time, my reading and friends were white middle-class feminists, UU, and others.

I remembered bell hook's voice, as she often came to Atlanta to read at Charis Books and More (the oldest feminist bookstore in the southeast and maybe the US) and at Spelman College. Her litany of "imperialist white supremacist heteropatriarchy" as unforgettable as she meant it to be. Also in her book Feminist Theory: From Margins to Center, she raised the lack of inclusion of working-class Black women's lives in feminist thinking. Her many books made feminist theory more accessible to me and others. Sister Outsider: Essays and Speeches by Audre Lorde, especially her essay "The Master's Tools Will Never Dismantle the Master's House" was so powerful. "For women the need and desire to nurture each other is not pathological but redemptive, and it is within that knowledge that our real power is rediscovered." In another essay "Poetry in Not a Luxury," she wrote "For women, then, poetry is not a luxury. It is a vital necessity of our existence. It forms the quality of light within which we predicate our hopes and dreams toward survival and change, first made into language, then into idea, and then into more tangible action. Poetry is the way we help give name to the nameless so it can be thought." These were provocative thoughts for me.

For over 47 years Charis Books has been my local bookstore where I have volunteered and been a member of Charis Circle, the first programming and fundraising arm of the store. I met Kay Hagan, facilitator of the feminars, participated in book discussion groups, and met, listened to, and learned from feminist authors there. I found *Weaving the Visions: New Patterns in Feminist Spirituality* Edited by Judith Plaskow and Carol Christ there. Such helpful insights into spirituality for me in this collection.

My spiritual search slowly grew as I came to believe that humans can and must be willing to heal ourselves and care for others. My understanding of "we are each other's magnitude and bond" was a promise I made for all my future endeavors. This promise was confirmed as I later became involved in the Women and Religion Committee (W/R), the Unitarian Universalist Women's Federation (UUWF) and the Feminist Theology Awards (FTA) process.

In 1985 Denny Davidoff, President of the Unitarian Universalist Women's Federation (UUWF), came to help start an Atlanta Chapter at UUCA. Over 40 women joined, and we began a book club, gathering together to consider our spiritual journeys, using ideas from Women Spirit Rising: A Feminist Reader in Religion (more on this book later). Later we gathered at a retreat in North Georgia to further develop our friendships and to support for each other. My best Catholic friend, Mary Ellen, joined us and together we created a ritual of connection. We used a ball of colored yarns, connecting each woman in the circle with time to share her wisdom. We became a "quilt" of many stories within strands of yarn.

Using the new curriculum Cakes for the Queen of Heaven, developed in 1992 by the Women and Religion Committee, the Rev. Sidney Wilde-Nugent and I provided training at UUCA. The curriculum was a creative way to think about religions, creating space for dialogue of paganism, Goddess religions and other forms of spirituality.

In 1994 Qiyamah Rahman and I were co-trainers for the curriculum Rise Up and Call Her Name, created by a grant from UUWF. This curriculum further expanded our ideas about ways women in other countries, especially those from the southern hemispheres, envisioned their lives through rituals, chanting and honoring their Goddesses/Gods.

In 1995, I co-facilitated with Dazon Dixon Diallo, (a human rights trainer with whom I later formed Human Rights Atlanta) the Unitarian Universalist Service Committee (UUSC) curriculum Gender Justice with a group of 25 women and men at UUCA. This curriculum felt radical, allowing me to more deeply discover and include the relevance of justice for women and girls as part of my spiritual practice. In the late nineties, I trained with The National Center for Human Rights Education with Loretta Ross and Dazon. I became a human rights activist as that felt like a way to integrate my feminism with a broader perspective.

Three memories that reflect my best work at UUCA. I coordinated Sunday Services for nine months in the absence of a senior minister. Speakers, other visiting UU ministers, lay leaders- all were invited to the pulpit. After one service I coordinated, a young couple approached me with a request for me to marry them. Sadly, I could not as I was not an ordained minister, although I did contemplate attending theology school. My finances prevented that dream. I was a single parent working full time to support two teenagers.

Although I created many Sunday services, the one I most remember: my service Honoring Mothers/MotherMentors. Elders Betty Pirkle and her family as well as Mary Lou Skinner Ross were honored. Both were important mentors and friends. Members of Atlanta UUWF read from *The Image of a Garden* by May Sarton, *In Search of Our Mothers' Gardens* by Alice Walker and *Tapestry* by Lucy Hitchcock, a UU woman from New England. Mary Lou was a nudge for me, always reminding me to take care of myself as I did my justice work. Betty and I traveled to Washington DC to attend a March for Economic Justice; I remember dipping my toes in the long pond listening to the speakers.

The third highlight for me was coordinating a Vesper Service titled "The Peace to Which We Aspire" with two young people (daughter and son of friends) who had recently returned from India and the Soviet Union. I had just returned from Japan as a UUA delegate to the International Association of Religious Freedom (IARF). We shared stories of what we had each learned, finding that participating with and listening to people about their aspirations for peace powerful. We learned that an international perspective was eye opening for each of us. Many years later, I was acknowledged by Mary Anne Chew in a beautiful program honoring my many contributions at UUCA.

I do not remember which GA I attended where I heard Carol

Gilligan, author of *In a Different Voice: Psychological Theory and Women's Development.* Just the title called me. Her research was based on "the thesis that women assess moral responsibilities from an entirely different frame of reference than most men." Gilligan's description of ethics of care as "expressed by one's sense of responsibility to the community, to the interdependent web" allowed me to envision another expression of my UU journey.

Since UUCA was a large congregation (over 700 members) many of us were involved in the Mid-South District of UUA. I volunteered to be the first district Women and Religion (W/R) Chair. The first W/R conference I attended was at the Catholic Women's Center in Grailville Ohio in 1979. I did not know anyone and often felt lonely. Few southerners attended. But I loved the women centered space. A Sabra service (using the imagery of a prickly pear, soft on the inside but prickly outside) by Joan Mendelson and Denise Tracy touched me deeply as I began to recognize myself. I also loved the space for the ritual, an old barn created anew by the Catholic sisters living at Grailville. Their model of vocation encouraged me to reflect on the many ways that women could live. I offered a workshop on creating feminist ritual and language in UU congregations.

And I took my first Myers Briggs test. It turns out that I am an Extroverted, Intuitive, Thinking, Perceiving (ENTP) kind of person. I was not radically so, as my measures were all near the middle.

I also got Cris Williamson's new album "The Changer and the Changed." That blew me away and I still listen to it, especially *Song of at the Soul* with this verse "Trying to survive the strangeness and the dying by learning to listen to my own voices, my spiritual Guides."

The next W/R conference was in East Lansing, Michigan, where I soaked up the ideas from Carol Christ and Judith Plaskow, taking their book *Womanspirit Rising: A Feminist Reader in Religion*, home with me. I really resonated with their ideas that theology is rooted in experience, with an understanding of my reactions to my experiences of misogyny and patriarchy. Another interesting message for me was Carol Christ speaking about goddesses, suggesting that these symbols of female power be seen as an independent power. Back home, I became a part of a feminar, yes, feminar. Our small circle of women very different from me (class and sexuality) became a place of pagan rituals, goddess celebrations and a conscious raising group. We met for several years. My favorite story from this time occurred after my teenagers moved out. One of our members, dressed as a witch, arrived with a basket full of garlic to detox my home. Many years later when I sold that house, I found pieces of garlic in the corners.

While W/R chair, I did workshops in Nashville, Tennessee, and a mountain top retreat in Alabama where we had to check our shoes to be sure no biting spiders were hiding there. In Jackson, Mississippi, I co-lead a workshop titled Women's Stories: Hearing Ourselves into Existence with the President of the Mid-South District. My worship service there was titled Out of Our Mother's Attics. Women in this small congregation expressed appreciation for the ways stories could enrich their lives and relationships to each other.

I attended the next W/R Conference was in Albuquerque, New

Mexico. My community of UU friends all over the USA and Canada increased and the groundwork for joining the UUWF Board of Directors was being built.

In 1983 I joined the UUWF Board, serving six years, after finishing my last year as the Mid- South W/R district chair. I connected my work as a new UUWF board member, delegate from UUCA and role as W/R chair at the UUA General Assembly (GA) in Vancouver, Canada. I will not be a delegate for three institutions again at one time. At a workshop led by Rev. Linnea Pearson, she offered this definition: "Feminism is both an alternative to other modes of religious thought and experience and an added dimension to the experience and expression of traditional religious modes. In many ways, feminist theology is akin to process theology ... it is linked to liberation theology, black theology, and the theology of hope." Now I am clearer about my favorite description of myself "I'll be a post-feminist in post-patriarchy."

Sitting on the floor in a gymnasium, I, along with others, facilitated a discussion on why The Purposes and Principles were critical to the well-being of UUA, using a feminist perspective. Ministers and lay delegates surrounded me. Other small groups were also doing this work. The W/R Committee had trained us as facilitators prior to GA. Many questions and probably concerns were likely raised as feminist thinking was new for many folks. The Purposes and Principles were approved at a later UUA General Assembly. Sadly, the UUA booklet describing The Purposes and Principles was written to exclude the relevance of feminist thinking, instead inserting environmental language.

My first international conference was in Japan. I attended the

International Association of Liberal Religious Women (IALRW) conference with several members of the UUWF board in 1984. My spiritual education included cultural education on this trip. I learned flower arranging and how to tie a belt on a kimono. Several of us slipped out to find the Kamakura Buddha, an exciting train trip with no signs in English. A friendly person speaking English helped us find the right station. This conference was held prior to the International Association of Religious Freedom (IARF) meeting where I was a delegate from UUA.

When the IARF meeting adjourned, many of us started our tour on a bullet train as it rushed by Mt. Fukushima, with stops in Osaka, Kyoto, and Hiroshima. We viewed lots of castles and shrines. We slept on futons, used Japanese baths, danced at the Odori fall festival and ate all sorts of food that I did not recognize.

Incredibly powerful for me was attending the ceremony at 8:45 AM, as that was the moment the first atomic bomb was delivered to Hiroshima on August 6, 1945. After the ceremony, many of us gathered near the river, and each one of us, hand in hand with a Japanese person, sent paper boats with candles in them to the memory of the victims, a traditional way of honoring the spirits of the dead. (Later that night we had to exit our hotel when tremors from an earthquake rattled the hangers in the room closet).

For me there are several remembrances of being on the UUWF Board. First, I met and was mentored by Bernita Cogan, a UUWF board member from Dallas, Texas. It had always felt to me like UUWF was a New England organization so her knowledge and support as a fellow southerner was very important to me. We became close friends, visiting each other's homes; best of all she made date filled cookies just like my Norwegian grandmother.

While on the board, I remembered that our responsibility of the Clara Barton Camp for Girls with diabetes was moved to a separate corporation. The UUWF Board was free to focus more on programing, involving women in churches, and feminist concerns that were rapidly developing, in part, due to the W/R committee leadership. One of my strengths is programing and my major contribution, while on the Board, was chairing the Program Committee for three Biennials in Atlanta, Georgia, Little Rock, Arkansas and Minneapolis, Minnesota.

Dr. Schussler-Fiorenza 's book *In Memory of Her: A Feminist Theological Construction of Christian Origins*, was one of the first books I really began to understand feminist theology. I was so curious about "hermeneutics of suspicion," that raised questions about religious practices. Her work helped clarify my search for a spiritual path and helped me begin to understand the work of other feminist theologians I had heard at W/R conferences. Feminism had been defined as "a particular lens of perception" that has influenced my consideration of new ideas in this literature. Schussler-Fiorenza's work seemed to offer some generative ideas for UU women and men. I proposed to the UUWF Board that we invite her to be the keynote speaker at the UUWF Biennial in Atlanta; they agreed using the theme "Struggle is the Name for Hope." Three UU women were respondents to her talk: a lay woman, a minister, and a scholar. (I can't remember one name, but The Rev. Judith Walker-Riggs and Dr. Betty Hoskins responded to her talk). We met at Agnes Scott College (a small women's liberal arts college) in Decatur, Georgia, a suburb of Atlanta. The crowd was very large, I believe, because Schussler-Fiorenza's theological work invited an imaginative reconstruction of history that was of interest to many UUs.

Special for me was that Gene Pickett, UUA President, attended. I had missed seeing him regularly after he moved to Boston. I learned that he met with Bernita Cogan, encouraging her to keep the attention on women's issues at UUA. I also believe he suggested my name for the UUWF board. Later visiting Boston, I occasionally met Gene and Helen for lunch to catch up with each other. I also managed to check out The Brattle Street Bookstore, not far from the Boston Commons and Beacon Street, locating women's theology, sociology, and ethics books for my study to learn more and more.

After reading Beverly Wildung Harrison's book *Making the Connections: Essays in Feminist Social Ethics*, her essay "The Power of Anger in the Work of Love," I determined to meet her. Her thoughtful analysis helped me to understand my dilemma as I dealt with my inability to become angry. When I was a delegate representing UUWF at the Catholics for Free Choice Meeting in Washington DC, I met Beverly and invited her to be a keynote speaker at the Little Rock, Arkansas UUWF Biennial in 1987. She agreed after we had an informal chat at breakfast. A conversation between Beverly and a UU scholar was created to consider her ideas. She helped us to understand women theologians as they reconstructed the origins of faith traditions, and focused our anger toward action.

As UUWF liaison with the Religious Coalition for Abortion Rights (RCAR), I gave a short speech about the necessity of abortion availability with RACR at the 1992 March for Abortion Rights in Washington. I attended with my college age daughter, and we marched with the UUA Delegation led by President Bill Schulz. My support and involvement concerning reproductive choice continued through my entire career with UUCA, UUWF and UUA. It was an ongoing part of my feminist journey, putting justice for women in all my work.

At the Biennial in Minneapolis, Minnesota in 1989, there were some changes and some challenges. The planning committee agreed that we needed to focus on what was happening, or not happening, at UUA. We also agreed to the conference title Women Bringing Justice to the Work of Theology. The Feminist Theology Awards (FTA) were introduced for the first time by the chair, Betty Hoskins. This biennial was also a beginning effort to tackle white privilege. I am not sure that we were successful, but it was a badly needed start. It was a challenging conference.

The First Universalist Congregation hosted the Biennial. A formal church, there was some distress when we moved chairs around on the podium in an effort to be more conversational. There were also some food issues as many women requested vegetarian meals and were served a plate absent the roast pork (a traditional meal in the Midwest). And I had floaters in my eyes, making concentration very difficult. Dru Cummins, the local host committee chair, connected me with her physician and that helped but I was not on the top of my game.

For me, my time on the board was sometimes difficult. because I was struggling as a single mother of two teenagers—no support, again. It was a challenge! Additionally, I did not always receive support from other board members. But I know that my contributions, while on the board, were significant as my programing skills were critical to the success of three biennials. I completed my six years on the board in 1989, relieved that my term was over. That Saturday night I created a ritual of reflection in preparation for my departure. I felt resolved, separating from UUWF, and woke up early to a gentle snow fall. I wrote these haiku verses.

> Serene
> as snow gently
> surrounds me.

and

> Waking up
> gentle white light
> white sound
> ah

Much later, one of my sister board members, sent me a turtle shell with a crack, and a note that was so generous "please remember that though wounded, you are still whole."

Bernita Cogan, along with Claire White, did the initial fundraising for Feminist Theology Awards (FTA) and it was agreed to and implemented by the UUWF Board. I met Betty Hoskins, a feminist scholar who was the first chair of the FTA at a UUWF board meeting. I joined that committee in 1993 for three years. I was appointed by the UUWF board as Chair in 1996. The new FTA Selection committee working with me was composed of six lay women, ministers, and scholars. We met at Collegium in the fall of 1993, honoring Betty for her leadership. Mary Lou Skinner Ross, a dear friend from UUCA, was so helpful as she kept me focused on my internal compass and yes, spiritual search. I am often more aware of my feelings when Mary Lou is near me.

The new FTA committee learned to work together as we explored two questions. What do we mean by UU theology? Do we mean thealogy? Or both? What is specifically UU about a proposed project? While at Collegium, we participated in and observed models of presenting papers followed by critical responses. We also networked with other UU scholars exploring ways to mentor, support, critique and improve feminist thinking in the FTA process. The original FTA vision requested that proposals were both scholarly and accessible to the UUWF and greater UU community. We wished to continue those criteria and revised the application to be consistent with The UUWF Mission Statement and the UUA Purposes and Principles. We insisted that we include the difficult dialogue to difference, and our search for justice. We sought new understandings as part of our feminist and theological search for truths. We desired a generous spirit, in relation to each other's works. We struggled … to listen to the diverse voices, the varied strands of our denomination, our communities, and our society."

By 1993, 14 FTA awards had been given. That year, at the GA in Charlotte, North Carolina, no awards were given. Project proposals did not meet the application requirements. There was both disappointment and frustration about that decision as well as heartfelt thanks for the integrity of the Selection Committee.

During my tenure as chair of the FTA selection committee, we gave awards to several UU women who wrote histories of seldom recognized UU women. Since all 75 pounds of my FTA records had been sent to UUWF for historical research, I have relied on my journals and notes to recall our work. I do remember two large awards. One went to Betty Donaldson, in Calgary, Canada for her site centered Goddess ritual. We also gave an award to Shirley Ranck for a curriculum "Feminist Theology for the 21st century." Due to several issues, the curriculum was never developed.

One FTA award given before I came on the committee continued to help me on my spiritual journey: Gail Ranadive's Creative Writing: A Spiritual Quest. In many periods of my life, I have journaled to deal with the chaos of my life. In the last few years, I became more reflective and deeply personal as her work helped guide me. Journaling in this intentional manner reminded me of my desire to be a journalist. I joined a writing group, producing several reflections, maybe essays, dealing with the loss of friends and of my mother. I began to do Haiku after I retired. And for my maximum satisfaction, I served as editor of "The Dancing Fox" for my cohousing community for over a dozen years.

When in Boston, after grandmother visits, I often traveled with Betty to visit her home in Worcester, Massachusetts, loving the used bookstore, where I found a copy of Nelle Morton's The Journey is Home. Her story of struggle with the Methodist Church resonated with me, along with her wonderful stories as she continued her work with other women. Although I was becoming a vegetarian, the Polish Kielbasa purchased on Water Street and superb bagels with lox and cream cheese from a Jewish deli was just too much to resist. Betty encouraged me to further enlarge my understanding of feminist theology and ethics. Although I had a master's degree, it was not in a liberal arts field. Under her guidance, I became a much more thoughtful reader and eventually claimed the role of feminist scholar activist.

In 2001 I spent time in Amherst, Massachusett, home of another UU friend Prill Hinckley. We checked out apple orchards, Emily Dickinson's home and a great bookstore. Later we attended The Women's Alliance for Theology, Ethics and Ritual (WATER) conference with Mary Hunt, Dianna Neu, Elizabeth Schussler-Fiorenza and other Catholic women, including some I remembered meeting at Grailville. It was my first encounter with WomanChurch, founded by many of the women at this conference. I was and continue to be in awe of the resistance of these Catholic women.

In Atlanta, I was fortunate to get to know Qiyamah better. I recommended that she join the UUWF board. Even though she was in graduate school working on her doctorate, she joined. Later I recommended that my friend and neighbor the Reverend Marti Keller join the FTA committee. She has shared with me that her time with UUWF had been most satisfying. Qiyamah and Marti, along with some other Atlanta UUWF friends, developed a piece "Reflections on Feminisms." We wanted to articulate clearly that there was more than one feminism. We defined feminisms as "including part of life, woman aware, world view perspective that supports and includes moving from margins to center, clarifying liberating visions, forming resistance ... using feminisms to shape perspectives." We then explored the ethics of caring and the use of both/and as a working concept. We also spent time sharing our journeys, focusing on their spiritual aspects.

One other UU woman became important to me: Loretta Williams, Director of Social Justice for UUA. At the Vancouver GA, we slipped off for lunch at a restaurant under the bridge leading from Vancouver Island to Vancouver. She shared her favorite saying "In the struggle for justice is the hope." We later traveled together in Japan, sitting side by side in very small Japanese buses. After she left the UUA, we lost contact but found each other again at the United Nations World Conference Against Racism and Xenophobia in Durban, South Africa in 2001. We attended a local theater performance about color lines: black, white, and colored. The laughter of locals amazed us as we could not recognize the funny part; we probably the only Americans there, three Black women and me. We headed for the pastry shop nearby to deconstruct the play and our responses to the laughter.

Loretta asked me to join her as a book reviewer for the Gustavus Myers Center for the Study of Bigotry and Human Rights. I joined, specializing in southern history, feminist, and labor books. I loved doing the reviews and participated several times in the consolidation process; we reviewed over 100 books and selected ten for awards each year. It was one of my most satisfying experiences, especially working with Loretta. I loved expanding new areas of interest as a Northerner living in the South. Also satisfying was holding the 2006 awards ceremony at the Auburn Avenue Research Library in Atlanta, the first ceremony not held in Boston. Many local human rights activists had looked forward to the ceremony but were unable to come at the last minute because they were in Jackson, Mississippi to address the chaos of Katrina.

Still, I was able to give an award to my human rights mentor Loretta Ross for her editing with others *Undivided Rights: Women of Color Organize for Reproductive Justice*. In the many reviews done, this was the first book that emphasized collaboration of women of color in their work. And it was groundbreaking, introducing of concept of reproductive justice.

I loved seeing Loretta (Williams, not Ross) on my way home from grandmother visits in Boston as she lived in Jamaica Plain. When her family was not available, she joined my family on special occasions. After she became ill, my daughter stepped up, taking her to doctors' appointments and the pharmacy. The last time I spoke with Loretta, we were planning our usual lunch and she said that would be lovely. She died later that evening. My loss of that close friendship was very painful. Later I attended her Memorial Service at the old African-American church, located not far from UUA headquarters. A UU friend came up to me and said that Loretta told her how helpful my daughter had been.

Several years after I left UUCA due to an unfortunate counseling session. I now realize this session was so misogynist that I did not know how to respond. It has taken a long time for me to recognize this hurtful attack, when I thought I was being counseled.

I joined the Thurman Hamer Ellington Unitarian Universalist Congregation (THE) as a charter member in 1990. Qiyamah and I often coordinated services, served as co-chairs, and struggled to keep this small congregation going. In the end, we were too small to maintain THE and notified UUA that we would no longer continue as a congregation. For all of us, it was a sad and deep loss.

Instead, I have increased my activism locally. It is probably not a surprise that I connected with Project South: Institute for the Elimination of Poverty and Genocide at a book group. An author presented their work, and both a scholar and an activist responded. That was new for me. I worked on learning popular education training methods and was asked to join the Leadership Team. Fund raising was also a new skill I developed there. Project South staff became my extended family. The same building housed The Georgia Citizen's Coalition on Hunger. I promptly joined the planning team for Poor People's Day, often doing human rights training. Work on the Living Wage Campaign began. At one event I was asked to give a Unitarian Universalist prayer, followed by a Muslim and Christian prayers. In one of our marches around the Georgia state capitol, to be followed by entry, the police stopped us from entering. Those of us at the front dropped to the ground. Fortunately, we had cell phones, contacted our state Senators, were rescued, and allowed to enter as citizens. Wearing my feminist and human rights hat, I became a trainer with Amnesty International-Southeast Region. Connecting with Glory Kilanko, Director of Women Watch Afrika, we trained students at all the universities and colleges in Metro Atlanta. I served on her Board of Directors. I also joined the Board of Directors of Refugee Women's Network. There, I met my first political asylum person and became her American mom. Though not successful in teaching her to drive a car, I did show her children how to carve a pumpkin and the benefits of trick or treating on Halloween. I joined their Diwali ceremony, enjoying that tradition with a great deal of food and dancing.

My UU journey ends as I am no longer a member of any congregation although I do hold to my UU faith. Many rewards of my journey include receiving some necessary mentoring; reading books to heal my patriarchal wounds and a felt powerlessness, as I developed my personal, spiritual journey: meeting new friends and finding many rewarding friendships; international travel leading to an expanded vision of human rights. I found myself and my place in my communities. My spiritual journey had become a human rights journey reflecting that "we are each other's bond."

My modeling caregiving has been a modest success as evidenced by my children now. Since the pandemic, my son Rich has become my primary caregiver, running errands, driving me to appointments (though I still drive to the library and see friends), and helping with chores at home. My daughter Karen flies in from Boston as often as she can to check on me and of course, we talk about all the books we are reading. I continue to write haiku, finding the reflection a quieting and spiritual way to focus my journey. I will soon be back in my writers group.

Now at home, I focus on hummingbirds, butterflies, and the beauty in my neighborhood. I greet my neighbors as they pass by. My time at East Lake Commons CoHousing is where this story resides, sheltering in place on my rocking chair on the front porch.

Huge old tree standing
Leaves scattered around the yard
So calm, beautiful.

To honor the memory of
The Reverend Doctor O. Eugene Pickett
Minister Emeritus, Unitarian Universalist
Congregation of Atlanta
Former President, Unitarian Universalist Association

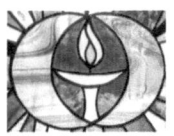

My MRE Story

Liz Strong

WHO AM I?

Elizabeth May Strong – birth name

Betty Strong – childhood name to match my semi-identical twin sister Barbara's name

Liz Strong – name I used in college

Elizabeth May Taylor – married name

Elizabeth Strong Taylor – after the divorce name

The Reverend Elizabeth M. Strong – ordained name

The Reverend Doctor Elizabeth M. Strong – doctorate name

The Reverend Doctor Elizabeth M. Strong – Minister Emerita

I was born June 17, 1940, twenty minutes before my semi-identical twin sister Barbara to my parents, Ashley Walter Strong and Marie Elizabeth Miller Strong, in Cooperstown, NY at the Mary Imogene Bassett Hospital around 9:00 am. My brother

John is 5 years older. I graduated from The Richfield Springs, NY Central High School, Syracuse University with a BA in Liberal Arts (a,k.a.—an Mrs. Degree) and was married at the end of my junior year. I raised 4 children who were 11, 9, 5 and 3 at the time of my separation in 1974. The divorce became final in 1978 and I learned quickly how limited my freedom as a divorced woman was. I needed my former brother-in-law to sign for me to buy my first car. I earned credit by taking over the mortgage payments on the house my children and I lived in those four years.

During that four-year interval (1974 to 1978) I volunteered in the religious education program as a teacher and a member of the Church School Committee and the Curriculum Committee at the First Unitarian Church in Rochester, NY. In 1974 I began to aspire to become a professional religious educator and applied to and was accepted into the Unitarian Universalist Accreditation Program. I enrolled in a Master's in Education program at Nazareth College in Pittsford, NY (a suburb of Rochester, NY) and earned a MS in Elementary Education as part of my studies in the Accreditation Program. I was supported by the First Unitarian Church congregation in this endeavor and received scholarships and praise for this work. I also taught a junior high class on Biblical Jesus to great acclaim. During this time, I served on the St. Lawrence District Religious Education Committee and became the Chair in the mid-80s. As the Chair I attended the UUA Conclave for the District RE Committee Chairs and in the process met religious educators from around the country. The District RE Committee consisted of 5 women from congregations around the District. At one point we discussed inviting a well-qualified man to join the Committee but wondered how we could continue to stay in one another's home during our meetings. Where on earth would he sleep? And would we have to stop meeting in our pajamas! We had become a tight knit group and felt that a man in the mix would break those bonds. We did eventually include him, and he proved to be no problem to our deepening bond as religious educators. We did stop meeting in our pajamas though.

As I met more religious educators, I learned about the Liberal Religious Education Directors' Association and soon joined. This broadened my scope and connections with career religious educators and enhanced my vision to become an Accredited Director of Religious Education. In 1978, after I earned my MS degree in Elementary Education, I was hired as the Church School Director at the First Unitarian Church and asked the congregation to expand my responsibilities to include youth programming and to change the title to Religious Education Director. It was an approved position for a woman and a parent of four children to take and by all standards, they did all these things and paid me a reasonable salary. It was a very rewarding experience and a time I cherish for the impact I made on the youth and the children in the program. We had nearly 500 children and youth in the RE program at the time, and I grew professionally at a rapid rate. I joined LREDA and became more active in the St. Lawrence District religious education activities that included youth programming for their District Conferences. I do believe I slept on the floor of every church in the District during those years!!

During this time frame of the late 1970s the Accredited Directors of Religious Education began to understand their work as

a ministry with children and youth. What I have come to understand in the ensuing years is that the process followed by the DREs
did not start with the parents, teachers, children, ministers, and
lay leaders of the congregations. It emerged from the experiences
of ministry work being done by the DREs who then advocated for
that work to be recognized as a full ministry with Ordained Ministers of Religious Education within the denomination and the congregations. It was a top-down process that was articulated within
the ranks of the DREs but did not reach the understanding of the
lay people or the ministers. They were internalizing their understanding of what they did with the vision of Sophia Lyon Fahs and
Angus MacLean. Following the belief of Fahs that children needed
their own minister in a congregation and in the denomination (as
espoused in her book, *Today's Children, Yesterday's Heritage*) the
work began to create the Ministry of Religious Education. I was
at the mid-point of my accreditation program at the time and had
to make the decision to complete the Accreditation Program to
become an Accredited Director of Religious Education or enter
the Independent Study Program on a path to ministry. I chose to
become a Minister of Religious Education.

Fahs writes (pages 198 and 199) "To be granted the opportunity to have one's faith mature in intellectual and emotional freedom
is something to be enthusiastic about. The present upsurge of
concern among liberals about services of worship, and the apparent yearning for more ritualistic forms, are an expression of this
realization that we all not only need to be convinced, but also to
have our feelings warmed.

"For generations of adults a service of worship once a week has been the outstanding feature of the church's program. This Sunday morning service has been the one uniting emotional experience which has kept congregations of adults loyal. 'In these church services,'" Dr. Angus MacLean writes, "we measure ourselves against the best we know." It is the only place where we go to acknowledge privately and publicly that we need to be wiser and better people, the only fellowship we join specifically to get what I cannot describe better than as a God's eye view of ourselves.

"If such services have been so significant for adults, can they not have a similar value for children, provided some adaptations are made to children's immaturity? This is the question and the hope that have led to special services of worship for children."

As a result of this new understanding of the depth and scope of the faith development of the children in my congregation I began holding Family Worship services each Sunday before the adult worship service and religious education program. These services were held in the Susan B. Anthony Lounge not in the Sanctuary. I encouraged teachers to lead a Chalice Time in their classes and provided readings, poetry, and songs to open these times for sharing and creating a sense of wonder in the children. I continued to grow in my understanding of the work I was doing and listened to my colleagues of many years (Roberta Nelson, Mary Nelson, Ellen Nelson (now Johnson-Fay), Christine Wetzel, Elizabeth Anastos, Ann Fields, Barbara Marshman, Caroline Fenderson, Junella Hansen, Midge Skwire, Carol Brody, Beth Ide, Rev. Betty Baker and Rev. Eugene B. Navias) to name a few—who began to verbalize their vision of a ministry of religious education. They articulated the ministry they were doing in their congregations and how it encompassed the components laid out by Angus MacLean and Sophia Fahs. And so, my quest began to become a Minister of Religious Education.

My developing understanding of what the impact of a Minister of Religious Education in a congregation could be grown more from my Universalist heritage than from the understanding of the work I was doing as a religious educator. Growing up in the Old Stone Universalist Church in Schuyler Lake, NY. I always knew I was a child of the church. Coupling that deep sense of belonging to the church family with the teaching of Fahs and the experiences of my religious education colleagues, I believed—and still do—that children develop and deepen their faith when they have a minister whose main purpose is to minister to them and their faith development and needs.

At first the congregation in Rochester, NY was supportive as I began my studies at Colgate Rochester Divinity School. They provided me with scholarships and expressed pride in my striving to become a more informed religious educator. But it soon became apparent to them that I was going to seek to develop my ministry there at the First Unitarian Church. Whiplash!!! Now I was stepping out of the traditional women's role as the church school lady. Women were still an anomaly in the ministry overall, and even more so in the minds of our denomination and congregants for a Minister of Religious Education. While they approved of my course work at the Divinity School and completion of the Independent Study Program, they balked at the idea my being Ordained and Installed as their Minister of Religious Education. Suddenly, I was deemed as being on an ego trip that was inappropriate and unwelcomed. I believe now that neither I nor the denomination articulated what a Minister of Religious Education would do that was different from, deeper in faith formation, or providing an inclusiveness for the children in the congregation than a DRE could. At the time there were only a few Accredited DREs in the denomination and the understanding in the congregations was of a lay leader taking care of the children while the adults worshiped in a Sanctuary that the children rarely if ever entered. The children were separate entities within our congregations. I, and those who envisioned a Ministry of Religious Education all sought to bridge that divide and bring the children into the fullness of the congregation through their role as a Minister specifically for the children but who also had standing and authority within the congregation. This connection did happen for me, and I mourn that the Minister for the children who could make it happen is no longer an ordained minister position within our congregations.

It was during my four years at Colgate Rochester Divinity School that there were more women studying for the ministry than men. This had a tangential impact on the efforts of religious educators to become, to be recognized and empowered to become Ministers of Religious Education.

From 1978 to 1983 I served the First Unitarian Church of Rochester, NY as their Religious Education Director while I completed my Independent Study Program. The discussions by the Board of Trustees began addressing my request to be Ordained and Installed as their Minister of Religious Education. During a Board meeting one night I was asked to leave while they discussed my request. I went to my office to await their decision. After more than an hour (several actually) I thought I would venture out of my office to see if there was any indication of their deliberations. What I discovered was, they had finished their discussions, and all gone home without anyone coming to tell me they were done or if they had come to any conclusions. My heart sank and I was sure that they had either voted to deny my request or had not come to a conclusion. Either way I was in complete despair of becoming an ordained and settled Minister of Religious Education. In the long run it took the UUA to intervene and have Reverend David Pohl come to talk with the Board of Trustees about the Ministry of Religious Education and that I, as a minister, had options just as they did. I can still see their faces when they began to understand that I held comparable power concerning the decision of where I chose to serve.

Throughout the late 1980s and into the 1990s as women and one or two men became Ministers of Religious Education more resistance to this ministry grew at the denominational level and within the congregations and among the established male parish-based ministers. The idea of shared ministry was almost anathema to them, and the congregations could not imagine how it would work amicably. Religious Education was still seen as "taking care of the children while the adults worshiped in the Sanctuary. There was no concept nor any interest in fostering an understanding of the children as the 'cradle of the congregation' where the children were to be the future adult members of the congregation as Sophia Fahs envisioned and recommended, and as the Universalist Church of America practiced. I am a third generation Universalist and was born into the faith and into the

Universalist Church of America. I grew up believing and being treated as if I was a cherished member of the church and that I would become an active adult member into the future.

During the first wave of Ministers of Religious Education it was the norm for us to remain in the congregations we served during our studies for the ministry. This presented so many difficult realities on so many levels that it is a wonder this ministry ever came into being. First was the change in our relationship with the congregation. The majority of the people did not understand that I was seeking to become one of their ministers and how that would impact that relationship. I think the majority thought I would serve in the same capacity as a lay professional with a fancy title and a tad more money. (Ah, yes, the money!) The effort to earn their vesting me with authority was never fully achieved in Rochester. This was an issue for most of us during the first two groups of Ministers of Religious Education. The second reality was the change in the relationship with our colleagues. I was fortunate to work with Reverend Doctor Richard S. Gilbert, a fellow Universalist who served as the religious educator with Angus MacLean in Cleveland early in his ministry. That was a huge help!! The third reality was the resistance from the UUA. It was expressed clearly many years later that the women who were becoming Ministers of Religious Education were seeking to share in a finite power reality within our congregations. There was little to no effort to educate the ministers or congregations about shared ministry and how that would enhance and strengthen the overall ministry of the congregation. I want to acknowledge Kay Montgomery for her support during that time and responding to our request to rename our work as lifespan faith development from the long used religious education. But with all those realities facing me and the congregation of the First Unitarian Church of Rochester, NY they Ordained me and installed me as their Minister of Religious Education. During the five years I served as one of their ministers I never felt I had the level of respect, support, or understanding of what a ministry to children and youth was about, or even why it was needed. The congregation did not support a shared ministry model even though my collegial relationship with Dick Gilbert was excellent and we thoroughly enjoyed working together. Because he had served as a religious educator in his first settlement, working with Angus MacLean, he understood the value of religious education and of how a ministry to children and youth would strengthen the congregation. He was always open to coming to a class to lead a Chalice Lighting while I led the opening part of the worship service for the adults. Then we would switch, sometimes with breath-taking last-minute sprints on his part to get back into the Sanctuary before I would need to launch into an unwritten sermon and before I was needed back in the classroom. But the congregants began to resist my continuing to teach a junior high class on Sundays and were increasingly critical of my administrative skills (which I have little ability nor love of doing). It became increasingly clear to me that they still saw this position as an administrator of the church school and the youth programming. They did not empower me to be a minister among them or to them. If I visited a member in the hospital, for example, I was asked if Dick was coming to see them too. Or they would complain to friends that The Minister had not bothered to visit them. When I wrote a particularly good sermon

I was frequently asked if Dick had written it for me. I was given kudos for my voice and patronized for my short stature; and of being considered "cute."

During this time, I became a mentor to minister of RE candidates Donna Corbus and Patricia Hoertdoerfer and talked with them about being a new ministerial colleague within the congregation where they served as DREs. I shared with them the realities they would face and in one case, advised her to seek ministry elsewhere because her congregation would not support her request for Ordination. Also, at that same time, my two youngest children were heading off to college, I extrapolated their leaving to 'grow up' as being what I also needed to do. And, so, I, as did so many of the Minister of Religious Education colleagues, understood the need to leave my first settlement and seek a calling elsewhere. In 1988 I went into search and was called to serve May Memorial Unitarian Society in Syracuse, NY. as their Minister of Religious Education with Reverend Nicholas C. Cardell, Jr. This was a time of collegial ministry that I cherish to this day. Nick was very comfortable in his understanding of himself and of who he was as the minister of the congregation. He was not threatened by the addition of a second minister to share in the overall ministry and understood that my ministry was focused on a segment of the congregation that he did not have expertise in being present with. He knew that with my ministry with the children and adults, coupled with his ministry to the adults, we made a powerful team that would enhance the faith development of the congregation as a whole. He already worked with the previous religious educators to hold Family Services on the first Sunday of each month to bring the children into the Sanctuary. He was always open to coming into the children's worship services for a brief time whenever I asked him to come. One day we realized that if we both showed up to visit someone in the hospital it might cause extreme consternation on the part of the patient and even go so far as to cause a heart attack thinking a double whammy visit by both ministers was a sure sign of a dire prognosis. So, Nick and I agreed that if I have a primary relationship with the person I would visit in person and he would make a phone call. If he had a primary relationship with the person, he would make the personal visit and I would make a call. It worked perfectly.

During my first year in Syracuse, I was asked to speak at the Annual Canvas Dinner. I remember asking if Nick was also going to speak and should I coordinate my words with him. The man said, "No, we are asking you to speak." Boom, I immediately understood that I was being given authority and I had better damn-well take it or I would not be offered it again. What a shift in my understanding of the power and authority of ministry and the incredible impact it had when a congregation invested authority in that ministry. It was during my time there that a little girl about seven years old overheard her mother talking about someone named Liz. The little girl said, "I know Liz, she is my minister. You probably don't know her." It was times like this that sustained me throughout my ministry.

And so, I began to thrive, not only in my congregation, but in the denomination and the Syracuse community. My children were all sort of out of the house, but on their own. I served on the Board of LREDA (which had changed its name from Liberal Religious

Education Directors' Association to Liberal Religious Educators' Association to reflect the Ministers of Religious Education addition to the ranks) as Vice President from 1978-1989 and President from 1989-1991. It was during my Presidency that the first Parish Minister was accused of ministerial sexual misconduct. David Pohl removed this minister from Fellowship and from the ministry. The LREDA Board wrote a letter of support to David citing that we believed he had done the right thing. Several members of LREDA received scathing letters and phone calls from Parish Ministers because of this. As the offending minister's behavior escalated in the numbers of women, he had abused the backlash from our action diminished and finally ceased.

As this was going on I was called back into service on the District RE Committee to serve as Chair from 1985 to 1989. I was part of the UUA Futures Curriculum Committee's Unitarian Universalist Team and wrote the pamphlet, "Can I Believe Anything I Want to? And the curriculum, "Messages in Music" with the others on the team. This was the first curricula written expressly teaching Unitarian Universalism to our children. My further branching out included becoming the President of the Iroquois UUMA/LREDA Chapter in 1988 till 1990, and on the Board and President of the St. Lawrence Theological Foundation from 1989 to 1996; the Board of Unirondack 1985 to 1988; UUMA nominating Committee 1990-1993 and again 2000-2003; UUA/ISP Envisioning Committee 1989-1993; Meadville Lombard Board 1988-1995; Modified Residency Program Committee 1995-2001 (chair 1997-2001). In the community I served on the board of the then Planned Parenthood Center of Syracuse from 1990 to 1998 and as President from 1995 to 1998.

I have continued to serve my faith and was the contract minister at the First Parish Unitarian Universalist Church in Ashby, MA, and am now retired and honored to be the Minister Emerita of that congregation. I am deeply saddened to have had to watch the Ministry of Religious Education fail and I have sometimes wondered if my ministry was in vain. I believe we have lost that connection of the entire congregation to one another across the ages with a minister on a team of ministers who understands children and is dedicated to their faith development along with the faith development of the adult membership in a seamless garment of Unitarian Universalism. If there is ever to be an Ordained Ministry of Religious Education again it must come up from the lay members who understand what a minister for their children would mean to all of them. I believe it is when the children ask the questions that they need in the process of developing a faith that will sustain them through the harsh and tender times of their lives, and their parents struggle along with them to find the answers; that is when a Minister of Religious Education can be of profound help and significance.

In the last two years I have been heartened by the number of former religious education students who have become Friends on Facebook with me. I find satisfaction and joy in knowing my ministry did reach them in a profound way. Not so bad after all.

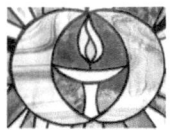

A Ministry of Institutional Change

Denise D. Tracy

"Like a ship in a harbor. Like a mother and child.
Like a light in the darkness, I'll hold you a while.
We'll rock on the water. I'll cradle you deep.
And hold you while angels, Sing you to sleep."

THESE WORDS FROM A LULLABY by Cris Williamson describe my image of what the church should be. A harbor. Ministers are the mothers that hold us in safety.

When I was 5 years old, our family lost our home in a flood. 11 people on our street died. My Dad had driven my mother, sister, and me to a friend's house. He went back to spend the night in our home. Later that night our neighborhood was destroyed. My father was missing, presumed dead, for four days. In those four days, my mother, sister and I took refuge in my Dad's church. There was a soup kitchen, a clothing depot and women from the church took the children, read to us, held us as we fell asleep on the velvet covered pews, for our naps. I look at my life and I find that this traumatic time gave me my calling to ministry. What I received, the love, the safety and the comfort, let me know that the church was both, as scripture says, a refuge and a strength.

We were homeless. My father was returned to us. I don't know how we survived. I only know that the church continued to be my anchor. At age 10, the first signs of a life-long kidney disease appeared. Weekly radiation scans and a diagnosis that I would not live beyond age 25, meant that I needed bed rest part of every day. This shocked me into future thinking. If I were not to live long, what would I do as Mary Oliver says, with my "one wild and precious life?"

I could only be on my feet 8 hours a day. So, Monday-Friday I went to school, then I rested. Saturday and Sunday, I went to my place of refuge—church. On Saturday, I sang in the children's choir. On Sunday I went to my own early church Sunday school and then I was an assistant in the second service Sunday school. I spent my free time at church activities. In the fifth grade, I decided that I wanted to be a minister. It never occurred to me that I could not do this. The fact it was 1960 and I had never met a female in professional church leadership did not enter my consciousness. My church taught us that God saw everyone as equal, and I believed this. For over a decade I volunteered. In high school, I taught Sunday school. During my college years, I became Advisor to the 40-member Youth Group.

In 1971, I finished college in 3 years. I applied to theological school. My church gave the scholarships for aspiring theological students to two men, with whom I had gone to high school. I knew that both of them were applying to theological school because they wanted to avoid the draft and Viet Nam. It should have occurred to me that not getting any money from my church after my many years of service, was a clue. It did not. I was about to get the shock of my life.

I had three weeks between the end of college and the start of theological school. Still, with the end point of my life expected to be age 25, I went to Europe. By letter, I made arrangements to have a key left for a room because I was arriving after midnight from Europe. I arrived safely at Andover Newton, found the key for my room, and went to sleep. The next morning, I woke up. I needed a bathroom. I found it, entered and there were at least 8 naked men, showering and shaving. We looked at each other. I turned around and went back to my room. I waited until 9:00am. I walked across campus to the administration building. I returned the envelope with the key and said a mistake had been made. The woman behind the counter said, "There was no mistake. This key was for Dennis Tracy." I said, "No, the key was for Denise Tracy. I am Denise. I need a different room. You have cashed my check. I am going to be a student here. I need a different room."

Every woman I know who attended theological school during the '70s has some version of this story. We felt called to ministry and the world tried to wrest our dream from our hands, minds, and spirits. We were met with micro-aggressions or bold assaults. Every woman I know from this era has the scars of battling the supposedly kind and loving male dominated church.

Each class began with a professor saying, "Good Morning or

Good Afternoon Gentlemen." During my psychology exam, the Freudian examiner said with his Austrian accent, "Don't vorry. You vill not haff to graduate. You vill not haff to finish this program. You are very pretty. You vill get your M.R.S. degree." I was on the Faculty/Student governance committee. The same professor asked me if it was my time of the month when I disagreed on some point.

I went to theological school a 21-year-old, pretty and smart girl. Within a week I became an insecure woman who was enraged by the treatment of the good men of the church. I had paid my tuition in full. It was non-refundable. How could I have been so naïve? Salvation was nearby, however. I was told about a class down the road at Boston College, taught by Dr. Mary Daly. I signed up. She was the most intelligent and the angriest woman I have ever known. Boston College tried once a year (despite her multiple degrees and the many languages she spoke) to fire her. She was saved each year, by the protests of students. Dr. Daly entered my life and helped me study the story of *The Church and the Second Sex*. For my class paper, I interviewed every professor at Andover Newton. I asked a series of questions, trying to measure their feminist quotient. Afterwards, I visited them all and told them the score I had given them and why. The Freudian gave all the "right" answers, but I failed him and told him of my experiences with him (the Mrs. degree and my time of the month) which said that his actions and words belied his correct verbal answers. I visited and gave a copy of my paper to each faculty member, so that everyone knew the grades that others had received. Every faculty member knew my name and I got an A on my paper from Mary Daly!!!

In Daly's class at Boston College, I met students from other Boston Theological Schools. I discovered that there was a committee made up of women from each of the 8 Boston theological schools. I applied to represent my school. Our advisor was a woman named Mary Lou Thompson, a Unitarian Universalist, editor of the book *Voices of the New Feminism* and a UUWF staff member. (I had grown up in Connecticut and my only knowledge of Unitarian Universalism was driving by our local UU Church on my way to my voice lessons one summer. The sign out front said, "God Trusts Us—See You In September!" My father only harrumphed when I asked what the sign meant.)

I took a class at Harvard Divinity School. There were a few women and together we bought whistles and whenever the professors used sexist language (man, mankind, or God the Father) we blew our whistles. We made both Time and Newsweek magazines with our experiment. However, I could not convince the women at Andover Newton to buy and toot whistles at offensive sexist language.

In the spring of 1972, I went to my denominational "check in." It was there I discovered that they would only "allow" me to work with the children of the church and not to preach or become a minister. I left that meeting in a state of extreme distress. I was going through a living hell, not to become a minister? I arrived at the Women's Theological Coalition meeting. At check in, I talked about my upset as a result of my denominational meeting. Afterwards Mary Lou asked if we could talk. She listened to me. She said, "I have known you for a few months. I think you might be a Unitarian Universalist. Our denomination is as sexist as the others, but we permit women to be parish ministers. It won't be easy, but I think you would fit right in." We talked more. She found a phone, called the UUA and made an appointment for me the next day at the Department of Ministry with Dr. George Spencer. I traveled to 25 Beacon St. (Mary Lou had written a letter of reference, which she had delivered by hand on her way to work at the UUWF that morning.) I was interviewed and became a UU candidate for ministry that day.

Becoming Unitarian Universalist brought the various pieces of my life into a unified whole. My illness, my seemingly radical choice of career and my desire to live the fullest life possible, all were affirmed by Universalist Unitarianism. Reading and studying liberal religious theology affirmed my belief that I had shared this faith all my life and had just not known that our denomination existed. The Universalist theology that all people are loved and saved by God gave me a joy that allowed me to explore my faith fully. The Unitarian belief that God was One force in the universe and all divinity was in that power delighted me. I felt that I could explore my own faith and affirm my own and the choices of others, freely. I saw a vision for what my ministry in the parish might offer.

Because of Mary Lou, I learned that Allies are crucial. Over the next several years, I became very close friends with Mary Lou Thompson and her husband, Max. Mary Lou talked with the then UUWF Director Libby Scarlatos about programming at the 1974 New York City, UUA General Assembly. Libby and Mary Lou wanted me to be ordained at the General Assembly, in an all-woman ceremony to affirm women's increasing role in the UUA. The UUWF Board approved their plan. The Bedford Massachusetts congregation, where I was youth group advisor, voted to ordain me, and send representatives to GA for the ceremony. It was quite a wonderful celebration. All the speaking parts were filled by women important, either to me or the UUWF. I did not know this was unusual. It was only the second ordination I had ever attended. The highlight for me: Gloria Steinem was the Ware Lecturer that year. I was introduced to her a few hours before my ordination.

I took my first job as a Campus Minister in Hartford, where I went to college. When I took the position in 1974, I was told that I was the 8th woman employed in ministry in the UUA. There were more women ordained but not currently working.

That fall, I attended my first UU Minister's Chapter meeting. Connecticut Massachusetts District ministers met once a month. I still remember sitting in a circle. I was the only woman. I was 24 years old, and I was the only person in the room under the age of 50. I learned that this CMD UUMA Chapter began their meetings by every member telling the best dirty joke they had heard since the last meeting. One person over from me, a colleague, started telling a joke about a boy named Jose, from Mexico, who was attending his first American baseball game. Jose was impressed that the players, each one of them, had four balls. There was loud laughter. (Oh joy, sexist and racist, I thought. I was so shocked that I don't remember the next few jokes.) I knew if it got to be my turn, I would have no joke to tell and that I could not be silent. Then it was the Minister of the Unitarian Church of Hartford, Nat Lauriat's, turn to speak. He was quiet for a long, long time. He looked up at me and said, "I have a daughter your age. I would not want her to be in this position. This dirty joke telling isn't going to work anymore, is it?" "Not if you want me to attend," I replied.

In one fell swoop the group gave up their beloved custom. They changed because they recognized that my presence required them to do so. These 8 guys became my allies. Over my two years in campus ministry, every one of them invited me to preach from their pulpits. They gave me wedding referrals and created classes that I could teach. I spoke at UUWF meetings in their churches. I learned about ministry in our discussions and listened to what particular struggle each one brought to our meetings. Every one of them gave me respect and helped me launch my ministerial career. As I interviewed for positions in Parish Ministry, they helped me understand the search process. When I left for my church in Greater Lansing, I knew I had 8 ministers on whom I could call, should I ever need help or advice.

In the future when denominational change was impossibly slow or impeded by arguments on wording or phrasing, or timetables, I remembered my experience with my CMD colleagues. They had let me into their circle and changed their very way of being collegial to welcome me. Later when it took 8 years to pass the Purposes and Principles, I conjured the kindness of those 8 men and had faith.

Being the first to fill any role is exciting. It is also threatening, both to the person who is first and to those who are experiencing the "first." As I traveled around Connecticut and Massachusetts, every time I preached, someone would come up and say, "I have never heard a woman preach before." Or "This is a first for me!" I would often laugh and reply, "Oh?" or "And?" They, too, would smile and laugh. By my presence, I felt that some future woman minister in Massachusetts and Connecticut would have an easier time, because I had been there before them. At least I hoped so.

I was filled with denominational zeal. I learned about congregational health. I studied how to explain our faith to strangers in anticipation of ministering to a growing, thriving congregation. Unitarian Universalism had clarified my faith and affirmed my pastoral aspirations. I wanted to return these gifts in full measure by having a successful ministry in a growing parish.

When I left for Greater Lansing, I was 26 years old. I had visited my Doctor for my usual kidney check-up. The results were surprising. My kidney function, although low, put me into a category where I could put away any fears of dying. I could never carry a pregnancy to full term, but if I was careful, I could live a normal life. The Universalist Church of Lansing had ordained Augusta Chapin in 1863. It was not an event they remembered. They were proud that in their 138 years of history, they had called over 50 ministers. I pointed out to them that from a clergy point of view, this was something to be alarmed about. Their longest tenured ministry had been one minister who had stayed for nearly 6 years. A few ministers had been in the congregation for only months before leaving and one had been dumped in the river after a congregational disagreement. It was a surprise to them that longer ministries pointed to both the stability and health of a congregation.

The Lansing church had merged the Unitarian Fellowship of East Lansing and The Universalist Church of Lansing before the denominational merger. As with the denominational merger the Unitarians were dominant in the congregation. Many Michigan

State Professors and State Government employees, who had to have a religious affiliation in order to teach or work, found Unitarianism the least offensive of protestant denominations. As a congregation it was not strong. The salary was $10,000 a year, with a few benefits.

When I arrived in Greater Lansing, it was a congregation of about 60 on a Sunday morning. They had no music. None. Not even a piano. No hymnals, either. How could anyone worship without music? I took my autoharp, printed some paper hymnals and we sang girl scout rounds and '60s Pete Seeger and Holly Near songs. They rolled their eyes a bit, but they sang along. Eight years later, by the time I left this ministry, attendance on Sunday morning was 225. We had a baby grand piano, a part time choir director as well as a 40-voice choir. We had to build a new sanctuary to house the larger worshipping congregation. (I was in Lansing from 76-84, for 8 years. I became their longest tenured minister. A record I held for another 20 years.)

I had to take classes to learn how to minister to a growing church—how to run a Capital campaign, how to finance and build a new sanctuary. The Alban Institute saw me once or twice a year. I took classes in mediation because my church was quite argumentative, with each other more than with me. Members argued about everything. When our new worship center was just about finished, a church member who was a well-known artist in the community, wanted to hang a very large prism, that would reflect a 6-foot rainbow on the sanctuary wall when the sun shone brightly. I advised him to not tell anyone and just install the prism. I told him it would take months of discussion and arguments for permission. (Next to

Seattle, Lansing had the second highest number of cloudy days each year in the USA.) He hung the prism. One Sunday, suddenly a huge rainbow lit the sanctuary, it was a beautiful surprise, and it was met with applause. Sometimes it is better not to ask but to act.

There were issues with my being a woman, however. The worst of these issues was someone, who for the last four years of my ministry, left me bizarre and threatening letters. I took them all to my Committee on Ministry. We went to the police. When I announced that I was engaged and going to be married, the tone of the letters increased in their anger and threat. On the day of my wedding, a plain clothed police officer and two men from my congregation were ready to intervene should this unknown person try to harm me. This is the primary reason I began to think about leaving Lansing. I felt off kilter and unsafe. The final incident, however, was startling. While I was on sabbatical, the church hired a "wanna be policeman" to be our live in sexton. Upon my return, I came into the building late one night to get a book I had forgotten. Suddenly I heard the words, "Put your hands up, or I'll shoot!" There he was gun drawn in the stairwell. His pistol, aimed right at me! I looked at him and said, "You're fired! Be out of the building by noon tomorrow!"

I called the UUA the next day and activated my name. The individual who wrote the anonymous threatening letters, continued doing this to the next several women ministers at the Greater Lansing Church. When he was finally seen putting a letter under the door of the minister's office and was confronted, the congregation had no mechanism for severing the relationship with this member. He was never asked to apologize to either the congregation or to any of the women in ministry that he had hurt and harassed.

During what would be the last two years of my ministry in Greater Lansing, (1982-84), I was asked to be Vice President of the UUMA Executive Committee. I was to work on a new portfolio called Center, which would support a conference on some aspect of ministry. It was the first time that ministerial renewal and excellence would be explored by the UUMA. Wellsprings was the first such conference sponsored by the UUMA. The program had both female and male speakers and the issues we explored were work/ life balance and self-renewal and resilience in the challenging field of ministry. What I experienced in my time on the Exec was sacred collegiality. We worked with the deepest issues of ministry, ministers and the UUA. I would return home from meetings, inspired by the professional strength and support of my colleagues.

One issue I remember quite clearly was a well-known UU Minister had lied to the Department of Ministry about taking CPE. He had asked for approval to work with a therapist and have a practicum experience in lieu of traditional CPE. Problem: The therapist he had supposedly worked with had lied for him. He never completed the work and therefore did not satisfy the CPE requirement for being fully credentialed. The UUMA received a report after the UUA had struggled with the situation and had taken no action. Our UUMA Exec took exception with the lack of action from the UUA. It was the first time I saw our denomination in a light that was problematic. The UUMA's job was to hold all ministers to a high professional standard. Sometimes this standard differed from the one held by the UUA.

The UUA was a typical white male denomination. At the time

of merger, the 1961 UU Theological statement of the Fatherhood of God and the Brotherhood of Man reinforced both the male dominated relationships and processes of the denomination. As a young man entered ministry, there was a track. There were starter congregations. A male minister took one of these and if he did well, then there was a second level church, then a third. There were exceptions. The sons of well-known ministers could skip a level and move to a larger more prestigious church, and no one would object. The Department of Ministry had a tight hold on the lists of ministerial candidates given to open congregations. General Assembly was a time when the person in charge of creating the lists for Open Pulpits was courted and lobbied by male ministers who wanted to change congregations. One person was responsible for all this work. This staff person was the most powerful person in the UUA. There was no way to ask questions, challenge or to examine either the process or the bias of that person. To do so was to risk offence and not have one's name put on desirable church lists.

There was also another invisible level of bias. The UUA had six District Executives. The Continent was divided into six large areas and one UUA staff person worked each area. For the most part the largest churches received the benefit of these staff persons' time. But the DE's could prevent or promote a minister's career track. After I became a DE, one told me, "Anyone that I don't want to be a minister in my District, will never become a minister in my District." By either working with the UUA Department of Ministry or by providing references to search committees, there was undue influence in the search process by the District Executives. The

Department of Ministry and the DEs had a closed power system.

It worked mostly because everyone agreed to it. If a guy was doing pretty well in ministry, he could move up the church scale, without too much trouble. In 1978, however, one guy upset the apple cart. The name of a new graduate was placed on a search list that would have been a church for a ministerial candidate with 20 years of experience. The church was a plumb placement with a salary of over $100,000 plus an equal amount in generous benefits, making it one of the most desired churches in the UUA. Somehow a new male graduate's name got on the list of this church and the search committee called him. The issue was brought to both the UUA Board and to the UUMA Exec. Because of congregational polity, and the will of self-determination of each congregation, there was nothing to be done. But the cracks of invisible bias in the search process were becoming visible and therefore questions were surfacing.

Added to the bias in the search process was the end of the Viet Nam war. When the war ended in 1974, all the young white men who were holed up in seminaries dodging the draft, suddenly had no reason to hide there anymore. They left en masse. As a result, theological schools lost approximately half their students. What to do? Women had begun applying to these same schools. In 1975, the incoming class of students at most theological schools was 50% or more, female.

Up until this point there were a few women in each year's theological school class. Before 1974, there would have been one woman on each list for open pulpits sent to search committees, but by 1978 there would be 3-4 names of women on the list of "starter" congregations. This was a new experience for congregations.

Suddenly there became a Tsunami of women preparing for ministry. Women were not content with the secret process of the UUA search process. The young male theological student who had jumped four levels of congregation to the plumb assignment also added to the questioning of the search process. While I was on the UUMA Executive Board we worked with the UUA on a proposal that each District would have an Executive, a UUA staff person. In the beginning, the UUA would pay more of the salary and costs but as the congregations were better served it was the hope that congregational contributions would increase and take over expenses. The new DEs would work in Building Programs, Ministerial/Congregational Relationships, Conflict Resolution, Religious Education, Fund Raising and Growth. There were two rules for the new DEs. The DEs would have nothing to do with the search process. DEs would not even be allowed to provide references for potential candidates. The second rule was: "DE's were to visit every congregation in their District at least once every two years." The plan was to strengthen the relationship between the UUA and every local congregation, no matter their size. The plan was also to increase the financial support by the congregations to the denomination. Every District would raise the equivalent of the salary and expenses of their own District Executive.

The new District Executives began to be hired in the spring of 1984. I had activated my name. I was one of the two new DE's hired in the first year of the program. My contract was an 8 year, "terminal" or not to be renewed agreement. This was different than the original 6 DE's, several of whom had been in position for long years of service. The new DEs were not to be involved in the ministerial search process from either congregational or ministerial side of the process. But until all the original DEs were gone, there were DEs who saw themselves as "in control" of the ministers who could fill "their" open pulpits. DE meetings were interesting. The conversations between the "old" and the "new" DEs were sometimes spirited. The long-term DEs had a wealth of experience and knowledge. They were in their late '50s or early '60s. If a name of a lay person, congregation or minister was mentioned, there was a cache of knowledge constantly shared. The new DEs often had a different sense of ministry and power.

I was 34 years old. The first woman to ever hold a DE position. When I accepted the DE position for Central Midwest District, there was no blueprint. There were vague notions of a job description. My husband left his job and career to move with me to Chicago. Through connections he found a job as a Fortune 500 Company Executive Trainer. He traveled Mondays to Thursdays two to three weeks every month. I traveled the five states of Central Midwest District, Thursdays to Sundays three to four weeks of every month. It was both hectic and fulfilling.

When I arrived in Central Midwest District, the dues for each congregation were $2 per person. Over my eight years, the dues were increased to $23 per member. (By the end of my 8 years, the amount collected was equal to the equivalent of my total salary and benefits.) As I traveled, I worked on congregational growth. I helped with about 19 building programs. I matched Meadville Lombard theological students with small congregations so students could have hands on ministerial experience—MITs were

Minister's in Training. Small congregations and ministerial students both benefitted from this program. We started the Midwest Leadership School. I also counseled and mediated arguments.

I remember two arguments particularly:

One was a minister, who had a visual disability. The congregation knew and said they accepted this when he was called to serve them. After a few months one woman insisted that the minister had ignored her when she tried to talk to him during coffee hour. She was enraged at being ignored. In listening, it seemed to me that the noise of coffee hour had interfered with this minister's ability to hear. He had simply had not heard her and since he could not see her, he had walked away. The church board was caught between this angry woman and their new minister. They did not speak up and support him. In some way his disability made it difficult for them to connect with him. Within months, this minister was gone.

The second was a Board President who was uncomfortable that her minister was openly gay. She felt that people would not want to join a church that had a gay minister. I conducted a process. The minister, in a private session with me, listed the characteristics and vision of the ministerial/congregational relationship. That night the Board did the same activity. During a break, I took the newsprint sheets and hung them next to each other. The vision and characteristics of the ministerial/congregational relationship were nearly identical. No place on either sheet appeared any mention or concern about the sexuality of the minister. Everyone studied the sheets. One brave person said, "We are well matched. This is a non-issue." Many years later this minister retired from this same congregation.

There were other situations where roadmaps for mediation or assistance had not been created. There were several cases of married ministers, who discovered they were gay. They left their spouses and their congregations. The spouses often remained in the church. In these cases, both persons and institutions were wounded and suffering. Trying to help was difficult. There were ministers who needed to leave ministries because of alcoholism or sexual involvement with congregants. Negotiations were part of the DE portfolio. In a negotiated settlement (the ending of the relationship between a minister and a congregation) as DE, I was the UUA/congregational representative. It was my job to represent the congregation and to as much as possible keep the church from being harmed. Often, I was in the room with a UUMA representative whose job it was to protect the minister. There are still ministers who have not forgiven me for the role I filled as a DE. This was before any rules of sexual boundaries had been adopted by either the UUMA or the UUA. At that time ministers were allowed to move from one place to another (to protect the minister). I did not see how quietly moving a minister helped our congregations, since ministers who acted in this way would most likely repeat these very actions. At DE meetings the truth would be revealed in conversations over dinner or late at night with a glass of wine by the fire. I was heartbroken by the pain in our congregations, often caused by unaware and unconscious ministers, aided and abetted by a secretive process.

There were apocryphal stories that were repeated in groups of

women-only clergy. The New Hampshire Vermont District had 19
ministers. Their retreat site was a lodge with 10 rooms with a set
of bunk beds in each room. Adding the UUA Staff person to the
19, meant there were 10 rooms and 20 beds for 20 people. This
was fine, as long as there were only males attending the UUMA
Retreat. When the first woman minister joined this chapter, the
19 ministers and UUA staff member, Gene Pickett, arrived at the
Lodge. Perhaps someone had thought about this situation, but no
one had taken any action. The first day, there was a lot of awkward-
ness. "Who would 'sleep with' the woman colleague?" At the end
of the day, Gene Pickett pulled her aside and said, "I have three
daughters. How about if we share a room?" They worked out who
would change and when. Gene Pickett was a man of elegance and
trust. He saw the awkward moment and thought about being a
father. He modeled how to transform a flawed process by being
kind. He used the power of his Department of Ministry position
for good.

Women struggled silently. One woman, who was not well
enough to write a paper for this book shared her story with me. "I
was the first woman to ever attend my UUMA chapter meeting.
After one of our sessions, I was walking across the lounge. A group
of male colleagues was sitting and one of them was lying on the
floor. As I walked by the prone man called out. 'Why don't you
come over here and sit on my face.' The men laughed. The next
day as I was walking by some phone booths, an arm reached out,
grabbed me, pulled me into the booth and felt me up. It was a
terrible experience for me." Women shared our stories whenever
we were together. We had a conference at Grailville (the first 40

women in UU ministry were invited to attend, 29 did.) UUA Department of Ministry staff person, Leon Hopper, was an ally providing funding ($20,000) for a grant Marni Harmony and I wrote. It was startling to listen to stories and share music and worship. I still remember our last night together, during a lightning storm, the one woman who was nursing gave some of her milk, and as the thunder and lightning crackled overhead, we shared a mother's milk communion. We swore each other to secrecy. Since this tale has been shared elsewhere, I share it again.

Being sexually "hit on" by male colleagues was part of the life of women in ministry. Learning to retire early, deflect touch or hugs in an oblique way, listening to sexist jokes, this was terrain that women in ministry learned to endure and/or smile at. It was too distressing to take it seriously or too arduous to confront each time these behaviors occurred. But the question remained, did these guys do this in their churches at home? Over time, the behaviors changed. When there were more women in meetings, we could speak up, sit together, and respond and support each other. When the UUA and the UUMA began establishing guidelines for both acceptable interpersonal behavior and appropriate boundary conduct, the world for women ministers became less fraught with male sexual power dynamics.

Being an employee of the UUA was mostly wonderful. There were exceptions, however. At General Assembly, all UUA employees were expected to be in the "Bull Pen" during plenary sessions. If a member of one of our congregations needed to consult with us, we could leave for short times with permission from our supervisor. It always worked out that I had my period during GA.

One year there were a number of people that wanted to talk to me during plenaries. I kept asking my boss Bob Hill, Chair of the Field Staff Department, for permission to leave. I finally sat down and discovered that the session was being extended. I needed to change my tampon. I asked Bob if I could leave to go to the restroom. He said, "You've been out a lot." I felt snappish and said, "Bob, is it okay if I go to the women's room? I have my period. I need to change my tampon." This was never an issue again.

When I adopted two special needs daughters from Thailand, I became the only member of the cadre of DE staff (both old and new) that had school age children. DEs were asked to be on the road 15-20 days a month. To make parenting work, my husband and I had overnight sitters and schedules that were complicated. One June, when GA was in Boston, I drove with two kids in the van (1,400 miles) from Chicago to my parents' house in Vermont. I left my children with my parents for 12 days. I drove to Boston for a 3-day, pre-GA DE staff meeting. I then attended Ministry Days, followed by GA and then a three-day post GA meeting. I returned to Vermont, picked up my children, drove home to Chicago. I arrived home, did laundry, repacked for everyone and within 24 hours was in Wisconsin for the Lake Geneva Summer Assembly. I was on the planning council of the camp, this meant arriving early and staying late. I was on the road from June 1 until July 12th.

There are two contributions I feel that I have made to our faith of which I am proud. The first of these is the many conferences I have helped to plan.

— The Women Minister's Conference at Grailville in1978. (The first gathering of the second wave of UU Women Clergy)

— The first Women and Religion Committee Conference at Grailville in 1979. (The Purposes and Principles were begun at this conference.)
— The first Continental Women and Religion Conference in East Lansing at MSU in 1980. It was the first conference of its kind, held with the support of both the UUA and Beacon Press.
— Wellsprings, a conference for ministers, which began the CENTER- conferences for ministerial support and excellence.
— WomanSpirit, the continental conference for 500 women, which was to set the agenda for feminism's future in the UUA, held at Lake Geneva, WI in 1990.

At these conferences feminist ideas were articulated. As a result, in the months and years after each event, the work to change our denomination continued. At these events worship, learning and deep interpersonal connection happened. Women were strengthened and our vision for the Unitarian Universalism was sharpened. We envisioned and sacrificed our life's energy to create and reveal a new denomination. I had an unshakable faith in the friendships of women in our denomination. I also knew that the divine power of equality would sustain me through anything.

My second contribution is support for the presence of children in our worship services. During my years in New England and when I arrived in Greater Lansing, there was total separation between the adult worshipping congregation and the Sunday school for children. This was true in most congregations at that time (1970s). I wondered how could children grow up to be church members in adulthood if they never entered the sanctuary for worship? I started having the children attend worship for 20 minutes one Sunday a month. I created resources and stories for these services. Other ministers heard what I was doing and as a result, I taught workshops at conferences. I published four volumes of Stories for Worship called *The Stream of Living Souls* series. These books are still used today. Most congregations invite the children into the sanctuary for part of the service now. I feel that I was part of this change.

In 1991, I was starting the last of my 8 years as DE. (In January, the 6-month sabbatical that was part of my contract, would begin, so I could look for another ministry.) During Thanksgiving break, I had a routine mammogram. I was diagnosed with breast cancer. The screenings showed three additional metastatic sites, giving me a stage four diagnosis. Instead of the contracted sabbatical, I asked the denomination if this could be turned into a medical leave, so I could receive necessary treatment. The UUA granted this. There was a prominent laywoman in my district who said I was taking advantage of the District. The UUA went to bat for me and approved the medical in place of a sabbatical leave, over any stated objections. I was scared and exhausted. I did not have the energy for an argument that I felt was pointless. I left my position in the winter of 1992 on medical leave in place of a sabbatical. I received almost 700 get well cards and letters.

I had two special needs children. I was not able to think about interviewing or moving. The idea that I might die, leaving my husband with two children to raise alone, humbled me. A rule had been put in place that as a DE I could not be in conversation about ministry with any congregation that we had worked with in the previous three years. I also could not be in contact with any Central Midwest District congregation. This meant if I followed the rules, I could not preach or minister in any congregation in my former District. I also could not attend any UUMA gatherings. I felt isolated and cut off from my community. I also believed in keeping my covenants with both the UUMA and the UUA. I did so.

The day I was to start chemo, I had an appointment for a third opinion with the head of all Women's Health at RUSH Hospital. I brought all my scans and reports. She spread them out. "As a teen, you had radiation for kidney disease?" Yes. She looked at the metastatic sites and asked me, "What sports were you active in?" "Gymnastics and skiing." "What injuries did you have?" I told her I had some cracked ribs along my spine and … she stopped me. Pointing to my scans she said, "My dear, these are not cancer spots. These are where the radioactive material has gathered in the healed cracks in your bones. We can give you chemo today, but you are not at stage 4, you are at stage 2. Most probably the radiation to treat your kidney condition years ago has caused this cancer." (I had just finished radiation for my breast cancer.) "With the radiation you have had, you are now at a 95% cure rate. With 10 chemo treatments, we would destroy your health and gain another 2% to 97%. Go home. Enjoy your life. Be happy, this will do more for your health than anything we can do here." It was May. My UUA job had ended. I had a new life before me.

I needed to keep my agreement not to work with area UU congregations in my District for three years. That fall, in 1992, I accepted a position with a church consulting firm who worked with other denominations and faiths across the nation. This became my work for the next 17 years. I consulted in the areas of growth, finance and fund raising, building programs, conflict mediation and boundary violations. To date, I believe I have the record of consulting with a church in Chicago where there were 75 complainants against their minister for sexual misconduct. I worked with this congregation for three years. My role as a District Executive had given me skills that prepared me for the new world of church life.

From 2007-2011, I returned to the UUA to do Interim Ministry. I loved this work. I retired and now do Law Enforcement and Hospital Chaplaincy. Over the years, I have watched the work I did to build up my District gradually go back to the large District system. Nearly every Sunday I preach at small lay led UU churches. I love their courage. Recently, one of them was having some financial troubles. I suggested they call their District. There was confusion. "Why?" "Well, they are there to help. How long has it been since someone from your District has been here?" "Over a decade," was the reply. "How much money do you give to the UUA?" "We don't," came the response. The years I tilled those fields are forgotten. Yet the UUA is still my faith.

One of the gifts I have been given in Unitarian Universalism is the opportunity to work with astounding people: ministers, lay people, artists, and musicians. Musician Holly Near was a program guest at several conferences I helped to plan. As a result, I was able to be her contact person for these events. She is a model for me of faithful and justice filled living. She wrote these lyrics:

"We are a gentle, angry people …
We are a justice seeking people …
We are a gentle, loving people …
And we are singing, singing for our lives."

I am still singing.

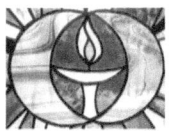

Anecdotes of a Feminist Minister

Alice Blair Wesley

IN THE EARLY 1950S I was one of 2600 students at an urban high school. I played viola in our symphony. I took plane and solid geometry, physics, chemistry, Latin and French, plus required English and history courses. I planned to become, and after college did become, a high school teacher. Unless a middle-class American woman wanted to be something really far out, like—say—a foreign missionary, she could be a secretary, nurse or teacher. Nobody ever told me; I just "knew" that. I never even wondered, "Who said?" Other women knew it, too. Foolish as it now sounds, I did not start seminary for 20 years after high school because it just wasn't done except by a minuscule few. The point is I did not start out as a feminist.

Had I been born male; I likely would have gone straight from college to seminary. In my family a grandfather, my dad, a cousin and two nephews—all male, of course—have been Baptist preachers and ministers. The religious impulse in me was strong before and after husband Joe and I joined Louisville's First Unitarian Church at age 23. As a university student of literature, I was drawn to poets of the ineffable, importantly including Ralph Waldo Emerson. I was later for about three years obsessed with the religious drama of ancient Greece. And by the '70s I had been about as active as a lay member could be, for two years in the fellowship of a Houston suburb, and for ten years in our large and thriving church in Wilmington, Delaware. I don't know how any minister can function without prior experience in a healthy church. I eventually served two new and seven troubled congregations. For sure I made mistakes, but I did as well as I did because I carried in mind a model of what a vibrant liberal congregation can be.

I don't remember precisely why I began to think often of studying for the ministry. One day out of the blue, my Wilmington minister, Bob Doss, said, "If you are going to spend so much time at church, you may as well go into the ministry." I don't remember how I replied. I think I mostly just stuttered. But found out like that, I had to talk with Joe—who was about to be transferred again to Texas—and to apply to Starr King and Meadville/ Lombard for admission as a non-resident. Starr King's president, Bob Kimball, said no way. As it happened, Meadville's President Malcolm Sutherland and I were each close friends with Dr. Warren Busse, a First Wilmington member. Warren sent Malcolm a rather glowing letter of recommendation. Meadville accepted me as a special, mostly non-resident student.

So, in the fall of 1973, having moved to Texas in the summer, I began taking graduate courses in history, psychology and speech at Beaumont's Lamar University. And in January 1974, I made the first of many flights to Chicago so that I could spend the first three weeks of the winter quarter at Meadville. The Rev. Prof. James Luther Adams had begun his professorial career in Chicago before he was called to Harvard. Meadville and the U.C. Divinity School had brought him from Harvard back to Chicago for the '73-'74 academic year. Adams' scholarship, passion and generosity had done much to shape generations of UU seminary students. Within hours of my arrival, he was generously talking with me about Greek drama. He readily agreed that tapes of his winter course on Liberal Doctrine of the Church could be mailed to me. My work on covenant has influenced our Association. I first learned from Jim Adams the significance of our 17th century New England ancestors' understanding and practice of covenant.

The 30 hours graduate credit I earned from Lamar were not cheap. Nor were my many round-trip Beaumont-to-Chicago flight tickets. But Meadville charged me no tuition, and I paid nothing for the dorm apartment I used for two or three weeks of every quarter until ordination. The library even let me carry home a suitcase full of books every time I left. I only learned later how controversial I was. A friend and I were chatting in a hallway before some General Assembly event. When another person joined us, my friend introduced me to a Meadville board member. "Alice Blair Wesley!" he exclaimed. "We talked about you by the hour at every meeting for three years!" I had found the faculty personally very supportive, but one professor was adamant that my special treatment would prove to be a disastrous precedent. Of course, we didn't have computers in the '70s. Once everybody had one, "distance learning" could become the norm, letting more women with families than ever before study for our ministry. Now all Meadville's students spend only a short period of each term in Chicago. I could not engage every day by computer with faculty and other students, as they do. Otherwise, their student days look much as mine did. Nobody then guessed that would ever be the case.

Even so, in the '70s some Unitarian Universalist men saw the rightness of getting more women into ministry, however it might be done. I would never even have got into seminary, nor become the particular minister I did, without the empowering help of UU men who were feminist before I was. I have named some on whom I depended because I want you to know who they were. While I was yet a student, more ministers in the Southwest Conference than I can now name—all men—invited me to preach from their pulpits, as did lay led groups. And thanks to Russ Lockwood of the UUA field staff, I was called to serve as student minister of a fellowship.

A little story illustrates my way of doing feminist ministry. I was an intern in a Houston hospital. After a stroke, a patient was brain dead. His brother, who would shortly have to tell the staff to take away life support, was in a waiting area. I approached, introduced myself, and put out my right hand. "I am Chaplain Wesley. I understand you face a hard decision." The man did not stand or extend his hand. Still seated he said, "You women are going to take over the world." As I sat down, I said, "Well, I don't want to take on the world. I just want this chair here beside you. Tell me, please, about your brother." He dropped at once the sexist gruffness and let me help him lighten by a little the terrible burden of his grief.

Ministry is about meeting people's needs. It is not about the minister's identity, nor about the authority given the minister, or not. And it is not about sexism, which nobody needs. Good ministry can require getting sexism out of the way, and the same is true of racism, regionalism, and even dogmatic humanism of the sort that bad mouths every faith except its know-it-all self. A focus on real needs is the best way to make-isms go away. Granted, the needs to be met are seldom so easily discerned as in my anecdote. Still, good ministry—to an individual, a congregation, an institution, or the general public - requires a primary focus on meeting real needs. It can't happen if the minister is more concerned about something else.

I was ordained by members of our Beaumont Church at the Sunday morning service following the 1977 Annual Meeting of the Southwest Conference. The service was supposed to be outside, but rain in a subtropical area can come down hard, indeed. Because of predicted rain I was ordained in a Jewish temple. The invocation was danced. A jazz combo provided instrumental music. Joe sang songs from Bernstein's "Mass." Bob Doss gave the sermon. Conference ministers laid hands on my head. It was all fabulous, as was the lunch Beaumont members served to 300. Because Joe's position in Beaumont lasted another year afterward, I worked with the fellowship and also the Corpus Christi Church for another year. Then Joe's firm moved us East again.

I give you a quick summary of my ministries. I served nine congregations. I was with two, each for a three- year term, because we were part of the UUA Extension Program (long since ended).

My time with others varied from one to seven years. Two were small because they were new. One, five decades old, had only about 60 members. Two had 200 and 240 members respectively when I left them. All save the new groups were in trouble when I went to them. I helped one congregation to add a much-needed adult meeting room, two to buy a used building, and one to finance and construct a new building. Having no previous training or experience, two RE Directors began their life-long careers with me. One of them went on to be for many years the RE Director of a large and growing church in another state. The other one became an MRE who was eventually the senior UU minister in his District. Membership in one of the smaller congregations I served now exceeds 400. Another one has not grown but is strong and influential in a small and poor town.

My reasons for working with so many weak congregations were three: family, money, and mission. Very young, I married a very young and smart guy. We had two daughters. I would never have left Joe and our children. He had made career commitments long before I was ready for seminary.

So, he was geographically mobile in his career, as I never was in mine. So, I never earned a salary anybody could live on. But then Joe earned big money. I could let it be known that I would gladly serve any UU congregation, so long as the members wanted to grow and would put me up in their homes, and so long as their meeting place was within a two-hour drive, or flight, from our house. (I flew on little puddle-jumper planes to Corpus Christi, Texas and to Cumberland, Maryland.) Joe's lay ministry merits honor. His salary paid for my theological education; he repaired a bunch of stuff, built pulpits and other furniture, helped to erect a new building, and subsidized the inadequate budgets of all my congregations. I felt privileged to work full out to strengthen our churches because they were crucial.

I thought so because I had found utterly persuasive James Luther Adams's scholarly convictions: That the covenantal form of several state constitutions and the U.S. Constitution derived directly from the covenants of the 17th century New England churches, from which our UU churches also derive. That other inherited features of democratic society have come to us from the Puritans' radically left-wing readings of Hebrew and Apostolic scriptures. That a church's purpose always follows from the members' ownership of their history, or—as Jim called it—their "whence and whither." Knowledgeable members will want faithfully to keep truly living and lively the best of their past, and also to reform past deficiencies and failures. Thus "the culture flows from the cult." Our members were ignorant of any connection to our Puritan ancestors, much less our derivation. Most had never heard of a contemporary covenant. Not only was it inconceivable to them that a liberal church might be constituted by the members' freely entered promise of affection and fidelity. A few in the '70s and '80s vehemently rejected all "commitments." They thought relationships for personal fulfillment only. These of course vigorously objected to "pledge" campaigns for the church's support.

Ignorance of our history was very far from the only factor, though, in their troubles. Production plants had closed in two towns, taking away leaders, jobs, and sound finances. Half of one congregation partied every Saturday night in a couple's home.

Because their church was important to them, partying members naturally talked often of church business. The other half of the membership felt shut out of decisions by "the in-group." An architect's poor design cost a church tens of thousands of dollars, setting back programming and growth. A rankly prejudiced city Council denied Unitarians a downtown building permit; angry and wounded members floundered afterward for a generation. Other problems resulted from incredibly dumb member doings having to do with money and buildings. One congregation had sold their building lot. In a wildly inflationary era, the money sitting in an account was losing value by the minute. A church really subsidized a large singles organization with an absurdly low rental fee. The singles seriously abused the building and were also responsible for the church's reputation as a "meat market." But who belongs to a church because they want to be in charge of budgets and buildings? The few who do may viciously fight an "outsider" minister who threatens their control.

I was not so much shocked as surprised to learn, in my first two congregations of the havoc wrought in members' lives by a male predecessor's lack of sexual ethics. People come to a church needing and expecting to find trust. When trust is betrayed at church, the emotional pain is intense. Unwarned, I thought I had happened into exceptional situations, but they were not exceptional. I had to deal with these problems in four of nine congregations. One minister's evil behavior went on for years. Though he used and exploited others, too, he provoked tragedy in at least one family. When he was at last fired, some twenty members withdrew and met separately for five years.

We UUs, however, had no tradition whatsoever of gatherings in which the members of several congregations wrestled with church problems and offered one another good advice. That never happened. I had been on two District boards. From 1968 on, I was a delegate at every General Assembly. As a minister I attended dozens of ministers' chapter meetings and study groups.

When Carolyn Owen-Towle was president of the UUMA, the UU Ministers Association did finally begin to deal with ministerial sexual ethics. But in not one of those settings did we ever bring up the many issues of our many little weak groups. Members could call on UUA field staff. Some of could be helpful; some decidedly were not. E.g., I had months ago finished a 3-year Extension term with a church that had seen hard times but come through them. The church had an able support staff and a small but solid RE program, serviceable buildings on acres of land in a fine location, plus good instruments, and really good music. My successor had been called. He and his congregation had a promising future. Then, I was asked, though we had as yet agreed on no details, to consider working with a brand-new congregation. The group, currently renting dank space at a swim club, wanted soon to move to the college town where they lived, 35 or 40 minutes away by car from the church. Absurdly, the church's minister told the UUA field staff person that people might abandon his church for the new group if I were serving it. The field staff man called the new group's president and told him, "If you call Alice Wesley, you'll never get a penny from the UUA."

No wonder we have barely more than a thousand congregations in the country! Whatever assistance I had rendered our congregations at whatever personal cost, this UUA staff guy did not think me worth his time; he did not even call. I had not known of such stupid, underhanded maneuvers in our "democratic" Association. I mourned for months. The new group later died. That very populous county still has only one UU church.

We are sometimes well served by UU institutions independent of the UUA. A small fellowship I used to know well was eventually transformed by what happened to one lay leader at a summer institute. Back home, other members teased him saying he had gone to SWUUSI and "got religion!" Truly, when they can be got to attend, members of a small group may be religiously awakened by sermons and workshops of a quality they had not encountered. In this instance, because one member found a summer institute wonderful, he took others with him when he went back. Before long, changes in their congregation meant it was growing rapidly. That I knew such a story was part of the reason I helped Morris Hudgins to found UUMAC, and every summer for years preached or lectured or taught on Star Island or at SUUSI or Ferry Beach.

Ministry is about meeting people's needs. People in congregations I served had plenty of needs, none having to do with my gender. Yet I would not for a moment seem to imply that gender issues were not important. Indeed, I think most now could hardly imagine the tizzy our Association got into over the women's movement of the late 1970s and 1980s. The Joseph Priestley District board asked me to chair the new District Women and Religion Committee. Our committee of six or eight men and women discussed how we might go about our task. We then asked the board to let our committee plan and run the Fall Conference, an annual

District event. I swear I think to this day that the board feared we might do something scandalous. We were told the answer was no because the Fall Conference should be on a subject of "wider interest."

So, we planned a Women and Religion Conference without board endorsement. The next spring on a Saturday morning, the Rev. Dianne Arakawa read a clear and cogent paper on feminist theologies, to which two women theologians from other communions responded. The 200 participants, who stayed for a choice of afternoon workshops, made our Conference the largest District event in living memory. The next spring's participants numbered 300, with some turned away for lack of space. After that the committee ran spring conferences at two, and then three different locations. Numbers afterwards declined rather precipitously because, I surmised, UUs actually decided pretty quickly that women ministers, and other supporters of the women's movement were not terribly fearsome after all.

Even so, for a while gender issues were big in congregations and for longer in people's personal lives. They could elicit very strong feelings in that learning to see and address sexism is, like peeling an onion, unpleasant. One may feel good about correcting a false assumption and reforming some unjust behavior. But every time a layer is removed, another and then another layer appears. Confusion, resentment, divorce, money troubles and/or suffering children may follow.

Not immediately but eventually, I could laugh at some ridiculously strong feelings. Once at a General Assembly I did not agree with some position advocated by the UUA Women and Religion

Committee and voted against it. That afternoon a couple of members of the very District Committee I had chaired pounded on my hotel room door. When I opened it, he yelled furiously that I had turned into a man! Again, when John Buehrens was running for UUA president, he spoke at my church. I soon received a letter from this same fellow on his lawyer's letterhead, threatening me with a lawsuit.

Usually, I just smiled when a parishioner could not forebear asking who fixed Joe's dinner when I had evening church meetings. At other times I couldn't smile. One day at my last congregation, a very well-respected member, a male attorney, showed up to let me know he was not at all pleased. He asked, "What are you trying to do?" He was upset that I had invited only other women ministers to be guests in our pulpit. I honestly had not noticed. I wish I could yell back at him now, "For crying out loud, so what?" I wouldn't want anyone to think, though, that my ministry was all about the problems I have described. It was also about beautiful and moving organ and choral music, about utterly delightful children, about gratitude for pastoral counseling and teaching sermons, and about the truly good-hearted, interesting, marvelous people in our churches, lots of them. Dealing with the problems was, however, wearing. In 1996 I retired from parish ministry, worn out. Before long Joe and I moved to dwellings in Washington State and Pennsylvania so we could alternately live near grandchildren.

Although not in a congregation, I wound up working as hard after I retired as before. I had once edited dozens of other ministers' papers, especially those given at UU Advance events while I was Advance's president for five years; I had edited my own papers and a book, and friends' books. Retired, I was helping Peter Hughes edit contributions to the new Dictionary of UU Biography. As Berry Street Scribe, I was getting transcribed and posted online scattered Berry Street essays which had been delivered almost annually since 1820. Then, my direction was much affected once more by a male colleague.

Joe and I had been having monthly lunches in Seattle with two other retired ministers and their spouses, never running out of things Unitarian Universalist to talk about. But one day Dick Henry called and asked that we have lunch without the others. Once I was more or less captive in a restaurant booth, he began insisting that I should apply for the Minns lectureship because, he said, the Association needed to hear from me on covenantal theology. I would never have thought of applying but for Dick. He kept pressing on other days until I did. Then, my application having been selected by the Minns Committee, I was obliged to research everything I thought I knew and more, and then to compose and deliver six essays in three cities during the church year 2000-2001.

The Meadville Press published the six essays as a book titled *Our Covenant* in 2002. Because of the book, I was asked to give the keynote address at two District Annual Meetings, to lead three ministers' chapter retreats, to address the UUA board in a Boston meeting, and to publish another paper or two. With nobody's asking, I dozens of times wrote about covenant on our ministers' email chats.

I am past 84 now. Nearly all those of whom I have written about are no longer alive. Robert Bellah years ago gave the Ware Lecture at a General Assembly, his title, *The Broken Covenant*. I was in my working years a feminist trying to persuade any who would listen that ours is, by every right of inheritance and sound thinking, a covenantal religious tradition. If I could, I would do those years over and hope to get more things right. Because of the world's needs, I pray ours will become, with others' efforts, a much stronger living and lively tradition.

A Worthwhile Struggle

Carolyn Owen-Towle

I WAS CLEARLY A WOMAN SHAPED by the expectations of my era.

After completing college in 1957, I eagerly awaited my marriage just days beyond my graduation. Moving from the support and tutelage of my parents, I welcomed the embrace of my husband.

As a young woman, married and expecting to be a housewife, raising kids would be my primary vocation. Nevertheless, I found interests and commitments leading me into community organizations where, as a "privileged" person, I could give back. Somehow, although most often I would begin by sitting at the side of the table, frequently, I found myself gravitate to the end of the table, taking on greater responsibility than I had initially anticipated. Learning a lot, community service fulfilled my need to make some difference in the world.

Our family was growing. I came to realize that my lack of

knowledge about religion made me want to look for what I could honestly share with our children. As good fortune would have it, the first place we visited was Neighborhood Unitarian Church in Pasadena, California. That was it! In a short time, we joined.

For 15 years, my marriage was pretty much what I needed and desired. While comforting and comfortable, we never really grew one another. We began to suffer from a divergence of common language and a poverty of spirit. Estrangement crept up silently. At some point, I recognized that we had little of substance or depth to say to one another. By then, I had become a feminist and was looking at the world differently. I sought counseling.

Given my upbringing and moral strictures, what happened next was out of character and, perhaps, more profoundly, out of loneliness. I fell in love with another man, Tom Towle.

In the very process of my opening up and coming alive, my capacity for intellectual and spiritual growth expanded. And my world quite literally crashed around me. I made the wrenching decision to go to the *light*. That choice brought great pain and anger to many in our family, congregation, and among my friends. I chose to leave my marriage to join forces with Tom, as co-partners in all we would be and do. Painful as the transition was, we were beginning the road toward an egalitarian bond.

Tom, my mate, has always seen women and men as equals. He has literally never been competitive with me in any way. He grew up with a mother who went to college, after three years of high school, worked professionally as a social worker before she was married, and set an example of feminist evolution for her two sons.

Tom remembers my father, early in our marriage, putting his arm around Tom's shoulder and with tears in his eyes, declaring how moved he was that Tom could have me work *alongside* him. Clearly, it was not yet my father's understanding and acceptance of equality. My mother served Dad, helping him achieve unimaginable success.

Increasingly, over a number of years as a layperson, I realized that fellow parishioners came to me for various things: advice, sharing, comfort, and questioning. Grounded in my Unitarian Universalist beliefs by then, I was startled, at one point, to simply know that "I was a minister" and that I'd better become one. It was definitely a call.

I was one of the lucky ones in the early 1970s. We moved to Iowa, where Tom became minister of the Davenport Unitarian Church. One month after we arrived, we learned that the UUA had begun an Independent Study Program for parish ministry. It was intended for women who could not practically access theological schools.

Lo and behold, the University of Iowa, just 65 miles away, was the oldest Graduate School of Religion in the country. Its standing was a prerequisite for the program. I enrolled and studied there for three years, followed by a year of independent study of Unitarian Universalism, in addition to CPE training. Rev. Thomas Mikelson, minister of the Iowa City UU church, and one of the designers of the program, served as my preceptor.

Once my studies were complete, Tom and I applied to several congregations as a team of equals and were called as co-ministers to the First Unitarian Church of San Diego, in 1978. I was the first woman minister in its 105-year history. Tom and I served there for 24 deeply satisfying years.

A confident feminist by then, we intentionally challenged conventional gender stereotypes, with Tom working on the religious education program and my being the ministerial support for the financial operations. Nonetheless, there were moments when parishioners pushed back, such as when I preached on inclusive language, and several male parishioners told me: "You know, Carolyn, when people say 'mankind,' they mean women and men." Really? I learned, then and there, we would aspire to embody inclusivity at every turn and moment ... in everything we said, did, or published.

Looking back, I've no illusion, even though by then there were many feminists in our congregation, that acceptance of me was partially predicated on the fact that there were two of us in the pulpit, and one was a male.

As I began to accept leadership roles in our Association, however, the climate out there was not uniformly accepting. During my tenure as the first woman President of the UUMA, a minister of our UU Church in Santa Barbara, was revealed to have engaged in sex with a large number of female parishioners. It was an awful, troubling scandal with huge continental consequences.

As the UUMA official I was, after the MFC removed him from Fellowship, I was taxed with letting this colleague know that he was also being removed from membership in his/our professional organization.

I remember that day vividly, as I mounted the stairs to my hotel room, wondering whether I could simply jump out the window rather than call him. Call him I did. His response: "Will I lose my insurance?"

As a result of this episode, a number of male ministers, around the continent, became really angry. Back in my church office, I began receiving calls and letters pouring out their anger at me. One letter, in particular, I'll always remember, from a colleague I'd considered a respectful friend, excoriating me up and down for the foul thing the UUMA and I had done. I recall reeling around my office, holding my innards, aching with hurt and feelings of being misunderstood and attacked. Following that, the UUMA began critically teaching ethical responsibility to groups of ministers, making absolutely clear our movement's evolving moral standards and boundaries.

A closing story. When I ran for the UUA presidency from 1991-1993, both women and men supported my candidacy. However, my loss by 99 votes revealed that our progressive movement was not yet ready for a woman as its foremost leader. And it took us until June 24, 2017, before our Association elected a woman President (from among three "women" candidates): The Rev. Susan Frederick-Gray.

Sorely disappointed, at first, we returned to San Diego, where we were met at the airport by a crowd of church members bearing flowers, food, balloons, hugs, joy, and song. After six months of re-appraisal by church leaders and ministers together, we settled back in for nine more years of fruitful co-ministry, with our beloved San Diego congregants ... until we retired.

Questions of Feminism
How Did Being a UU Feminist Change Both You and Your Faith?

Some Answers

Dianne E. Arakawa

WERE YOU BORN A FEMINIST? I was not born a feminist. But I came under its influence from childhood. The first was my mother, who as a nisei (second-generation Japanese American) in Hawaii, experienced the transition from her parents' immigration from Japan to settling in the Hawaiian Islands in 1905. Although she (and her siblings) expected the traditional practice of educating the eldest son then the younger children, this broke down. My eldest uncle chose not just to get only a bachelor's degree but also a master's degree in Chicago then to get married, which somehow tripped up the possibilities and timing for his younger siblings. This included my mother. After I, a girl and the youngest in a patriarchal family, was born and was being educated, mother gave me every opportunity just as with the eldest and boys. She showed no prejudice in offering me every kind of support that they received.

Who were other influences in your growing up? Apart from

the feminist influence of my mother, I was persuaded to become independent, self-reliant, confident, religious, and critical (of patriarchy) because a number of teachers and pastors affiliated with the school that I attended, the Punahou School in Honolulu. This independent school was founded by Congregational Trinitarian missionaries from New England for the education of their own children. The nearby United Church of Christ, Central Union, became a sort of home church for me as an adolescent. Together, the impact of Punahou's teachers, chaplains, staff, and students on my life was significant. In particular, two were art teachers, whom I worked for separately—washing and drying paint brushes and containers and organizing and cataloging art history slides. One was an English teacher, Betty Thrasher, who became a visiting teacher from the Chicago area at my school and invited me to coordinate a Chapel service for my class, based on Genesis 1 and the Kumulipo (Hawaiian creation poem). Another was an American history teacher, Robert Torrey, who cast a critical lens on American politics and later taught President Barak Obama. Still another was Rev. Ray Akin, a Disciples of Christ pastor, who was asked to teach world religions based on Huston Smith's The Religions of Man and asked me spiritual questions.

What happened when you attended a women's college? I entered Wheaton, then a small women's liberal arts college outside of Boston, established by Mary Lyon. Mary Lyon was an educator dedicated to the advancement of women and a Congregationalist. There I found myself in an all-female learning environment, to which I had to adjust, but also where I grew comfortable. Unsurprisingly, I took courses in Art History and Religion—Old & New

Testament, Church history (ancient to the present), Jewish history, and theology. More important, I was taught by three challenging professors—Prof. John Martin, the founder and chair of the department, professor of the New Testament, theology and world religions, and a Congregational lay leader; Rev. Dr. Charles Forman, professor of the Hebrew Bible, Jewish and early church history, and a Christian Congregational-Unitarian Universalist; and Rev. Dr. Harold F. Worthley, professor of European and American church history, and the College Chaplain who was of the UCC. All, who held doctoral degrees from Harvard Divinity School, in time encouraged me to attend divinity school to continue my studies and/or explore Congregational ministry. Some of their mentees had also entered divinity or rabbinical schools. I recall one returning to preach in our Chapel then leading a workshop on religious feminism. Others were pastors or priests in the United Church of Christ or Episcopal Church or served Jewish institutions.

Why did you go to divinity school and how were you changed? As a result of attending a women's college, receiving majors in both Religion and Art History, and being encouraged by three Religion professors, I made the decision to apply to divinity schools but only after a year of employment and discernment. So, that summer I found an apartment in Cambridge, made new friends, took Theological German at Harvard Divinity School, and volunteered at the Museum of Fine Arts in Boston. In the fall I located a position in research at the Houghton Mifflin Company in Boston, worshipped at King's Chapel in Boston under the ministry of Rev. Drs. Carl Scovel and Charles Forman, and soon afterwards explored a couple of divinity schools and seminaries. After a year, I entered Harvard

Divinity School. It is the oldest Congregational-founded divinity school in the country. In some ways, due to my mentoring, it was not very different from my college environment; perhaps, larger, more demanding, with a wider variety of professors (from Roman Catholic to Unitarian Universalist), more diverse, and with a few more feminists and Unitarian Universalists. I had always taken for granted that UCC and UU women clergy had been ordained as early as 1853. But I was still one of a few women and one of two Japanese Americans (the other was male) there.

I took the requisite courses, began to explore ministry in the Unitarian Universalist Association. Other formative steps on this path included interning at First (& Second) Church with Rev. Drs. Rhys Williams and F. Forrester Church in Boston, exploring the Program on Religion & Education at the Harvard School of Education, student-teaching religion at Belmont, MA, High School, and serving as a summer chaplain in Clinical Pastoral Education with Chaplain Allen Reed at the Massachusetts General Hospital in Boston. It was during those three intense years, that I also studied and became conversant with Christian feminism and women's liberation as an anti-dote to Christian patriarchal thinking. The early Prof. Mary Daly, Rosemary Radford Ruether, Phyllis Trible, and Elizabeth Schussler Fiorenza became invaluable guides, and remain so. As a result, I could never read Scripture without remembering Galatians 3:28 (There is no longer Jew or Greek, there is no longer slave or free, there is no longer male and female, for all of you are one in Christ Jesus.), wondering about any hidden or missing textual message, and how to employ a feminist critique on any message. Although my concept of God had always been broad (due especially to having Japanese Buddhist/Mahayanist grandparents and being raised in the Emerald Isles), it widened even more in worship, practice, and language. No more God, he. I received the American Bible Society Prize in reading Scripture before graduation and was offered (preliminary) fellowship in the UUA.

What about the start of your ministry in the UUA? After divinity school, I began ministry at the Community Church in New York City in 1978 and was ordained there. It was the church founded by Rev. Dr. John Haynes Holmes and ministered to by his colleague-successor, Rev. Dr. Donald S. Harrington, and Rev. Vilma Szantho Harrington, the first woman ordained in central Europe. The congregation held a broad theist theology, unlike other humanist UU churches, a robust social action ministry, and was probably the most racially-ethnically diverse congregation in the denomination. With that was a spectrum of notions about feminism, but no outright resistance. The congregation celebrated and grew in diversity (including feminist language) rather than repressed it. I remember representing the church to the Manhattan interfaith clergy meetings; the UUA to the Asian American & Pacific Islander Clergy Women's Caucus in Berkeley, CA, with Rev. (later Bishop) Roy Sano of the United Methodist Church, and to the National Council of Churches' (NCC) Women in Ministry meetings. I met wonderful feminist colleagues including Revs. Denise Tracy, Leslie Westbrook, and Diane Miller. During that period, my spouse, Stephen C. Washburn left teaching at an independent school in New York City to graduate from Union Theological Seminary and be ordained at the same church.

What happened in ministry afterwards? After New York, Steve & I accepted a dual call to the Congregational (UCC) Universalist Church in Woodstock, IL, in the Greater Chicago area. It was outside our comfort zones, as they say, but it was the only church that, despite its whiteness, seemed willing to call "an interracial clergy couple." It held a broad theology (Christian to theist to humanist) and had some great lay leaders. We modeled and managed a gender-balanced co-ministry, used the Bible and other readings from world religion, and were able to address social issues. I became more active in denominational feminist groups, like the Women & Religion Committee, coordinated national meetings, and wrote more. I continued to represent the denomination at Asian American Clergy Women's Caucuses and the NCC Women in Ministry group meetings. At the time, new neo-pagan, Wiccan, UU women clergy began to assert their new-found freedom in the denomination. This began to put exclusionary pressure on Christian and theistic women clergy. (Several had already left for the UCC and other Christian denominations.) To me, the arguments of the neo-pagans were small-minded and tiresome. (For example, I, a Japanese American whose family had been interned in the U.S. during World War II and who had been recognized by the National Council of Church's Women and Religion Committee as the first Asian American woman to be ordained in the U.S., remember being blamed for the Crusades, King Phillips War, then the New England witch burnings.)

Why did you leave UUism after twenty years? The inclusive UUism that I joined after graduating from divinity school was that with the older Purposes & Principles, which affirmed Christianity, theism and humanism, respected world religions as well as thoughtful dissent. At that time, some UU churches in New England seemed to still have a connection to their liberal Christian roots and appeared more broad-minded and forward thinking. They used and even preached from the NRSV Bible, christened children and baptized adults, recited the Lord's Prayer in different forms, and offered Communion with a symbolic understanding of the Real Presence of Christ at least once a month. There was theological engagement, even feminist, eco-feminist, Womanist, Asian American, and Latina. But informally in the 1990s and formally by 2005, the UUA adopted a new set of Principles & Purposes. As I understand it, these essentially let go of their past traditional theological ties in order to prepare for the future unknown. So be it; after all, it was affirmed democratically by a majority of 5 humanists. However, I describe it as "liberal fundamentalism." To me, this felt like saying, "Let's strip down what was an important and inclusive religious tradition until it surprisingly resembles any other sectarian, secular and humanist group in its exclusive fervor." While in the Chicago area, I received a second master's degree this time from the University of Chicago Divinity School. Studying with Profs. Lawrence Sullivan, David Tracy and Jane Carr. I came to value Chicago's historical-anthropological method in studying religion. This encouraged me to embrace religious particularism over general universalism.

Where have you been for the past twenty years? Needless to say, by the end of the '90s I, still a feminist, returned to Congregationalism in the United Church of Christ in order to remain connected to the Church Universal. Ever since, I have been serving MA and CT churches in this denomination from which UU's separated in the early 1800s in MA. Galatians 3:28 still guides me: "There is no longer Jew or Greek, there is no longer slave or free, there is no longer male and female; for all ... are one in Christ Jesus." We still study and preach from the Bible, baptize children and adults using traditional Biblical words to connect us to the wider Church, offer Communion, say and teach the Lord's Prayer, and educate, all using feminist standards, and dissent. Plus, we network with people of other religious faiths—Christians, Jews, Muslims—as well as the unchurched. In the UCC we also say and mean, "Whoever you are, wherever you are on life's journey, you are welcome here." (And this includes everyone, of whichever racial ethnicity, background, sexual orientation, gender identity, religious upbringing, Christians, theists, seekers—plus feminists like me, of Christ.)

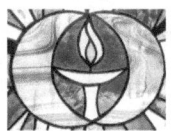

Spirituality Beyond Words

Emmy Lou Belcher

ONE DAY I AWOKE TO SEE MY PICTURE in the Detroit Free Press. I was standing on the steps of the Michigan state capital building. I looked frozen in my hood and mittens, and I was. The weather was abominable, sleeting with a wind that pierced my winter clothes. My eyes were watering, but I proudly held up my sign from the Religious Coalition for Abortion Rights, supporting pro-choice stance on this issue. I was ready to go inside and corner State representatives and senators in their offices, on the elevator, in the hallways to let them know how many religious groups supported the pro-choice stance on abortion Anything to get out of that cold wind. Soon after this, the US Supreme Court ruled in favor of Roe in Roe vs. Wade declaring that abortion was a health concern to be decided by the woman involved. We thought our long struggle was over. How little we knew.

After spending my high school and college years active at the

Ann Arbor UU congregation, I started attending the Women's Alliance at the Detroit church with a friend whose child was the same age as mine. She told me about this wonderful women's group that had childcare during its monthly luncheon and discussion sessions. I asked her where it met. At the Unitarian church was her reply. I told her that I was a Unitarian and we started attending together.

The group soon invited me to speak to the congregation on their behalf and to represent them in the Religious Coalition for Abortion Rights, to which they belonged. I discovered how much I liked being involved in these areas—speaking and social action. Meantime, I became more involved in the church itself, teaching in Religious Education and eventually becoming the Director of Religious Education. My interest in theological issues began to emerge as I met with ministerial colleagues (as the RE Directors in Michigan did in those says) and as I worked on the District RE and Development (growth) committees. That growing interest in theological depth and the encouragement of the women's group propelled me toward studying for the ministry.

But there was no seminary in the Detroit area for me to attend. The nearest liberal seminaries were in Chicago or Dayton, Ohio. I had a child still at home. My husband urged me to follow my interests in studying, but not in acquiring any debt. I also didn't want to break up our family by moving to Chicago or Dayton. Many years later, at my retirement celebration, Rev. Charlotte Cowtan, who became a friend in those early years, preached a sermon where the refrain was "Why were you hanging around ministers all the time?" She and another colleague, Rev. Joan Kahn Schneider, helped me to put together a program for meeting the "equivalency" requirement of the Fellowship Committee: If I could prove I had developed skills and covered topics equivalent to that gained in a seminary, I could be considered for Fellowship. That way I could pursue my goal of studying for the ministry and still maintain my responsibilities for my child and my marital relationship.

The Equivalency was a complex path involving workshops, General Assemblies, experience as staff at the Detroit Church, consultation with colleagues, university courses, etc. I found a program for a Master's Degree in Religious Studies at the University of Detroit, a Jesuit college less than a mile from my home. While there, I continued to work at the DRE job in Detroit. I had childcare available in my neighborhood which enabled these long hours of study and work. One of my advisors at U of D was Dr. George Pickering, a Unitarian who had graduated from Meadville/ Lombard School of theology in Chicago. He taught Ethics at the U of Detroit and lived in my neighborhood. When I balked at taking Biblical Studies from a Christian professor, Dr. Pickering took me to lunch and talked about the difference between scholarly work and Christian conversion. The professors at University of Detroit were scholars and he declared that I would probably enjoy the classes. He was right. I loved it. My Biblical Studies professor, Dr. Jane Schaburg, was a feisty ex nun, a feminist, and a scholar who specialized in the birth narratives and Mary Magdalene. We ended up as friends, and I ended up with a dual major in Biblical Studies and Theology. Dr. Pickering also encouraged me to write a thesis so I would grapple with a concept in depth. I wrote a comparison of the ontologies of James Luther Adams and Karl Rahner, the

Jesuit theologian. I communicated with Adams about some of the questions I had and ended up visiting him in Cambridge when I went before the Fellowship Committee. The Jesuit on my thesis committee was an admirer of Rahner. Lots of good discussions there.

I also attended several of the Women in Religion conferences put together by Rev. Denise Tracy. My sense of spirituality was enhanced by acknowledgment of the feminine as divine as the male. Rev. Tracy and her cohorts brought in scholars to teach us and created worship that included ritual and female imagery.

While I was still studying, I left my job as DRE in Detroit, did a CPE at Children's Hospital of Detroit, and began an off-site internship at the Universalist Unitarian Church in rural Lyons, Ohio. The church was 100 miles from my home in Detroit. The congregation paid a small stipend that covered my gas and provided a place to stay at a member's home. My off-site supervisors were Stan Aaronson, the minister in Detroit, and Rev. Carol Brody, who was the Religious Education staff person in Ohio Meadville District. It was not felt that doing an internship at a large church would be particularly beneficial to me as I had worked for eight years on the staff of First UU in Detroit, including a stint as the only UU on staff between ministers. I met with the supervisors periodically, sometimes at their offices and a few times in Lyons.

The small church in Lyons (about 53 members) had survived for almost 100 years, sometimes with and sometimes without a minister. It was felt that since I had attended and worked with only large congregations, this would be a good learning experience for someone who would probably be placed in a small congregation when I began my own ministry. The congregation was supportive and taught me a lot. They listened closely when I came to the Committee on Ministry to talk about the troubles my son was having back in Detroit. We made arrangements for me to be in Detroit most of the time, doing work with the Board and pastoral care on weekends. I don't think this would have been usual had I been a male ministerial candidate.

After my internship, I was finishing my thesis. I was hired by Emerson Unitarian Church in Troy, Michigan, to do preaching, advising the Board, and some pastoral care. I also taught at least one adult RE class. During the spring, I traveled to Boston to meet the Fellowship Committee. They gave me a "2" with the stipulation it would become a "1" when I finished my thesis and graduated. While at the UUA headquarters I was able to see packets put together by ministers in search. When I got home, I began assembling my own packet. One of the first items I chose to include was a copy of the Detroit Free Press photo of me at the state capitol holding the Religious Coalition for Abortion Rights sign. I was ordained by First Unitarian Universalist Church of Detroit in June of 1989 and was called to the ministry of the Unitarian Universalist Fellowship of Grand Traverse to be their first full time minister.

We began in rented space, outgrew it, moved to a larger rental, (all within three years.) then realized that we were running out of rental spaces in the area. The church began a capital campaign and built its own place on land donated by a member family. It was the first of three capital campaigns in which I would be involved in my career. The new building was planned for one and a half times the size of our then congregation. We outgrew it in two years. A team of six was put together to attend a conference on growth done by the Alban Institute. We loaded into a van and took off. When we returned, the team proposed going to two services on Sundays. The congregation agreed to a trial year, and finally accepted the proposal. It remained so until I had left.

When I started at Traverse City, I began a youth group to which our teens brought their friends. One of the reasons Traverse City wanted to call me was because of my RE experience. When I came, they had 77 members and 12 children and teens. When I left, fifteen years later, they had almost 300 members and over 100 children and teens. We gradually hired staff until there were three other staff, including a full-time music director. One of my concerns was not to increase the salary of the senior minister so much that it would be impossible to hire more staff. We raised the salaries to UUA standards for all of us. Part of my predilection in ministry was to broaden the leadership within the group. It was not a hierarchical system, even though I did supervise all staff for the Board. I believe that each person brought a gift to the church and was interested in having lots of leadership or committee places for those gifts to shine. It was ministry as a tapestry of community energy and creativity.

I also brought a new attitude toward worship services to the congregation. I had a degree in Art and a teaching certificate in that field before I went into the ministry. I was interested that the Sunday experience incorporate as many of the senses as possible, not just auditory ones of sermons and readings. The large number of artists attracted to the congregation were recruited to provide settings, often quite elaborate even taking up space throughout the sanctuary, and orders of service covers, each growing out of the topic for the day as each artist envisioned it. The music director and I met for a couple of hours each week to create a sound pattern for the service—hymns, Preludes, offertories, etc., that reflected the moods and topics of the service. Kevin Tarsa, the music director, (who went to graduate from Meadville and become a parish minister) put together not only a choir but also smaller ensembles of singers and musicians to enhance the worship ambiance. In each service, sound, sight, and even taste and smells were woven together. A couple of times per year we had an orchestra, made up of whoever wanted to play that day. Kevin arranged music etc. to make it possible. It was an exciting place to worship and an exciting place to minister.

That congregation had always been involved in the social action of the community, but mostly as individuals. I immediately began associating with reproductive rights and civil rights, sitting on boards such as Planned Parenthood and the Human Rights Commission. We also raised money to buy endangered land in the area for the Land Conservatory. We participated in actions to support reproductive rights. I had Dr. Pickering from University of Detroit come to town to give a public lecture on the ethics of Pro-Choice in the abortion issue. (I received a couple of death threats when that was publicized.) When a conservative congregation put on the ballot an initiative to ban civil rights for LGBT persons, our congregation formed teams and trained to work door to door to inform people on the issue and how anyone's rights were limited by limits placed on another. Both I and the congregation became known for our support for reproductive rights. Other ministers such as Methodists and Presbyterians were not as free as I was to speak on these issues as their congregations were more divided by them. They often remarked how they wished they had my freedom. The Congregational minister in a nearby town joined me in my endeavors, as did at least one of the American Lutheran ministers. In Northwestern Michigan, this spunky little UU congregation reigned in these controversial areas.

One of the other areas that I feel I have been helpful in my ministry is my admission of my own mental problems. I have a low-grade depression [dysthymia]. With treatment, both pharmaceutical and therapy, I have been able to operate as well as anyone without this ailment. My disclosures allowed many to come into my office seeking help. Often these people spoke of how my openness had given them permission to seek help for their own problems. Many were seeking validation that having such an affliction did not bar them from a normal life.

After 14 years at UU Congregation of Grand Traverse, I felt a need to search for a larger congregation. I felt I had done about all I could do there, and more money from a larger salary going into my retirement funds would be a good thing. While at Traverse City, I had divorced my husband of 27 years. I was now on my own to provide for retirement. So, I again prepared search packets. My first year of search did not find a match. All the congregations where I was asked to pre-candidate chose younger males for the position. I was by then 59. I assured the search committees that I would be working until I was 70 in order to have enough Social Security income to afford to retire, and because I was nowhere near wanting to retire. Without a successful call, I did interim ministry for a year at Morristown, New Jersey. Before I came, the congregation had a year with Barbara Child as their first interim. It was easy to follow her as she did a lot of the confrontational work with staffing, etc. before I came. When I left, the congregation had called Alison Taylor to be their minister. It turned out to be a good match.

This time round, I received calls from two congregations. I chose DuPage UU Church in Naperville, IL, because I liked it and because it was near to my son who had settled in Chicago. It turned out to be a good choice for professional and family reasons. DUUC needed to expand their building, so as someone with two capital campaigns under my belt, they felt ready to call me and begin. We raised our money just as the recession of 2008 began. A good team and advisor along with a dedicated congregation pulled it off. The congregation already had a couple of social action commitments and was a big supporter of Planned Parenthood, demonstrating its support during a time of increasing anti-choice picketers. I joined in all of their projects but also worked interfaith issues. Naperville was starting to diversify, there were rumblings of anti- Hindu and anti- Muslim movement within the community. Interfaith leaders began gatherings for educating each other and the wider community. DUUC participated in every one of these various events. I was recruited to be on the board of an organization that supported LGBTQ teens. Several of the DUUC members took training and participated in this organization. Anti-gay sentiment was rising among the Evangelical population, so again I worked on cutting edge issues. I retired when I turned 70 in 2014 and was named as

Minister Emerita by the congregation.

I write this piece soon after the 2022 Supreme Court decision that the Federal government had no legislative backing to establish pro-choice as the nation's law, throwing the decision back to the states. Immediately several states made abortion criminal, but the state of Kansas decided to hold a plebiscite on the issue. The votes were tallied and by over 79% that conservative state voted against a proposal to make abortion illegal in their state. What an amazing breath of fresh air validating the pro-choice movement's stance that the majority of people want safe abortions to be legal. As we prepared to struggle again on this issue, a wind now blew at our backs lifting us to the challenges ahead.

Outlawing abortions is a matter of valuing fetal existence over the lives of women and ignores the many dangers of pregnancy both physically and psychologically for women. As the days and months pass with more states outlawing abortions, it has become apparent that the restrictions on abortion would be onerous for many. Planned Parenthood of Illinois, a state that preserved a woman's decision on whether or not to have an abortion and kept this procedure safe and legal, found their clinics expanding by over 20% after Indiana outlawed abortions. I felt immensely sad as though my previous work had been thwarted. In a recent guest appearance in Muskegon, MI, I preached about that feeling and how I re-charged. Comments came from many about how important that sermon had been for many, especially older women such as me who had worked so hard to make abortion legal. We need energizing and hope. I began to collect articles, poems, etc. that illustrated ways to see the world that would re-energize women. I hope, now that churches are re-opening after the trials of COVID, that I will be able to help with such messages.

My Feminist-Charged Ministry

Ellen Dohner Livingston

ALTHOUGH I GREW UP NEAR THE BOSTON headquarters, it was only later, as an adult, that my husband, Luke Dohner, took me to a Unitarian Church. We were living in Orlando, Florida; we both knew we had immediately found our religious home. No doubts, no conversion experience, and no troubles with family around renouncing the religion of my childhood. Unlike others who may have struggled to find a home in our faith, it was a smooth transition into my future as a Unitarian Universalist lay leader, Sunday school teacher, parent, and happy heretic from Christian roots.

My road to professional ministry started in an unlikely place: the border town of McAllen, Texas. We landed there, because of my husband's assignment to branch manager in an agribusiness. This locale, on the opposite side of the map from Boston, had no church remotely resembling religious liberalism. So, we decided to go through the process of starting a Unitarian (pre-merger) fellowship. Our classified ad produced around twelve folks who met in a nearby restaurant's back room. At that time, I was the mother of a baby son, expecting another, and although Luke was elected president, he was too busy traveling. And even though I was great with child, I became the leader by default and tacit approval.

At that time in my late twenties, I had absolutely no idea of the possibility of becoming a Unitarian minister. My dream scenario was that Luke would give up the corporation life, go to Harvard or Meadville to become a minister, while I would happily support him any way I could. Barring that, my son would grow up to become one!

Fast forwarding from the Rio Grande Valley through our itinerant life, Luke was transferred to other places; perhaps a good chance to see the USA, but all small towns with no Unitarian presence. And, by then, I was happily busy with three young children. I was free to do outside activities, only because of help from my widowed mom. However, I did get a chance to finish college at Pan American University in Edinburgh, Texas. It wasn't until we arrived in West Palm Beach, Florida that I began to work on a Master's Degree at Florida Atlantic University, majoring in Black Literature, and enjoyed writing my thesis on "Negro (sic) Women in American Novels by White Writers." My goal was to earn a PhD and become a professor. There was also, hurray, a real UU church for us to attend and have our children dedicated.

It was the late sixties, a most turbulent time in our society: the Viet Nam war and resulting protests; Civil Rights and MLK; as well as the burgeoning Women's Liberation movement. I participated in countless protest marches and meetings and sometimes got my children involved. However, not my husband, Luke, since he was afraid of corporation push back. I probably got my name on FBI lists, since I learned later that the organization that sent me to its convocation, *The Women's International League for Peace and Freedom,* was high on McCarthy's list of suspects.

During that period, our minister resigned under duress. Because I was active in the church and writing their newsletter, I was asked to take a part-time paid position as Executive Director *pro tem* ... "until we can get a minister." I was often exhausted but loved the job. Still no preaching or anything officially ministerial, but I planned Sunday services and thrived in that position.

I was also going to weekly "consciousness-raising" meetings, active in the local Women's Political Caucus, and was identifying totally as a Feminist. I took on public speaking for the League of Women Voters to overcome my entrenched fear of public speaking, and it was working. All the while, I was restless and perplexed about where my marriage was going.

We were planning to go back to visit my extended family and my birthplace in New England. Hmm, I felt a possibility brewing. I could check things out at the Department of Ministry in Boston. So, I made an appointment with the head, The Rev. David Pohl. David was his cordial self. Not totally discouraging, he informed me of *one* successful ministry of a woman minister named Joyce Smith, in the Midwest, as well as other female religious education directors. Pohl concluded our meeting with this caveat, "of course, Ellen, you will never have a big church." He was right about the way it turned out, but it wasn't a discouraging thought at the time, since I never aspired to one, anyway. Reality rules.

I left that meeting with a pounding heart and an optimistic smile, shadowed only by David's reservations. Yet hope was alive, because Pohl had informed me that since we were moving to Dallas, I could consider attending the Perkins School of Ministry there. And that's exactly what happened.

Meanwhile, I received an unexpected call to serve in an improbable cause. The chaplain of Southern Methodist University, Claude Evans, invited me to join a nationwide organization known as "Clergy Consultation for Problem Pregnancy." I agreed, not knowing then of the legal dangers of counseling women on their options for unwanted pregnancies, pre-Roe v. Wade, but I dove right in.

We were an underground group, illegally arranging through secret communications for troubled women to come to our homes by appointment. We would caringly listen as pastoral counselors but offer no advice one way or the other. However, we always provided them with information for out-of-state legal abortions. It was up to these women to make their own calls and arrangements. My feminist conscience had led me to commit this act of civil disobedience.

The words of the chaplain still ring in my ears: "I am for a woman's choice, because I believe in reverence for life." That wise and gentle man expressed my thoughts absolutely. Clearly, we're in need of this courageous kind of moral leadership in Texas right now. We disbanded after Roe v. Wade passed in 1973.

I was already on my way toward being a UU minister! My first application form asked a question that still fills me with frustrated amusement today: "Is your wife willing to be employed in order to support you financially?" Never doubt that there's such a thing as progress in our world.

As it turned out, I would soon be mate-less anyway, because we were on the verge of a divorce, propelled by my spouse, Luke, having a mental breakdown and disappearing to places unknown for several months.

During that chapter in my life, I had no financial support, including any emotional support from my family back East. I was plodding through seminary by filling in all the right blanks as fast as I could, while taking care of three teenage children. My daughter, Katherine, was diagnosed with serious scoliosis which required an eight-hour operation to fuse her spine. It left her in a cast for six months. We went on welfare, with no help from her disappeared dad.

I thank all the powers that be for the UU religious community of Dallas ... especially, for their generous help with my children. The Reverend Dwight Brown was supportive, to a point, of my efforts toward ministry, although he reminded me more than once that when women become UU ministers, everyone's pay scale would go down. Sorry, Dwight, that never came to pass but thanks for the warning anyway.

Looking back in wonder, close to disbelief, I know I'm not the only woman who has overcome even greater odds than my own to achieve a fervently desired professional place in her future. My feminist beliefs fueled that passion, but it was also my pure joy at the thought of actually, really, and truly being a real live minister.

A joy that has lasted, even unto this day.

I like to think I came to ministry with my eyes wide open, having been a person who has stood by our faith and grown in it, and having served Unitarian Universalism as an all-round liberal, scholar, counselor, activist, and performer. I'm also a *white* person, very privileged to have been born into a loving, trustworthy, New England middle-class family, never wanting for life's necessities. Unquestionably, there have been spaces, forward and backward, on my game board, entitling me to produce a winnable goal. I've been fortunate and blessed.

I was in pioneer mode as a female candidate: one of a small handful of my gender. I will never know how many search committees sent back my packet with a "thanks, but no thanks" because of my sex. One New England chair sent it back with an unlikely comment: "Looks like you might do better in California." What? I had never even been that far West. But bless his heart, maybe he was prescient after all, because that's where I eventually landed for good.

At GA, I started negotiations with a UU congregation in the South Suburbs of Chicago. During my first interview, I was asked by someone on the search committee what I would do if both a church emergency and a home emergency with my children happened at the same time. Before I could think of a good answer, another woman jumped in: "We would never ask a man that question!" Thank goddess for the bold feminist laywomen among us!

So, we said our goodbye to Dallas and drove north to Chicago. Our family landed on a storm-ridden, winter day that made it difficult to plough through deep snow to the door of our rented little house. Everything was so new and different; yet I was ready, at least that's what I told myself. I was facing life like single moms and alcoholics are counseled: "One day at a time."

As the first "lady minister" in the area, I received good publicity in the local papers. One reporter wrote that my son Luke called me *Rev. Mom*, a title that resonated and stuck, at least for a while.

It was in Park Forest that I was blessedly the first woman to be ordained in any congregation in the Chicago area, maybe the whole state. As a total surprise, I was given a black academic robe as a gift from my flock. The distinguished Reverend Jack Mendelsohn, then serving First Church Chicago and my mentor, gave the sermon. During the reception in the basement, a young girl came running down the stairs exclaiming, "Reverend Ellen, there's a rainbow up there, come look, come look!" Perhaps a cosmic message, because the rainbow above our Chicago Heights church became an ongoing symbol for the hope and many-hued promise of our faith. After rain, here comes the sun.

It also happened, at that time, that I started keeping company with a friend in Park Forest, an architect by the name of Nick Livingston. I met Nick when he brought his band to a New Year's service in our old building. We eventually became lovers; then we joyfully married.

Here's another signal achievement, once we were in our new building. In 1982, during the height of fears of nuclear attack, a woman named Jessica Merritt, a member of an established "Peace" faith, spearheaded an idea that captivated Americans across the land. Our assignment was to take a piece of white cloth, about 18 by 30 inches with strings on each corner, and create a picture or symbol using any art medium addressing this theme: "What I would most dread to lose in case of a nuclear attack?"

Because of my activity in the Nuclear Freeze campaign, I was chosen as state coordinator of the committee. Our Church collected these original and heartfelt banners, created by folks of various ages, and walks of life, from all over Illinois. This was truly an unforgettable happening in my life both as a minister and American citizen. We then took them to be displayed at the Illinois capitol steps, then onward to tie them altogether around the Washington D.C. Mall. Amidst lots of press, I had my picture taken with Pete Seeger. The Park Forest church still displays our ribbon banners with lasting sentiment and pride. Surely today, America needs a comparable outburst of shared national creativity, motivated by the realities of annihilation.

After almost ten years of continuing to serve those dear people, I was ready for a change. Guess what? We finally moved to California. I became the minister of our Pomona Valley UU Congregation whose church property needed ample repairs and renovations. As always, my husband, Nick, led us in those projects, using his skills and contractor connections. We also established a day care in our Sunday school area to help pay our parish bills.

Additionally, versatile Nick played the piano for services and parties, wrote scripts for skits, and gave away his paintings. And Nick never interfered with my ministry; he was the biggest fan of my sermons. The only thing we ever argued about was which hymns to play for worship. If Nick sounds like the ideal spouse to a woman minister, it's true. But I'm also confident, lucky as I was to have beloved Nick's help and adoration, I could have made it with that congregation or others without his help.

The two decades of my tenure in Montclair were highlighted by my tackling the challenging agenda of the Women's Liberation movement, in and out of the UUA. Right off the bat, we fought for more inclusive language in our services. There was plenty of push back. One day I was told that a male shared at coffee hour out of my earshot: "I'm getting tired of hearing Ellen complain that we men have made such a mess of the world." He made a point, alas, I needed to hear. Why should our "progressive" UU men come to church to be scolded for what they didn't personally perpetrate? Result? I was more tactful of my wording in regard to all genders. But I never abandoned my feminist-charged ministry. As noted earlier: "I am totally a feminist!"

I still heard rumors in the larger district that we were essentially a women's church. After all, it was often our Pomona Valley womenfolk who led conferences lifting up women's *herstory*, rituals and music, so soulful and moving. And our active Pagan group fed into that reputation, issuing from the primacy of Earth Mother and WICCA which featured female witches and crones.

Although, like all churches, we had more women than men, we never identified ourselves solely as a "women's lib" congregation. I was there to love, serve, and enjoy everyone regardless of their gender identity. I love men and show it—starting with my two sons, three brothers, and two husbands. Furthermore, I remain in admiration of all our males do, and sometimes some are feminists in their own way.

Yes, these were the Golden Years of my career, receiving accolades and enjoying celebrations. Concurrently, we grappled and protested as UU's in the ever-present issues of war, injustices, and racism. I was also awarded a Merrill Fellowship to study at Harvard Divinity School, enjoying their programs and auditing classes for a semester—a candy store for me—thus continuing my education in the very region where our faith started.

I also took a goodwill trip with other UU's to beleaguered Nicaragua and committed civil disobedience at the nuclear testing grounds of Nevada, getting arrested there—all with unwavering support from my parish. I always put my extra time into being a liberal faith presence in the public square, serving on at least ten community boards of trustees and committees, giving talks and pastoral messages, and protesting for liberal causes. I chose to place my primary energy into local causes rather than the larger denomination.

No big deal. That's simply what we, progressive clergy, and laity, aspire to be and do. Such activism exemplified the core my ministry as a feminist. Additionally, I toured the country, performing one-woman shows of the Unitarian reformer Dorothea Dix and the feminist Louisa May Alcott.

What kept me going all those thirty years of active ministry and still does, as I'm now Biblically speaking, "old and full of years?" I was inspired, often by fellow liberals, to practice Yoga, become a student of meditation, as well as engage Eastern philosophies and practices. These disciplines nourished my mental and physical health, and, yes, I'm fully aware of being the beneficiary of such privileged opportunities.

I aspired to follow my *credo* as being simultaneously a pantheist, a religious humanist, and heeding the Quaker ideal of calling on the light within myself. I have also carried deep in my heart the Buddhist ideal of relieving suffering and bringing joy, serenity, equanimity to all. And, needless to say, the Buddhist focus on "non-attachment" carried me through many a cumbersome pledge drive!

My ministry has brought me immense and enduring satisfaction, plus enough suffering to remain humble and learn deep lessons, knowing well that no one is ever promised a rose garden. Looking back, I'm sure I should have done some things differently, but I'm too old now to let those possibilities alter or mar my cherished memories.

How could I help but love this profession that deeply tested my womanhood and resolve. I thrive on the thought that I touched many people with my Unitarian Universalist faith and over-arching goal to connect with others. Always connect. Always connect. I have been reassured of my skillful means to that end.

Writing this essay has made me aware that the life which has been changed the most is my own.

So be it.

My Transforming Experience

Peggy S. Collins

THE VOICE OF THE UNITARIAN UNIVERSALIST Women's Federation (UUWF) helped to transform me in learning and living out my feminism in the UUA and my life. Their mission of Transforming Thought was to create a world where:

- Women and children are safe from abuse and violence,
- Women are valued and their history known,
- Women have full reproductive freedom based on their own moral agency,
- Women are included and expected to be part of the work of the world,
- Women's spiritual experiences are respected.

When I joined Chapin-Crane (District of Michigan Woman and Religion Team named after the first Michigan women ministers) in 1982, it was a most impactful part of an expansive time for me. New to UUism, I was finding I could enjoy my womanself more than in the Presbyterian Denomination where all the women were downstairs and, in the office, or kitchen. As I was also in intense therapy, it seemed that the times were introducing me and opening me to a new way to be, and I was questioning everything. As a struggling single mom, I found a place of welcome. Why there was even a Women's Group! And groups for singles.

There were three major currents coming together in our culture at the time: feminism, ecology, and spirituality and they all supported the same underlying values of nurturance and protection of all life, an openness to engage in the process of cooperation with each other and the earth. I was deeply engaged in all of it; it was claiming me and waking me up. The UUA was at the front of so many supportive movements where one could learn and grow and get involved.

By the time I joined the Team, the 1972 Women & Religion Resolution to change from masculine to gender-free language had been passed (as language gives shape and form to our thought). Hymnals were being updated with inclusive language and I was feeling included. Penny Hacket-Evans was the church Religious Education Director (although from another UU congregation) and a friend. She had been on the C-C W&R Team; her term was ending, and she was looking for a replacement for herself. I had kept two little pamphlets from workshops that had happened when she was on the Team—both featuring Carolyn McDade's music. Penny kept asking me if I wanted to join but I kept saying no because I had no experience in presenting workshops or even planning meetings and didn't think I would be any good at it. She convinced me that I could do it and when I finally said yes, I felt I was on a path of deeper learning.

Over my four-year term, I got a lot of support from other Team members and became more comfortable with offering ideas and speaking. The first workshop I lead was entitled "Are You A Closet Witch?" Pretty bold eh! It was for its time. Another friend, Barbara Rosilik (from an active women's group at Birmingham UU Church) and I presented a couple of workshops on defining terms like Pagan, Crone, Heathen, Witch, Patriarchy—to take the scare out of them. Questioning these concepts was new to me too.

We held two conferences a year—one larger and one smaller (if my memory serves me) and we packed the women in for several years. If you've been a part of a group putting on conferences, you know that there is a lot of detail involved, and I got to feel more confident and enjoy it.

I attended many workshops from other W&R Teams across the U.S. Went to the Annual District and General Assembly gatherings and a Convocation or two (one in Lansing, Mich. and one in Albuquerque, NM). Then later a UU Women's Retreat in Mexico where we watched fairies, and I was "fairy-flashed." I poured over newsletters from Foremothers like Rosemary Matson of the UUWF which was the continental membership organization. Lots to read via 'the Communicator, UUWF Mission: Transforming Thought." Denise Davidoff, Elinor Artman, Til Evans, Mary Lou Thompson, and Dorothy Emerson are other names I find in documents from that time that I saved.

From the beginning of my term, we all were encouraged to read.

A study and discussion packet that Denise Tracy (then Minister of the Lansing UU Church and the lead in our C&C, W&R Team) put together included a book: *Womanspirit Rising, A Feminist Reader in Religion"* edited by Carol P Christ and Judith Plaskow. It was an eight-week curriculum and, like the consciousness groups so successful in the discussion of women's rights and feminism, it was intended to provide an opening for a budding need. Being a reader (mostly Science Fiction) since teen years, I found that reading books by women and feminists was more relevant to my life story. I read lots of them—still do. Black Women and women of color, native women, Eastern, Asian, Arab, herbalists and shamans—I was discovering that women were speaking everywhere. That hasn't stopped either as over the years I've given away at least two bookcases of books that I know I won't be able to read again even if I did live that long. After learning of Carol Christ, I read everything of hers as they came out ("Diving Deep and Surfacing" stands out). I subscribed to her Online blog. Carol P. Christ is a leading feminist historian of religion and theologian who leads the Goddess Pilgrimage to Crete, a life transforming tour for women. www.goddessariadne.org It was a long-time dream of mine to go to her Goddess pilgrimage on Crete and I was finally able to do that—I think it was 2002. It was so satiating that I haven't felt the need to travel again.

Rev. Denise Tracy also published a lot and I have the *WomanQuest, Embracing the Sacred Expanding the Circle,* The WOMANQUEST Working Papers. A conference held at George Williams College where Lake Geneva, Wisconsin in April 1990. May Sarton (poet and author), Helen Caldicott (dealing with nuclear power threat), Carolyn McDade (I have sung with a McDade group for more than fifteen years and still do), Sonia Johnson (Housewife to Heretic), Naomi Goldberg (Changing of the Gods), Betty Friedan (The Problem with No Name), Elizabeth Dodson Gray (Green Paradise Lost). Other curricula created by UU Women are "Chants for the Queen of Heaven in Ancient Times" (A five-session religious education curriculum in feminist theology for adults and older youth by Shirley Ann Ranck), "Rise Up and Call Her Name" (a woman-honoring journey into global earth-based spiritualities by Elizabeth Fisher.) I took part in both of them and was greatly enriched. A friend and I presented the "Cakes" workshop to women at my church.

In looking through my archives for this offering, I see that I have quite a collection. Old Wives' Tales from 1982 and one older and undated. Several "Matrix" editions—Md-South District, Copies of "Reaching Sideways, Joseph Priestly District W&R Committee from 1982-8, "The Women's View—UUWF Pres in Dec 1989, copies of "The Communicator" UU Women's Federation Publication Flyers for some of the conferences that C-C sponsored, an invite from Aug 1992 from Rev. Ms. Denise Tracy to a workshop "Wellsprings." In 1995, I partnered with women from First UU in Detroit to open "The Center for Women's Culture." We held workshops, a support group, study group and a weekend retreat with UU composer Carolyn McDade. We held a "Maiden/Mother/Croning" Celebration. Much of our mission and events were published in "The Connector" Dec. 1997.

Being on the W&R Team was foundational to exploring 'alternative facts" and wanting to present views that I have found healing. My Community Access Cable 15 Station offered a course on the components of producing a show—camera operation, etc. After the components were taught. They asked for ideas for a show to produce. Since I had just taken a course in Community Mediation, I offered it as an idea. We produced it. It actually ran on the public station for a few weeks and Cable 15 provided me with a recording of it. It's still relevant.

I was emboldened to present a skit at the Detroit Women's Coffeehouse entitled "Phyllis Shaft (Schlafly) Speaks." It was the Presidential Election of Nov 1992; many friends claimed no need to vote as they were sure Clinton would win. I was taking a Feminist Studies Coarse and asked my Prof if my skit would count as credit. My Prof put it in YouTube format for me, but it didn't feel safe to make it public.

An epiphany—a sudden insight into an essential meaning of something—a change in perception—came to me during my time on the team that changed my life. Denise had returned from a trip and wanted to share a goddess figure with us that she brought home. Team members were encouraged to take turns with it in their homes. When my turn came, I placed her on my fireplace mantel. It was lovely to have her presence so available. I was house cleaning and thinking and she was right over my shoulder on the mantel. Suddenly the meaning of her—the essential meaning of her—filled me—the realization of women's bodies connected over centuries—millennium—by our umbilical cords. How we have continued life. She would never look the same to me again, nor would women.

I am proud of the contributions and opportunities I've taken and created that have enriched my life and deepened thought, awareness, a different view, an important view. As a former and long-time member of Northwest UU in Southfield, Mich., I have presented several sermons, meditations, arranged sermons with guest speakers. The topics and/or people are always of importance to me.

- The Music of Carolyn McDade, Spirit of Life Song.
- Food For Thought about nutrient-dense eating.
- Living With Pride, sermon by Dr. Kofi A Doma on Ruth Ellis (LGBTQ).
- No Man's Land presented by Irene Miller, Holocaust Survivor.
- Drumunity! Rhythmic Fun for Everyone by Lori Fithian
- Reflections on Labor Day with Mary Van Derzanden, Certified Electrician.
- Disability Rights with author, Janice Fialka.
- Seven Grandfather Teachings (Native American wisdom)
- Earth Day with Poly the Plastic Bag Creature (plastic problems).

Although Penny had retired her term on the CC W&R Team, she didn't stop creating workshops for women. I remember workshops on ritual, creativity, Earth Shine on reflection, book group and choir. The choir group turned into an invite from Carolyn McDade to participate on her next CD project. I've been part of three McDade CD projects over the years. I thank Rev. Denise Tracy for feminist leadership and for being a first in so many ways (talk about brave). I thank women who served over time to bring history/herstory to light and to inspire women to carry the flame forward. I have benefited from so much from these many experiences. The strength of women helped me survive (even thrive) 32 years with Ford Motor Company, Accomplishing a Master of Arts in Organizational Development. I created the documentation a classroom training and taught an in-house curriculum for health and safety personnel at Ford. I've served on boards and gotten involved in community and political projects. I've learned to value and take care of myself.

I don't know if I ever intended to be a forever student, I don't think so. I never felt successful in school. However, learning about the truth of women's religion, history, religion, culture, witch-burnings, women-hating, women loving women—all the information that was withheld and still is—I became a forever student.

In closing I quote Audre Lorde from her expression: "I have come to believe, over and over again, that what is most important to me must be spoken, made verbal and shared, even at the risk of having it bruised or misunderstood. That the speaking profits me, beyond any other effect. I am standing here as a black lesbian poet, and the meaning of all that waits upon the fact that I am still alive and might not have been."

I thank you for the opportunity to review what the UUWF and UUA has meant to me. We were part of a larger movement that was brave, and we helped to move it forward. To be asked to remember with thanks, the persistence of women, the support and camaraderie of women. I have more confidence to try things I never would have. At 77 years, I see no end to it. Bringing the values of nurturing and protecting life is part of who I am. Uncovering truth and its many layers continues to be my quest and purpose. Like Audre, I feel grateful to be alive—still.

The Making of a Black Feminist/ Womanist Unitarian Universalist (UU)

Qiyamah A. Rahman [27]

Introduction

... NINETEENTH-CENTURY BLACK WOMEN laid the intellectual and political cornerstone of Black feminism, but African-American women in the twentieth century brought Black feminism as a political movement, and Black feminist thought as its intellectual voice. [28]

In this essay I demonstrate how the core values of feminism/

---

[27] I use the terms feminist womanist interchangeably. I define feminism as a range of social movements and ideologies that define and establish the political, economic, personal and social equality of the sexes. It incorporates the position that societies prioritize the male point of view and women are marginalized by patriarchy. Womanism, according to womanist scholar Layli Maparyan (Phillips), is the restoration of balance between people and the environment/ nature and reconciling human life with the spiritual dimension.

[28] Patricia Hill Collins. *Feminism in the Twentieth Century in Black Women in America: An Historical Encyclopedia* by Darlene Clark Hine, ed. Brooklyn: Carlson Publishing Inc. 1993. p. 418.

womanism are evidenced in my life as a Black UU clergywoman and how I have been shaped by feminism/womanism and how UUism and the Unitarian Universalist Association (UUA) has been shaped by me as a Black woman in Amerika. [29] Furthermore, exploring my coming to consciousness as a feminist/womanist activist reveals some important milestones that ultimately led me to UUism.

Born in 1948 and ultimately the third of eleven children, I was preceded by my brothers' birth less than a year earlier. Born in the same wooden farmhouse in Hawkinsville, GA that our mother grew up in and delivered by the local midwife, my brother and I had similar birth experiences. However, his birth was marked by complications—fluid on the brain. The health disparities in segregated rural Hawkinsville sealed my brother's fate—irreversible brain damage.

> **"Shouldn't an important part of discovering yourself be discovering what your family was like? Whichever side you favor in the nature versus nurture argument, who your parents are certainly helped shape who you are."**
> **—Quinn Cummings**

The first few years of my childhood were spent in Detroit in an unfinished attic in my grandmother's house with my parents and three siblings. My parents migrated from the south in the

---

[29] Throughout this essay when using the term "woman" I am including female, transgender, feminine, womxn, and non-binary.

1940s. My father, a veteran with a third-grade education, worked at Ford Motor Company, until he retired in 1975. We lived in Cork Town, one of the oldest neighborhoods in Detroit. It was formerly settled by wealthy Irish and named after County Cork, Ireland. Cork Town became home to many poor ethnic families over the years. While my parents' approach to child rearing was biblically based, "spare the rod and spoil the child," my father's abuse of my mom reflected society's sanction of gender-based violence. My childhood memories included: exploration indoors and outdoors, bicycling, little red wagons and roller skating, church and dinner often followed by Sunday car rides, frolicking barefoot in the rain, homework at the kitchen table, an assortment of pets and falling in love with books.

Firsts

I recall the first time I was called the -N word around eight or nine. Or the time we were playing in a public park in Dearborn and a uniformed policeman told my dad that colored people were not allowed in the park. I have seen and heard some horrible instances of racism over my lifetime. I am fortunate. I have not had many experiences like these, mostly micro aggressions. None the less, my eyes were opened to a world that hated me for the color of my skin, the texture of my hair and the broadness of my nose and lips.

In 1967, my first airplane ride to Montreal, Canada for Exposition 67 found me at the Cuban pavilion. The handsome brown skinned man handed me my purchase and asked with a charming Spanish accent, "What are you?" No one had ever asked me that question. It had always been apparent by the labels we are assigned in Amerika. I stumbled over my words. "I am an American," I stated. The moment the words left my mouth I was instantly angry. I had completely denied my African heritage. I felt shame and shock. Where was the Black revolutionary that had been reading and studying about oppression and liberation? Where was she? It was the height of the Black power movement at Wayne State University, the year Detroit and other major cities imploded in fiery rebellions. Dr. MLK, Jr. called the fiery upheavals, "the language of the unheard."

One of my first consciousness raising experiences occurred in a Marxist-Leninist study group in the 1960s, my first year at Wayne State University. Reading C. Wright Mills, Power Elite and his explanation of military, corporate and political elites brought clarity about growing up Black and poor. I was slowly starting to connect the dots.

My mother and grandmother played a significant role in nurturing my spirituality and my sense of justice, fairness, and service to others. The Black Church was their survival tool that had helped them to withstand the day-to-day oppression heaped on Blacks. It allowed them and so many other Blacks to claim the bitter sweetness of their lives, and a deserving break from the aggressions of white supremacy. Church was where I gave my first speech, held my first office, and led my first meeting. It was an extension of family and one of my earliest experiences of community and belonging outside of family. But unlike some UUs that left organized religion, I was not damaged by it. I seized the best and left the rest.

My father, a brutal broken bully, whose redeeming quality was his strong work ethic was incapable of functioning as a loving parent after a lifetime of oppression. However, without exception, all the adults in my life espoused education as a way to make something of ourselves and to give back to our people. Unfortunately, racial pride was not taught in school nor in my home. So I spent years not loving myself or Black people.

The rich tradition of Black feminist thought has emerged out of Black women's sense of their experiences, anchored in knowledge claims in an Afrocentric feminist epistemology. [30]

Another study group, the Black Workers Congress in Atlanta, impacted my life in the '70s. This dramatic awakening and explosion were this time not in the streets, but in my personal life and my marriage. I was ready to spread my wings and push back against all the socialization that I had so readily accepted. I traveled to Cuba for three months, leaving my infant baby in the caring hands of my then husband. My blooming activism had been birthed, slowly, festering from a lifetime of oppression. I was making clumsy attempts to seize control of my very disjointed, dysfunctional, and distorted life, rather than continuing to acquiesce to parents, boyfriends, husbands, and society's notion about who I was. In retrospect, I realize that I was already a feminist/womanist by virtue of my lived experiences. I began to shift my faulty thinking with the help of theory and reflections from rev-

---

[30] Patricia Hill Collins. *Feminism in the Twentieth Century in Black Women in America: An Historical Encyclopedia* by Darlene Clark Hine, ed. Brooklyn: Carlson Publishing Inc. 1993. p. 349.

olutionaries to develop some clearer thinking and direction. And yet, I was still operating from so much internalized oppression and self-hatred. My life became an intriguing mix of spirituality, new age creativity and dysfunction in a search for the real me, not the colonial clone masquerading as me. I worked to get off welfare, get back in school and to claim a career to support my family and to continue my self-healing journey. My later calling to ministry supported my increased efforts of self-actualization to reclaim my humaneness, pursuing a lifestyle that fostered justice and service to others.

Organizational Affiliations

In the 1980s during my formative years in the Battered Women's Movement as a survivor of childhood trauma, and an adult survivor of domestic and sexual violence, I worked in shelters, state coalitions, served on boards of state and national coalitions and eventually I directed the Family Violence Program for the state of Georgia. Currently, I serve as the Sexual Assault Response Team Coordinator for the Virgin Islands. I have made lemonade from the lemons in my life. In 1991 I enrolled in the Africana Women's Studies Program (AWSP), a doctoral research program at Clark Atlanta University. AWSP was the first Africana women's studies program in the nation. Historically Black Colleges and Universities (HBCU) like CAU teach their students to be independent and self-reliant, to develop a global perspective and nurture their unique potential to resist oppression. Ideas of fairness, equity and justice fueled my activism as a way to give back.

Around 1991 I visited the UU Congregation of Atlanta. The

visit did not go well when a gentleman standing next to my son would not take his hand during a hymn. I conveyed my experience to an individual that told me about Thurman Hamer Ellington UU Congregation (T.H.E.), an intentionally diverse new start congregation. And the rest is history. That was thirty years ago. At T.H.E. I served on the board and various committees, wrote, and delivered homilies and continued to deconstruct capitalism and Christianity—all the while dormant seeds of feminism/womanism continued to blossom.

Being new to UUism caused me to miss an important historic event, the African-American UU Minister's Pilgrimage to Philadelphia in 1992, a.k.a. as The Continental Congress. The purpose of the pilgrimage was to honor Frances Ellen Watkins Harper, a Black 19th century Unitarian woman, abolitionist, writer, and women's rights activist. My class papers and exams conflicted with the Pilgrimage, and I have regretted my decision to forgo the Pilgrimage ever since.

UUWF

The UUWF was one of my first organizational experiences as a new UU. As one of the largest and most visible UU organizations focused on women's issues the UUWF greatly contributed to my growth as a feminist/womanist UU. In the early '90s the UUWF funded a coordinator's part time paid position to conduct education and raise awareness about gender-based violence in society, an issue I was deeply involved with. UUs typically volunteer with shelters and rape crisis centers, make financial contributions, and serve on boards. However, the issue of gender-based violence appears to be less frequently raised from the chancel or even from the pews. Furthermore, the issue has not appeared to be a justice issue raised by UUs or the UUA. The fact that UUWF was doing so way back then confirmed that I had made the right decision accepting Rev. Marjorie Bowens-Wheatley's request to join the UUWF Board. During my tenure, I had the opportunity to connect with many UU women's groups around the country.

Dissidence in UUism

While my growth and development within UUism has for the most part been a mutually reciprocal process, there have been instances of institutional racism that have challenged my identity and loyalty to UUism as a Black feminist/womanist: Open Membership, the Black Empowerment Controversy, 1993 General Assembly and the 2017 Debacle:

Open Membership

One of the key issues raised at the 1963 General Assembly was the exclusionary practices prohibiting membership of African Americans in several rural southern Universalist congregations. This proposal, intended to exclude the congregations that were discriminating against Blacks, was defeated. Congregational polity, the right to self-governance and autonomy, was the cause of the defeat. The overwhelming majority of the UU membership opposed exclusion of Blacks, however, a more strongly belief in the free religious movement prevented UUs from taking further actions against institutional and individual racism within UUism.

To do so, some believed, challenged congregational polity. [31] While this GA took place before I became UU, this history was a glimpse into the faith community I had chosen as a Black woman. I was saddened and disappointed. And wondered if as a southern Black woman, I would have been able to stay, were I present at the time of that decision.

Black Empowerment Controversy

In 1969 and 1970 hundreds of Blacks and some white allies left UUism. The mass exodus occurred in October 1967 when our country experienced, "a summer of racially-charged riots and a perceived rending of American society." [32] In response, the UUA's Commission on Religion and Race convened an "Emergency Conference on UU Response to the Black Rebellion" at the Biltmore Hotel in New York City. The Black UU Caucus (BUUC), created during that conference worked over the next year on a proposal recommending an annual budget of $250,000, over a four-year period. The intention was to address racial injustices. The proposal was presented at the 1968 General Assembly in Cleveland and approved, despite the growing financial problems of the UUA. Mark Morrison-Reed's succinct analysis identified the factors that led to one of the major conflicts in UU-isms racial relations:

> "It happened because of the bigotry and mistakes of earlier generations of religious liberals, because society was forcing change upon religious liberals and change is difficult, because

---

[31] The Commission on Appraisal of the UUA, Interdependence Renewing Congregational Polity (Boston: UUA, 1997), p. 140.

[32] Ibid.

middle class Black UUs needed to redirect their priorities—and this meant, for some, leaving. These were all good people torn by competing loyalties and conflicting values, some of which ran counter to their deepest traditions of polity and individualism. It happened because of institutional immaturity, fear, and hubris. "It happened because it had to happen." [33]

1993 General Assembly

Thirty years after the 1963 General Assembly (GA), the 1993 GA, my first, was held in Charlotte, NC. The GA Planning Committee planned to host a "costume ball" in commemoration of Thomas Jefferson's 250th anniversary. Participants were invited to come in "period dress." The UU Women's Federation board discussed the Committee's ill-conceived plan at a board meeting. We drafted a letter to the GA Planning Committee articulating our opinion that the ball was insensitive to Blacks. The Committee response was a thank you. And the rest is history.

I was disappointed with the Planning Committee's response and its continued efforts to forge ahead despite ample warnings. At the GA I had the opportunity to participate in the Thomas Jefferson Ball Protest. There was a large contingent of BIPOCs and European American allies. The atmosphere among the protesters was high energy and celebratory. We were experiencing a "Ball" of sorts downstairs with drumming, dancing, singing and chanting while the TJ Ball took place upstairs. I was thrilled to be a part

[33] Mark D. Morrison-Reed, *Darkening the Doorways: Black Trailblazers and Missed Opportunities in Unitarian Universalism*. Boston: Skinner House Press, 2011. p. 229.

of something so significant so early in my UU formation. I was especially struck by the lack of rancor and the unspoken message that all differences do not have to be disagreeable. Early in my formation as a Black female feminist womanist UU I was being introduced to some of the glaring contradictions that I would continue to face in white centered UU culture.

2017 Debacle

In March 2017, news of the hiring of a white male minister to a regional leadership position within the Unitarian Universalist Association, sparked controversy over whether the UUA was living out its commitment to diversity. To learn that almost all the top staff positions were held by whites was devastating news to me. It shattered my confidence in white UUs ability to resist and transform white supremacy and to share leadership with BIPOC UUs. In the trenches doing the day to day work I was not checking in to make sure our efforts were making a difference. I just assumed they were. News of UUA's staffing patterns felt like a betrayal and one that was hard to accept as a Black UU feminist/womanist.

Womanism and the Women's Movement

Over the years I have grown to understand that womanism is characterized by some of the following assumptions that: [34]

— Privileges Black women's experiences, voices, and perspectives in the building of theory, theology and practice.

---

[34] This definition is a compilation of the various feminist/womanist scholars I have read and researched over years.

— Addressees the oppressions of racism, sexism and classism and maintains the necessity of racial solidarity between men and women.

— Emphasizes the need to resist and change oppressive conditions in collaboration with communities of Black people and allies.

A number of scholars contend that many white women in the women's movement during the second wave, 1960s, marginalized and often ignored Black women's concerns and issues. Prioritizing class, over race caused Black women like me to feel alienated and reluctant to claim the term, feminist. White women's initial failure to recognize the interlocking oppressions of race, class and gender, minimized important social relations and issues that acted oppressively against Black women and other women of color. Holding the dialectical relationship of race, class and gender as interlocking oppressions was central to formulating an analysis to guide Black feminists, which distinguished Black women like me from white feminists. Included among some of the early and most visible Black women's feminist organizations were: 1) Combahee River Collective; 2) National Black Feminist Organization; and 3) Black Women Organizing for Action. Their presence, along with other organizations challenged the mistaken notion that the women's movement was a white middle-class movement.

My Ministerial Journey

When Alice Walker coined the term "womanist" in 1979 it provided Black women religious scholars a way of "thinking, talking, writing about, and doing theology and ethics based on their own experiences and history ... a way of naming who they were and what they do." [35] I was influenced by womanist theology's links between healing, liberation and transformation, factors that emphasize the transformation and resiliency of historically marginalized groups.

Womanist theory is characterized by following:

1) mental and emotional strength;
2) self-determination;
3) a compelling sense of survival;
4) emphasis on women's collaboration
5) women's experiences;
6) a strong orientation and rootedness in community and family;
7) a global link to women's struggles.

My student years at CAU immersed me in womanist theory and practice which later spilled over into my ministerial formation as a seminarian at Meadville Lombard Theological School.

Feminism/womanism allowed me to act as the agent and instigator of my faith development upon encountering UUism. Initially, I reveled in the space of safety and lack of judgement in my new faith community, with no need to constantly debate the merits of what I believed. This provided the space and permission for me to explore theology more deeply. I studied, discussed, de-

---

[35] Rufus Burrow, Jr. *Enter Womanist Theology and Ethics* in the Western Journal of Black Studies, vol. 22, 1988. p. 1.

bated and wrote papers. I grew to understand womanist theories link to a liberating and healing praxis. It is a universalist theology that addresses and analyzes the tri-dimensional oppressions of Black women, that encompasses race, class, and gender. Womanist theology links the sacred and secular and views god as a liberating and sustaining god. Its sharp critique of racism, including white women's initial failures to acknowledge and address Black women's realities represented similar "missed opportunities" present currently in UUism. Instances of white UU's inability to share power and to eradicate racism, and to decenter whiteness continue to pose challenges as I struggle to maintain my presence as a Black UU feminist womanist clergy woman.

Conclusion

"Living as justice where our calling is a critical way of defining what it means to be human." [36]

As a Black feminist/womanist UU clergy woman I bring my lived experiences to UUism. As a result, I recognize that women's unequal access to and lack of control over resources, results in subsequent vulnerabilities that have placed them at greater risk essentially because they are women. This is even more so with females that identify as BIPOC. Furthermore, I recognize and value the role of Black women as "Disruptive Other," a tradition represented in a long history of resistance to disrupt not only the

---

[36] Rebecca Todd Peters. *In Search of the Good Life: The Ethics of Globalization.* New York: Continuum International Publishing Group, 2004, p. 31.

oppression of women, but also the oppression of all people that is necessary for gender equality & racial quality. Black women's sustained activism fighting against oppression and exploitation has afforded me a distinct perspective with survival skills that allow me to utilize adaptive behaviors and strategies of resistance. My survival has often depended on my acquired ability to use all the larger communities' economic, social, and cultural resources. [37] I have brought my Black consciousness and my still evolving feminist womanist self to UUism. That is the gift I represent. I have engaged UUism first as a supporter and a member of UU congregations, and now as a minister. My major contribution has been the gathering of stories of Black UU women and girls and lifting them up for the larger UU world and for future generations. This contribution chronicles not only the presence of Black Unitarian, Universalist, Unitarian Universalist women but establishes an oppositional body of knowledge forged from the struggles of Black UU women. This history of activism has continued through the existence of AAUU Ministers, BLUU and DRUUMM to name the most visible organizations.

UUism has contributed to my development as a womanist feminist through opportunities to engage with diverse UU women. At times the UUA and affiliate funding organizations have provided small financial support for my research and writing projects that contribute to the legacy of Black UU women and girls. I recommend the UUA develop a Research and Development component. Such important research should not be left to individuals but

---

[37] Gloria I. Joseph and Jill Lewis, *Common Differences: Conflicts in Black and White Feminist Perspectives.*

should have substantial institutional support.

UUism and the UUA have been supportive of my need to claim space, time and agency to explore and create the way forward that best allows me a vision that is liberatory and evolving. That has not always been the case for many friends and colleagues.

I am part of a "legacy of struggle, search for voice … interdependence of thought and action … that recognizes the significance of empowerment in everyday life." [38] I am part of a long history and tradition of activist Black women claiming agency and acting in opposition to their oppression. The dual consciousness, oppositional gaze, and resistance pedagogy and scholarship is my inheritance bestowed by a long line of spiritual warriors whose shoulders I stand on that shaped my feminist womanist identity. I have shaped and been shaped by my journey as a UU and I know that UUism has felt my presence and been the beneficiary of my feminist womanist presence. Though the journey has not been without its missteps, we are all the richer and wiser.

Aluta Continua! Blessed Be!

---

[38] Patricia Hill Collins. *Feminism in the Twentieth Century in Black Women in America: An Historical Encyclopedia* by Darlene Clark Hine, ed. Brooklyn: Carlson Publishing Inc. 1993. p. 418.

Toward a Revolutionary Man-ifesto

Tom Owen-Towle

"We, with love, shall force our brothers to see themselves as they are, to cease fleeing from reality and begin to change it."
—JAMES BALDWIN

I AM BOTH HONORED AND HUMBLED to contribute to this critical tome. As an 80-year-old elder, my life has been transformed—turned outside-in (reflectively) and upside-down (prophetically) by the invincible surge of "women rising" in our Unitarian Universalist ranks during the 1970s and '80s. What follows are inter-lacing truths garnered since my UU ministry commenced in 1970: power of the hyphen, the *whaamm* factor, brothering vows, and a benediction of hopefulness.

Power of the HYPHEN

Back in the early 1970s, a handful of Unitarian Universalist men at Neighborhood Church in Pasadena, California gathered to build an ark—what the poet Rumi called "a huge, foolish project, like Noah ..." We named our enterprise M.A.L.E. —*Men's Awareness Liberation Effort* in pursuit of deeper growth as kin and providers, fathers, and public servants. And while we were clumsy, often chided and parodied, the brash path we were choosing was the right one.

Women were rising; men were responding!

When Carolyn and I got married in 1973, we joined our last names to produce the moniker Owen-Towle, combining our personal and familial histories. As she phrases it: "If we could, we would capitalize the hyphen!" Our governing mission has been to sustain an egalitarian partnership, which would, in turn, animate relational justice as parents, professionals, patriots, and religious pilgrims. The hyphen has been the chosen theme of our pudding. Despite stumbling and falling short, we've stayed the course. The power of our hyphen has horizontalized the decisions and identities of my adult male voyage.

The hyphen picturesquely demonstrates balance, evenness, and parity whenever it is employed. The hyphen brazenly and persistently tears down walls and builds bridges among genders, races, generations, classes, and capacities. The hyphen's errand is to combat all forms of supremacy and domination. The hyphen, when embodied, produces more emotionally expressive and ethically worthy men.

The hyphen was instrumental in launching a gay-straight dialogue group in our Unitarian congregation in Davenport, Iowa in 1975. Moving to San Diego, our UU Men's Fellowship was unveiled in 1983, and remains, to this day, a vital and vigorous organization of over 100 active men—including 8 support groups (involving 60 brothers), monthly discussions, mentoring, worship services, service projects, bi-annual renewals, and a mailing list serving nearly 270 men throughout our Pacific Southwest District.

Once underway, the hyphen couldn't be halted. In 1993, the UUMeN, our continental enterprise, embarked and was staunchly grounded in these hyphenated principles: male-supportive, pro-feminist, gay-affirmative, racially inclusive, inter-generationally-sensitive, and earth-centered. UUMeN would sweep the Unitarian Universalist landscape, raising the numbers of local men's soulful and activist groups from a scant few to roughly 20%.

Oh, the stories I could recount about Unitarian Universalist men changing ourselves while changing our worlds.

I've seen transformation occur, with my own eyes, to hundreds of men; yea, it's happened to my own, crusty and gnarled, soul as well. I've seen men who have become a gentler yet stronger species at home. Men who have dared to quit their secure jobs, because the posts became too confining or incongruent with their values. Men who have exited all sorts of "closets" in exchange for closer encounters with authenticity. Men who have marched for causes they wouldn't even write checks for in earlier days. Men who have left unhealthy bonds, wobbled, whined, and wept for a while, then stood tall and forged ahead. Men who have agonizingly matured, right in front of us, into a more suitable sexual orientation or gender identity.

I've seen men massage men's backs, using their hands, for

the first time, to touch another man for healing, not hurt. And, afterwards, pledging never to do harm with their hands ever again ... to anyone or anything. I've seen men, who have been psychosomatically constricted most of their days, never stop bawling for the duration of a weekend.

I've seen men finally "get" the ravaging reality of transgenerational racism, often when unavoidably facing their own condition. I've seen men emerge from prison life to tell sagas of agony and restoration in our "safe" circles ... then, other men, converted by these brave confessions, stirred to go forth and work in brothering other men behind bars.

Can you feel the earth shake a bit and the heavens warble some when imagining such stories of salvation?

I could go on and on, and we will. We must never run out of opportunities for men—starting with the very ones in our own household—to unravel tales of bone-deep hurt and spirit-soaring hope in kinship circles that gladly harbor their hearts. Today, Unitarian Universalism, more than ever, needs to occasion ways for men to become brothers. For males—of all capacities, backgrounds, and identities—are truly served and saved ... brother by brother by brother.

Patriarchy, while granting men clout, has caused costly, oft-irreparable, damage to our bodies and souls—producing emotionally constipated boys, suicidal teenagers, miserable adults, and burgeoning violence within the self and against others. The carnage continues. Patriarchy remains a major human obstacle, and when doggedly diminished on the road toward dismantlement, everyone is freed. Women, children, plants, animals, men, and any and all deities will be duly rejoicing! Working as "yokefellows" (St. Paul's term), alongside all gender identities, to make the ideals of equality substantive exemplifies healthy and mature masculinity.

In 2021, we've only begun to approximate the mid-19ᵗʰ century exhortation of our Unitarian fore-sister Margaret Fuller: "A new manifestation is at hand, a new hour is come, when Man and Woman may regard one another as brother and sister, able both to appreciate and to prophesy to one another."

We have much work to do, and it won't be finished during any of our lifetimes.

The WHAAAMM Factor

The basic acronym WHAM has stood for multiple, diverse perspectives such as *Winning Hearts and Minds, Women's Health Action and Mobilization*, and *Wisconsin Hydrogen-Alpha Mapper*. Furthermore, one could be playful with each of the letters, when viewing this ellipsis and its relevance for Unitarian Universalist males.

For example, under W: how about well-heeled, well-spoken, well-educated, and well-settled? And H surely stands for heretical since we are choice-makers deluxe. And, at our best, we're hospitable, humane, and hopeful; while, at our haughtiest, we can be high-brow and holier-than-thou. As for A, considerable UU's are essentially agnostic about solving life's mysteries, as well as aspiring to be allies, accomplices, and advocates for justice. Authenticity sometimes seems to fit us as well. And under M, there is often a skirmish in our souls between being bona fide merrymakers and pesky malcontents. And plenty of us could be characterized as mavericks: notorious for taking independent stands.

Okay, onward to the explicit relevance of the Wham factor for men's demanding work amidst mushrooming feminism.

The overwhelming majority of self-identified male UU constituents are members of Whaamm: white, heterosexual, Anglo-American, able-bodied, middle class, males. When I first wrestled with this acronym, I could have added another M (middle-aged), but no longer is that true. But if it is for you, insert another *m*. As a constituent of Whaamm, I've personally been a carrier of unearned privilege and power and must labor to redress my situation. To do so, I've added ER or ever-reforming—employing the term *semper reformanda* ("always reforming") from our 16th century Unitarian fore-brother, Francis David—to become a 21st century Whaamm-er—trying to bring my practices and preachments into stronger moral alignment. Our particular *man*-date is to be a *semper reformanda* force—internally, externally, and eternally—in order to grow a cosmos of mounting justice and joy.

I start with an admission. When I, as a Whaamm-er, look into the mirror, my core identities are hardly visible, whereas men of color reveal that they see color before maleness, before anything else, experiencing its societally-induced stresses and prejudices. Hence, Whaamm members possess the unmerited luxury of emotional freedom, economic gain, and social advantage … enabling us to work directly on ripening our masculinity.

That's one reason why the men's movement—there are exceptions like the *Million Man March* in 1995—has been predominantly Whaamms fashioning our own development—pretty much an insider project. Yet, unquestionably, a sizable hunk of authentic moral growth requires our stretching to know non-Whaamms up-close and personal, then building relationships that are sincere, equitable, and mindful. The present-day demographics of our local UU tribes, especially in America's metropolitan areas, are starting, ever so slowly, to resemble the diverse colors, classes, generations, and capacities extant in the larger society. The hegemonic masculinity of European culture, while still in ascendancy in our liberal religious fold, is blessedly loosening.

There's more complexity. *Cisgender* is the current term for self-identified males, wherein a sense of personal identity and gender correspond with our birth sex. Yet non-binary folks don't always fall into one of the two categories male or female. Additionally, not all non-binaries classify as *trans*. Gender identity is extremely fluid and nuanced nowadays in our UU parishes. Therefore, whaamm-ers need to listen respectfully, then sincerely accept however anyone wishes to name him/her/themselves.

A final disclosure. My singular Whaamm journey has been quite sheltered and fortunate, as has that of countless other self-identified UU males. To be sure, I've known illness, relational misconduct, divorce, death of loved ones, bouts with insecurity and inadequacy, but the bulk of my torments have been internally generated, not externally imposed. One example. In 1965, as a San Francisco seminarian, I went to Selma, at the specific urging of Dr. King for "supportive whites" to accompany disenfranchised African Americans in the push for civil rights legislation. Yet I didn't live, as did blacks, with daily threats to my body and dignity. As a visitor, I was slandered and spit upon for a week.

But I don't wish to minimize the bona fide struggles of countless UU Whaamms. Some have been beaten and/or beaten others. Others have incurred the indelible scars of military trauma. Still others have lost their jobs in the ongoing quest for affirmative action, a program they often both understand and applaud. And their stories are stories to be heard, whenever they've chosen to join our brothering fellowship and unburden their oft-buried soul-aches. We turn no brother away.

At the close of our brotherhood conclaves, I invite those gathered to join hands, while I leave a space between myself and the next guy. Our circle is intentionally broken as a reminder that there are men who aren't physically present in our company: men too frightened to appear, men who feel excluded or unwelcome, men who possess neither the time nor the capacity, and so on. My closing words, before our farewell chant are: "May our circle always remain wide-open for yet another man circumnavigating the road toward authentic brotherhood."

We men are pledging to become whaamm-ers all the way to our graves.

Brothering VOWS

Unitarian Universalism is a covenantal faith, based not on creeds but on enduring commitments. To contribute toward a saner and more reverential universe, UU whaamm-ers are called to personify vows that major in results not merely ruminations and resolutions. As our Unitarian fore-brother Horace Mann (1796-1859) urged: "Be ashamed to die until you have won some victory for humanity." Or, at least, until you have entered the battle and engaged for the duration of your days.

I. Undertake a REVOLUTION

During the past several decades, men's attendance and leadership (both lay and professional) in our progressive congregations has been shrinking. Fostering viable boy-friendly programming has posed difficult challenges for our Religious Education. The bedrock hungers, hurts, and hopes of males go relatively undernourished in our ranks. We need a spiritual revolution to serve, if not save, the males in our midst.

The word *revolution* comes from a Latin term denoting "to roll back" or "to unroll." Consequently, the main objective of brothering is to roll back the assumptions, biases, and behaviors that suppress men's psyches, oppress women socially and economically, and wreak ecological havoc. Rolling back the negatives so that positives might be unrolled is the duty of practicing revolutionaries. Any robust revolution will keep Whaamm-ers burning, learning, turning, and churning all our days and nights. Life is a partisan fray, and the tests and tribulations facing self-identified males are monumental. To confront our stubborn prejudices and hidden injuries will require revolutionary honesty. To stop the psychic and physical harm we males perpetrate upon others and ourselves will require revolutionary courage.

Now is the time for Whaamm-ers to arise from our seats of entitlement and extend the realm of justice to every living creature. 2021 is the season to sustain a revolutionary *man*-ifesto. And dear fellows: it's never too late to join and suit up!

II. REJOICE in Your Own Identity

We whaamm-ers are summoned to revel in our masculine embodiment but never at the expense of other beings. Our rejoicing is grounded in humility not arrogance. We promise never to tolerate the bashing of women, children, LGBTQIA+ persons or BI-POC folks, and we refuse, as well, to scorn, belittle, or humiliate men *qua* men.

III. Live RELATIONALLY

Lone ranger-ism constitutes a damaging malaise cultivated from boyhood on. Self-ascribing males become brothers through intentional efforts to relate caringly and justly with all living creatures, starting with self (often the hardest challenge), other males, then branching out to include females, non-binary siblings, animals, plants, and the deities. Never forget: we UUs are placed on earth to *live* "the interdependent web of which we are a part" not just pay homage to it.

When men risk trading in patterns of aloofness, alienation, and abuse for bonds of affirmation and affection, we will contribute immeasurably toward the well-being of all creation.

IV. Be RE-CREATIVE of Body

Like the chimpanzees, we males play zestfully as little ones then taper off upon reaching adulthood. Why? Because there's always work to do at the office, household obligations to meet, and "masculine" roles to assume in society. There's little time left over for parades, amusements, and balloons. Yet daily life without a sufficient dose of fun is a puny and shriveled life. We animals exist on earth to work *and* play in alternating rhythm, to participate in both business and monkey-business.

Genuine re-creation entails playing for play's sake, not with a why in mind, or with an opponent or finish line, but simply to stomp and chortle, drum and dance. Brothers pledge to be silly, frolicking, and fun-loving creatures.

Remember we're a men's movement not a men's system!

V. Be RESPONSIBLE

Accountability means utilizing whatever status or muscle we males possess, both individually and collectively, to bolster the good of the cosmic order. In our stated UU Purposes and Principles, *responsibility* holds a high priority, being referenced twice: we affirm "the free and responsible search for truth and meaning," and we are called to "respond to God's love by loving our neighbors as ourselves."

Responsible men redress wrongs rather than ignoring, wallowing in, or perpetuating them. Brothers apologize for our malfeasance: making amends and daring to heal, whenever possible, any tormented or devastated bonds. We try to make sufficient atonement, as well, with our mistreatment of the entire ecosphere: sky, soil, water, plants, and beasts of the field.

But there's more to redress. In combating any injustice, we must also compensate for transgenerational wrongs our gender has perpetrated. Additionally, responsible men aspire to mend brokenness with those institutions we've either ignored or aggrieved … including our own Unitarian Universalist Association and local congregations.

I'm not interested in blaming or shaming my own gender but simply in calling us to accountability. Men made patriarchy possible, but it is not an immutable condition. Scholars remind us that in the 200,000 years of *homo sapiens*, patriarchy accounts for less than 5% of our evolutionary record. Just as there was a pre-patriarchal period in human history, there can be a post-patriarchal one as well. However, it will command the boldest and bravest work we men have ever done.

VI. RELEASE Your Heart

Whole men are both pale-blooded (brooding and sweet) and red-blooded (fiery and assertive) and exude expansive emotionality on a daily basis. As my buddy, Shepherd Bliss, puts it: "I wish all brothers both bubbles and lightning!" Yes, evolving men exhibit testosterone-with-heart.

One of the most prevalent yet almost completely ignored disorders in modern society is male depression. The best antidote is truthful sharing and purgative release. Brother Doug von Koss reminds men to let our tears fall from our eyes, unwiped, soaking the ground, so that something fruitful might be harvested from the soil.

VII. Bridge with RESPECT

Right relationship is the phrase the Buddhists use to describe being in just and caring connection with all existence. Respect entails companioning humans in kind, merciful ways, being stewards (husbandmen) of the earth's resources, and growing in sacred communion with the Eternal One.

At First UU Church of San Diego, in the early 1990s, we occasioned workshops for self-identified women and men to join together as allies in building bridges of thicker respectfulness. One of our numerous exercises was the *Fishbowl*. Women would create an inner circle with men remaining seated on the outer circumference. Women would then share honestly and deeply among themselves around a given theme, with the men merely listening. After the women have their "say" and the men their "hear," the roles are reversed.

Certain guidelines are essential for Fishbowl success: no cross-talk among the inner circle members or between the circles; no one speaks twice in the inner circle until everyone has had a chance, who wishes to speak; only I-language; absolute confidentiality; the participants are seated with their knees touching for connection and trust; and there is no follow-up discussion.

Clearly, feelings are oft raw and rife; so, after each specific session, congregational professionals are available for personal counseling and ongoing support. Given the reality of gender fluidity in our contemporary UU parishes, leaders might wish to configure the Fishbowl settings in fresh and caring manners. However, our primary mission remains fostering greater respectfulness among humans.

The first topic is: What do you *affirm* about the other gender identity? The second question is: what do you *fear* in relating to the other gender identity? Participants offer their responses without mentioning specific names. In practicing affirmation, we develop an appreciative consciousness with respect to "otherness." Regarding fear, Thomas Powers writes: "We fear each other ... fear of our neighbor's presence and power. We often judge or wish each other ill." Clearly, the case.

Our second ecclesiastical effort, also in the 1990s, at expanding the vow of respectfulness, was establishing a "Stopping Gender Violence" Task Force, comprised of an equal number of women and men as co-leaders. This alliance would plan educational programs and support experiences in our congregational life. One such healing group was for victims of sexual violence and a separate one existed for perpetrators.

In the latter group, I recall one male participant "legally" not being allowed to dwell within 100 yards of women or children while on church premises. Consequently, he could only attend his private, evening support group. Years later, after "Horace" had moved to another state, he called me, "out of the blue," to declare his gratitude for our church's respectful and supportive stopping gender violence work. Horace tearfully spoke over the phone: "Thank you, thank you, Rev. Tom. My time with your Church in San Diego began my rehabilitation toward becoming a more respectful male being. And I'm still making strides."

Respectfulness is our highest earthly duty.

VIII. RESTORE Your Spirit

Men are driven to do and to have, but we have oft forgotten to *be*. We recharge our batteries, as well as the greater world, whenever we restore our harried, dried-up spirits with intentional times of Sabbath, contemplation, and self-care. That's why we call our San Diego weekend get-aways for men: renewals rather than retreats.

IX. Sign on as a RESISTER

It's vital that Whaamm-ers play an unremitting role in women's ongoing battle for equality ... walking neither ahead nor behind but alongside our sisters. In the tussle for women's equality, pro-feminist men are bidden to labor sympathetically and supportively. The welfare and hardiness of our mutual destinies are interwoven ... exemplifying, once again, the power of the hyphen.

As men we will never realize full humanity solely by reclaiming our emotions, bonding with our brothers, and reconciling with our parents or ancestors. The way to recover our embattled masculinity and to repair the fractured globe is through serving the marginalized and suffering.

I often hear my UU male comrades saying, "I don't have the energy or time to be political. Furthermore, I'm hurting too much myself." I offer two plain responses.

First, I enduringly care about the personal plight of all my brothers and energetically invite those in need to join a male-based (not biased) support group within our Unitarian Universalist Association. I understand, even celebrate, the process of men venting long-festering agonies and woes. Wounded animals are the most dangerous, and mature men must forcefully care-front our own anguish.

But being wounded is only part of our story. We men are also wounders, and we must answer for that. We need to address the unbearable pain and horror that women and children experience, living in a world in which one in four women will be raped and one in six children is the victim of sexual abuse.

Self-identified females are never entirely free or safe, perpetually harassed, and always vulnerable.

Second, since we're incorrigibly social animals, we men can ill-afford to gaze contentedly at our navels without being public contributors. Our brand of liberal and liberating religion requires that whaamm-ers heal both the body personal and the body political. We must be, as Unitarian Universalist brother Jaco ten Hove invites—"both-and-ians!"

I grow weary of men, as well as women, in our movement claiming: "We've solved the sexism issue; our pulpits and lay-leadership positions are filled with women. And look, we've finally even elected a woman to be President of the UUA. Hey, we've arrived! Let's move on to other, more pressing, injustices!" No, dear ones, we haven't flushed gender injustice from either our personal consciousness or institutional behavior as Unitarian Universalists. Women are rising and men are responding ... but we have not yet reached any semblance of a Promised Land! *Semper reformanda.*

What our pro-feminist principle is urging is this: "Men, we invite you to hear women's anxiety and rage without commenting. Don't be paralyzed by guilt. Don't defend or retaliate. Don't grovel or pummel yourselves. Don't even take women's anger personally. Just listen, long and hard, to their stories. And then, choose, every minute of every day, to become a more responsible, respectful, and resilient man."

Benediction

The whaamm-er revolution (and its attendant vows) isn't another task force or *ad hoc* venture but rather a life-cause ... and one which we won't complete during our earthly jaunts. We will make strides and endure setbacks. Our aspirations will always outstrip our achievements. Yet we relentlessly march forward and onward with this prayerful hope:

> *O Spirit of Eternal Life, Love, and Liberation …*
> *May we become healthier and hyphenated siblings.*
> *May we unwaveringly serve the fulfillment of all beings.*
> *May we pledge to die whaammer-ing away.*
> *Amen, ashay, shalom, and blessed be!*

Turning Points

Marilyn Sewell

ALL THAT IS WITHIN ME
Bless the Lord, O my soul:
And all that is within me, bless his holy name.
—PSALM 103:1

THE SETTING IS LEXINGTON, KENTUCKY. The time is the '70s. I am meeting with my therapist, weeping copious tears because I have lost my marriage. And my community. My husband and I had been active in Central Baptist Church, but since I separated from him, I have become persona non grata in our social group there, the "Couples Club." Understandable, I guess. So, I'm alone in the world. Without a job. With two toddlers in my care. My therapist makes a prescient suggestion: "Why don't you try the Unitarian church—there are a lot of divorced people over there." And so, I did. And so there were. Well, it was second wave of feminism, and women were breaking free. I was one of them.

I met my husband-to-be, Frank, at a church book discussion group in New Orleans, just a block away from my apartment, on St. Charles Avenue. I had wandered in that evening because I was lonely—I loved my job teaching English at Franklin High, a school for gifted students, but I was fearful that I would fall into that most dreaded of conditions: old maid. I considered moving to Alaska, where there were 132 men for every woman. Excellent odds! I perused materials from the various chambers of commerce in the largest Alaskan cities. But ... Alaska is cold, and I was used to Louisiana heat. Besides, did I really want to marry a fisherman or a lumberjack?

I decided to reach out for help from one of the earliest matching services in the nation—I filled out an extensive questionnaire, sent in my $8.00 (not an insignificant amount in the early '60s), and was promised the names and phone numbers of at least 3 matches in the NOLA area. I waited ... and waited ... and waited for a response. After six months, the company wrote back, on a piece of graph paper with green lines: "We are sorry to inform you that there is no one in the New Orleans area who is a match for you." No refund. That's how I ended up at the discussion group.

So, when Frank showed up that evening and I learned he was a doctor doing his surgery residency at Charity Hospital, I saw my opportunity. As we parted that evening at dusk, I could tell by the way he was shaking the change in his pants pocket that he would never leave me. Oh, and what was the book we were discussing that evening? Betty Friedan's The Feminine Mystique.

I.

The next seven years were a revelation. I had two babies 16 months apart, and my days were filled with diapers and baby formula. I fell into the unhappy state of being the support person for a surgeon, a job that was not at all suited to my talents or inclinations. I began reading piles of feminist literature, mainly to find out why I was falling down the depression rabbit hole at an astounding speed.

I was married to a kind and generous man, had financial stability, had the prescribed two children. Wasn't that the way my life was supposed to unfold, I mean, at the very best? But my unhappiness kept gnawing at me. I began reading about the experiences of other women and found myself there.

Simone de Beauvoir's *The Second Sex*, published amazingly in 1949, was groundbreaking for me—I saw myself on nearly every page. Among other feminist authors, I read Erica Jong, *Fear of Flying*, Adrienne Rich, *Motherhood as Experience*, and *Institution and of Woman Born*; Marilyn French, *The Women's Room*; Susan Griffin, *Woman and Nature*; Dorothy Dinnerstein, *The Mermaid and the Minotaur*. It was only later that I discovered powerful feminist works by women of color: bell hooks, *Ain't I a Woman*; Audre Lorde, *Uses of the Erotic: the Erotic as Power*; *This Bridge Called My Back: Writings by Radical Women of Color*, edited by Cherrie Moragu and Gloria Anzaldua; Maya Angelou, *I Know Why the Caged Bird Sings*; the poetry of Lucille Clifton. I was unaware that I was cultivating a radical and dangerous change of consciousness. Once I had internalized a vision, been blinkered by the light, there was no going back. Or at least no going back without becoming a Stepford Wife, nodding, and smiling. I couldn't do that. Just couldn't.

The Unitarian Universalist Fellowship of Lexington supported my evolving self—many members were experimenting with lifestyles, joining self-made encounter groups, trying out open marriage—and getting separated and divorced at an alarming rate. Some of these experiments led to personal growth, others, to disaster for both marriages and children. Change, it is too rarely said, is not always for the better. And even when a shift is positive, there are always the goddamn tradeoffs.

II.

I had begun writing seriously as a high school teacher in New Orleans: my first nationally published piece was an article for the National Council of Teachers of English. When I married, I closed the folders on several writing projects and sequestered them away in the bottom of a little-used kitchen cabinet. I also stopped writing in my journal, a practice I had kept since I was eighteen. Intuitively, I knew that words were subversive, and I couldn't afford to let them out—what damage they might do! But please note: the subconscious always wins.

I did know that my brain was turning to mush from disuse—I needed to get out of the house and engage the larger world in some way. So, I signed up for a creative writing course with Wendell Berry, a poet, novelist, and essayist who was teaching at the University of Kentucky and was just becoming well known at the time. I had never met him, though, and was unprepared for the power of our first encounter.

When I entered class that first day, the students were gathering around a circular table. I plunked myself down just to the left of Wendell, and that was to be my place thereafter. Wendell was tall and lean and had the hard muscular build and the hands of a workingman. I soon discovered that he was a farmer as well as a writer and a teacher.

On that first day Wendell read to us from Paradise Lost and then read a short story by his friend Gurney Norman, an initiation story set in Eastern Kentucky. I was moved by this teacher, and I didn't quite know why. His voice was soft, all Kentucky, but he spoke out of some deep place within himself, from some place of integrity and purpose. When he laughed, that came from the depths of him, too. Here is a man whose life is given over. I knew that I must be with him for a while and learn what I could learn.

Our first assignment was to write a story. I had written for a number of years, and had published a few pieces, but always articles and book reviews, never fiction. I knew I was not a fiction writer. I decided, quite arbitrarily, to write an essay on ... examinations. I knew I had a way with words. I was confident that my long essay was carefully reasoned, well-constructed, graceful, and perfectly punctuated.

Wendell returned our papers at the end of the next class meeting. I could hardly believe his response—there was no grade, just a blanket rejection. He had written, "Where is your authority to make these statements? Give me something of yourself." The other students filed out, many no doubt similarly disappointed in Wendell's response to their work, but I stood there as if my feet were screwed into the floor, clutching my paper and staring, unable to stifle the huge tears rolling down my face. What did he mean, give me something of yourself? All I could say was, "I don't know what to do. I don't know what to do."

Wendell shifted from one foot to the other and blinked his eyes in discomfort—he hadn't intended to hurt me. "Come and see me," he said, "and we'll talk." Wendell kept sending my papers back, all that semester. No comments at all. I knew that he was asking for more from me and that he was right, but I could not articulate the change. I wrote feature stories for the Lexington Herald Leader. I reviewed Wendell's new book, *The Memory of Old Jack*. And I went regularly to Wendell's office and talked. I talked about my writing, and I talked about my life. Every time I went, some tenderness in me felt exposed.

All during my academic career in college and graduate school, I was the quintessential straight-A student. My other teachers had all told me how good I was. Wendell was the only one who asked me for more. And he was the only one who taught me anything about writing. Tell the truth about what you know, he said. That's all. But telling the truth was the most difficult thing in the world. I was beginning to understand what that kind of honesty means for a writer: the choice of a single word can reveal an old desperation still alive; a metaphor which takes you unaware can awaken you, can quite literally change the pattern of your life.

I began work on a personal essay late in the semester. The final day of class came too soon. I had been up all night in a last-ditch effort to finish my essay, something that would be from myself, something that would be honest. I was still typing my paper at 7:30 a.m., when my son Kash wandered downstairs for his morning hug, and breakfast. With him on my lap, I typed the ending of the piece on my old Remington Rand portable, the one my father had given me for high school graduation. It was that or a mutton coat, he said. I chose the typewriter.

I heard the waking-up sounds of my younger son, Madison, and went upstairs to change him and bring him down for breakfast. Amidst the milk and bananas and cereal, I finished the paper. There was no time for proofreading. My class was at nine, and I rushed to get dressed, but at 8:40 the babysitter had still not shown up. What could I do? I was suddenly struck with the clear necessity to go to class. Nothing in my life had ever been clearer. I will be in class today.

It was December, and snow was on the ground. I quickly bundled up the boys in their snowsuits, put them in the back seat of the station wagon, and raced off for the hospital, where Frank had gone earlier that morning to do surgery. I parked in the emergency room parking lot and took Kash and Madison on the elevator up to the fourth floor, to the surgery department.

I said to the receptionist, "Here are Dr. Sewell's two children. He'll have to look after them this morning." I kissed the children goodbye and left before the open-mouthed young woman could regain her composure.

Class began in the usual fashion that morning, Wendell asking if anyone wanted to read. He looked to his left, where I was scrunched down, trying to hide from his gaze. I demurred, saying only that I had a piece I could read, if nobody else had anything. Wendell then went all the way around the circle, asking each in turn, but it was final exam time, and no one had anything to read that day. So, he said, "Well, then, let's begin again. Marilyn, do you have anything to read?"

The floor was mine by default. I had no sense of whether or not my essay was any good. I knew only that I had at last tried my best to be honest in a piece of writing. I began reading about my severe depression after the breaking of my first engagement, about friends who tried to help but couldn't, about a husband who loved me from a distance, about my troubles teaching little English boys in Liverpool and my tenacious love for those students, and finally about my first pregnancy and giving birth. As I read, I began to cry, and I continued to cry all the way through the reading of the nineteen pages, not once raising my eyes. When I finished, I threw the paper at Wendell—half in spite, half in triumph—and said, "Here, that's what you wanted."

There was not the usual period of analysis and criticism—rather, after a few quiet moments, people said goodbye to one another, and each had a warm word or a hug for me. I had touched these individuals, it occurred to me, by simply revealing who I was. They were drawn to me, not because I was confident, strong, intelligent, superior—the way I had always tried to present myself—but because I was honest about myself: I was mean, generous, naive, confused, hopeful, determined, angry, and loving. I was all of these contradictions and more—and all that I was, was acceptable. And I knew that my marriage was over.

III.

So, I found myself convinced that I must leave my marriage—but leaving an intact home, financial means, loving in-laws—leaving all this with two toddlers and no job? Well, it was beyond daunting, it was f_____ crazy. I was a teacher, but the demographics were such that teachers were being laid off, so I had to prepare myself for some new sort of work—maybe I'll become a therapist, I thought. I got a degree in clinical social work just as Ronald Reagan became president, and social work agencies began shutting down. I had three jobs in two years. I found part time work at WKYT TV as an on-the-air personality giving advice with a strong feminist edge, but the pay was meager. I also became the editor-in-chief of a small magazine, Bluegrass Woman until the owner decided that the articles, I was soliciting for the magazine were too radically feminist. I bought a suit and a fancy briefcase and applied at IBM, the largest employer in Lexington. They offered me a job as a secretary. Somehow, even with all my education (an MA in English Literature and an MSW), I didn't fit anywhere.

IV.

I had followed my therapist's advice: try the Unitarians. I soon became thoroughly ensconced at the Unitarian Universalist church in Lexington, finding unconditional acceptance in the community there. The minister, Roger Fritts, who had studied at Starr King, told me all about the school—it sounded like an extraordinary institution. I was intrigued. Maybe I should consider seminary, I thought. I had always been religious, after all.

So, I flew out to California for the first time in my life, flew into that strange land called Berkeley to present myself at Starr King. I remember the interview well. One lay member of the committee asked me, "What will you do if we don't accept you?"

I said, "I don't know." Then in another interview, Ron Cook, one of the professors, asked me, "What is your goal in life?"

I blurted out, "I want to be all used up."

He said, "Well, parish ministry should do that for you." Before I left Berkeley, the school told me I had been accepted.

Deeply conflicted, I flew back home to think it over. I wasn't sure I wanted to become a parish minister. I knew only that I needed to make a living somehow and in some way be useful to others. My decision to go would mean leaving my boys in Kentucky with their father, who had established himself as a surgeon and had remarried. He was a good man and a good father who wanted to be with his sons. In a couple of years, Kash and Madison would be junior high age and needed to be with their father, rather than with a mother struggling to find herself. They needed stability. I knew all this. But rational thought did not comfort my heart at the thought of leaving them.

One morning about two weeks after I returned home, I was awakened before dawn. Something, some internal voice, told me to get dressed and go for a walk. Generally, I go to bed late, get up late, and have never seen a sunrise unless forced by an early flight. Nevertheless, that morning I felt compelled to put on my jeans and jacket and walk out into the dark, destination unknown. I just took one step after the next, finally ending up at Transylvania, a nearby university.

The campus was a broad expanse of green with one smallish

tree in sight. As I walked toward the tree, the darkness gave way to light, and I saw there amongst the branches a little brown bird. I moved closer and closer to the tree and to the bird in the eerie silence of the early morning, until I was standing right next to the bird. Strangely, it did not fly away. I stayed there with the bird for a few minutes, then walked back home. Without thinking—just moving automatically—I got out my old Remington portable typewriter and typed out my acceptance.

Now what was this all about? I don't know. All I can do is report my experience. Much later in seminary when I was casually thumbing through a dictionary of religious symbols, it hit me—of course! The bird is the traditional symbol of the Spirit. I remembered the dove descending when Jesus was baptized, I remembered the dove that told Noah land was near. My little bird was not so dramatic or so imposing—just a little sparrow, most likely, hovering in the dark and waiting for the dawn.

Years later I recounted this experience to my son Madison during a road trip we were taking together. He was in college at the time with a three-part major: mathematics, physics, and logic, so I was a bit reluctant to tell the story, anticipating that he might be skeptical. When I finished the telling, I paused dramatically and waited. He said, "Mom, that's the stupidest thing I've ever heard."

Well, maybe so, but I staked my life on it. Several months after my encounter with the bird, I left for Berkeley with a suitcase and two boxes of books.

V.

When a direction is right, all the pieces seem to fall into place. Upon arriving in Berkeley, I found everything I needed. A rent-controlled apartment up the hill from Starr King, in a grove of eucalyptus trees. A companion, a graduate student from Taiwan, who loaned me his old Ford Pinto, cooked noodles with black bean sauce for me, and invited me into his bed. He was ten years younger and wanted children of his own one day. That suited me—I wanted a lover and a friend, but not a husband. With Albert, I learned about a different culture, and I learned also about prejudice. I watched people being condescending to him because his English was not perfect. Not a coupling designed to last forever, nevertheless our relationship was marked by great affection. It was right for both of us at the time.

Most important, I found a school whose philosophy is to say "Yes!" to students. Starr King School for the Ministry is a unique institution. The school was founded on the assumption that students are adults who know what they need, so in consultation with their advisors, students choose their own classes. After finishing degrees in three conventional schools, matriculating at Starr King was like being in an academic candy store for me. I gobbled up everything that attracted me. Gandhi? Black preaching? Creative writing? Tillich? All these, along with the usual church history, religious education, and denominational polity. To say that I flourished under the positive philosophy of the school is a vast understatement. Starr King was made for someone like me. It opened the way not only for my professional development, but for my personal development as well, giving me a growing confidence that I had something good to offer.

All during that first year of seminary, I grieved terribly the loss of my sons. Many a night Albert held me while I cried myself to sleep. Playful and high-spirited, he became a friend to my boys. They took to him immediately—especially after that first Christmas, when he showered them with gifts. All during my Berkeley years, eight in all, the boys spent Christmases and summers with Albert and me.

After my parish internship at First Unitarian in Dallas, Texas, with John Buehrens, I went back to Starr King for a fourth and final year to finish my Master of Divinity. But by then I had realized that I wanted to do a Ph.D. I was taking a creative writing class with Ron Loewinsohn, novelist, and critic at the University of California. When I mentioned I was considering the Ph.D., he volunteered to be my dissertation director—a hugely significant offer, since my emphasis was theology and literature.

Edwina Hunter of Pacific School of Religion and Claire Fischer, a scholar and feminist who was a professor at Starr King, completed my committee. Claire knew the push and pull of the doctoral process quite well, and with her guidance, I finished the degree in four years of additional study. My dissertation was an original novel, plus a major paper on Maxine Hong Kingston's The Woman Warrior.

My son Madison came to spend his last two years of high school in Berkeley. Having him with me brought immense joy after our long separation. He and I had long conversations over dinner most nights—I watched him struggle at Berkeley and finally flourish. He and I graduated together in 1991. My first book,

Cries of the Spirit, an anthology of spiritual poetry by women, was completed the same year. Beacon Press wanted to publish it, but I had no money to pay for permissions. Bill Schulz, then President of the UUA, suggested I asked the Grants Panel of the UUA for financial help, and they came through: one day I opened a letter and found a check for $12,000. *Cries of the Spirit* was the first of its kind, eventually selling around 78,000 copies. Readings in UU churches had been drawn almost exclusively from male writers before *Cries of the Spirit* was published. Thereafter, never again.

VI.

My search for a church pulpit did not go well. Most ministers do two, maybe three pre-candidatings (three-day interviews) in order to find a church. The final year of my doctoral studies, I did five pre-candidatings all over the country, from Florida to California, but no church seemed right for me. The head of the UU Placement Department, Dan Hotchkiss, was irritated. He told me that I was "being aloof" with these churches. I told him I did not feel called.

I believed, and still believe, that ministers should feel called to a church before accepting a position. The call doesn't have to do with size or location of the church, or with salary. It is a love affair that is ignited during pre-candidating. I had not fallen in love. I had not been called.

On the other hand, I had student debt, and I needed work. I asked the Department of Ministry if I could do an interim ministry for a year. The Department agreed, and I began receiving slips of paper in the mail, letting me know of available interims. I kept throwing them in the trash. What is wrong with me?

Then one day a slip came suggesting the First Unitarian Church in Cincinnati. I knew instantly that I must go to Cincinnati. Without thinking, I called up the head of the interim search committee and said I wanted to take the position. I refrained from telling her that God sent me. Surprised at my assertiveness, she told me that they were just starting to look at candidates. She asked me to send my packet, and they would let me know in a month or two. As I suspected, God got it right, and I was chosen.

Cincinnati was the city where our family was living when my father snatched my brother and sister and me from our mother and took us to live in Louisiana when I was nine years old. My mother went into a mental hospital for a year, and I didn't see her again until I graduated from high school. I couldn't articulate exactly why I felt compelled to do the interim in Cincinnati—but once again, an internal necessity drove my decision. Once there, I realized that I was not ready for a call as yet: I needed to explore the loss of my mother.

I secured a psychiatrist, Madelyn, to help me with this work and saw her weekly for nine months or so. One day I brought in some artwork I had done. It was abstract, all in slashing red streaks.

"What does red mean to you?" she asked.

"Love," I said. "Passion, maybe."

"What about anger?" she said. Yes, what about anger. To avoid visiting that anger on some congregation, I needed to acknowledge it in myself. To look at the source. To see what was supporting my drifts into depression.

For much of that year, I struggled emotionally. The psychological work was demanding. But I was very much alive and present, and the church was a healthy one with strong lay leadership, so my ministry flourished. I continued searching, doing four more pre-candidatings. I was becoming very good at interviewing, so churches wanted me. But I did not want them. Why was nothing working out? I began questioning whether or not I was supposed to be a minister at all. Then First Unitarian Church in Portland, Oregon, asked me to pre-candidate. This was the tenth and last church I looked at.

I wasn't supposed to be on the Unitarian Universalist Association's list for First Unitarian in Portland—it was a large church of around 625 members, and I was just out of seminary, having never served a church as their called minister. The UUA's recommended list for the Portland church was filled with men, so in the Placement Department's wish to be egalitarian and inclusive, they wanted at least one female. I was a female with a Ph.D., so bingo! Was this the church I had been looking for?

I had never been to Portland—or to the Northwest, for that matter. As my plane neared the ground, I was captured by the bold landscape, with its mountains and towering trees. I found it daunting and, at the same time, compelling. My love affair was beginning.

I was met at the airport by two members of the search committee and driven around the city to look at typical neighborhoods, with their lush gardens and tree-lined streets, which I found charming. Then I was taken to the church. The building is a classic New England structure, reflecting the heritage of the founders, prominent individuals from the East who established the church in 1866. Unlike most Unitarian Universalist churches, it has a steeple. The structure of the building says something about respect for tradition and, with its raised pulpit, respect for ministry, as well. It is an elegant structure and beautifully appointed. First Unitarian is an urban church, located in the heart of downtown Portland. Since its founding, the institution had been a significant force for good in the community.

When I left the sanctuary that day, I knew I wanted to worship in that beauty, and I wanted to be a part of that tradition. Would the search committee agree?

The first meeting with the committee was in the home of a woman who lived in Eastmoreland, an area mostly of cottages built in the 1920s and '30s. The season was spring, and yards were awash in color: rhododendrons, azaleas, tulips, daffodils. The home was near Reed College, which along with most every other charitable and civic organization in early Portland, had been founded by Thomas Lamb Eliot, the church's first minister. The public library, the art museum, the Boys and Girls Club, the Humane Society—all had begun with the vision of Eliot and his congregants.

I had done my homework, and I knew that the church had been on hold for the past few years. The former minister had lost two wives to cancer in the last five years of his ministry, losses that had greatly affected him, as well as the congregation. A sadness prevailed. The church needed new life.

My conviction that this church was my call grew during the initial interview. First Unitarian was ready to flower, and I felt my heart open: I wanted to be in Portland, and I wanted to be with these people. I thought that I could provide the leadership they needed for their next phase. As the interview was winding down, I waited for the right moment, a silence that provoked attention. I looked at the committee members and said plainly, "This is where I am called to be."

My declaration was premature, of course—moreover, a unilateral one and not mine to make. Since I was the second out of five candidates in a nationwide search, the committee members looked around at one another and coughed politely. Finally, one of the women asked, "What makes you think so?"

My response rolled off my tongue. After all, the words had been waiting two years to be spoken. "I can offer you some things that you need," I said. "I'm a strong preacher, and a large church needs a strong preacher." I paused, then went on. "More important, you are a great church, and you have forgotten this. I can help you remember that you are great." I paused again, to let my promise sink in, then I continued. "And you can give me something I need: I need to be challenged to excellence, and you can do that for me."

I delivered my pre-candidating sermon at University Unitarian in Seattle that Sunday. Quite honestly, I can't recall the title, but I do remember the topic: I preached on the relationship between spirituality and the erotic. I thought that if the committee chose me, they should know what they were getting.

Just before I entered the church, my attention was drawn to a nondescript bush by the door. There was my little brown bird sitting amidst the branches.

I had to wait two months for the search committee to decide.

I knew that having had no parish experience, I was an unlikely choice, but that was just logic speaking—internally, I knew that I would be chosen. I was not surprised when the phone call came.

The candidating week went well, and the vote was 94.7% positive, as I remember. A minister hopes for 98 or 99% in the congregational vote, but I was the first female senior minister called to the church, and a group of long-time members quite frankly didn't want me. I didn't look like a minister to them, and I didn't sound like one, with my soft voice and Southern accent. Led by a member of the search committee, they lobbied against me. But the rest of the congregation was willing to take a chance on me. I accepted the call.

The installation service was at the First Methodist Church because our sanctuary was not large enough for the event. It was a grand occasion, attended by the mayor, the president of Reed College, and various dignitaries from the denomination. My sons Kash and Madison were there that evening, in their suits, all grown up. My work had taken me from them. That evening, they came to witness and to celebrate what their sacrifice had yielded.

Needless to say, I had a lot to learn about ministry. My challenges were complicated by the rapid growth of the congregation. Early in my ministry—in fact, before I ever stepped into the pulpit—we wrapped the church block with a red ribbon and declared ourselves a Hate Free Zone, as a witness against a state ballot measure seeking to overturn the civil rights of gays and lesbians. Local media featured the story, and First Unitarian became the go-to church not only for gays and lesbians, but for liberals who had been unchurched, but searching spiritually. The congregation grew nearly forty percent in my first year in Portland.

Overwhelmed, I became radically dependent upon the God that brought me to Portland. If I was truly called, I knew I would be held. And I was held during all of my seventeen years of ministry in Portland, partnered with the Spirit that brought me to the church and that had sustained me through the years: "Through many dangers, toils and snares, I had already come ..."

I brought little experience as a minister, but I brought all that time had wrought. My years of study in education, English, and social work. My work as a teacher and psychotherapist and writer. My learning as a wife, as a mother, as a lover and as a friend. And perhaps more significant than any of that, I brought the questions and doubts and the pain that flowed through the years I had lived. I put all of me on the altar. All that is within me. Redemption is possible, I knew.

The scripture promises "those who seek will find." Yes, we will find—but not necessarily what we think we want. And maybe not on our own timeline. Or in the way we expect. Or in the place we think. And every decision has its costs, for us and for others.

Notwithstanding, I had found my call at last. I had come home. I was fifty years old and ready to begin.

The Intersection of Feminism and Ministry

Kendyl Gibbons

IT WOULD BE IMPOSSIBLE TO PONDER the impact of late 20th century feminism on my life and ministry without acknowledging the influence of models within my family of origin.

My mother was an intellectually gifted, talented, and glamorous woman who in her youth aspired to a career in the performing arts as one of the few practical options available to a pretty young woman who was not averse to leveraging her attractiveness in the service of getting noticed. She traded that aspiration for the security of marriage to a young naval officer whose career ambitions consisted of scientific work as an electrical engineer for the military. As young parents living in the suburbs of Washington DC, the two of them readily agreed to dispense with the lukewarm Protestant religion of their own upbringings, while still seeking ethical structure and instruction in the values of justice and tolerance for their children. They discovered the ministry and outreach of A. Powell Davies at the downtown Washington church, and soon joined the nascent suburban UU fellowship in our sector of the beltway. One of their most fundamental shared values was education, and my mother quickly became a regular fixture in the first-grade religious education class. Over the course of my growing up, the congregation called a minister, bought property, and eventually built a building after years of renting facilities for our Sunday gatherings. By the time I was a teenager, both of my parents were practicing alcoholics, and I was furious. My mother's unreflective ambition found its vicarious outlet through the achievements of her children, but that was unsatisfying, and my first intuitions of feminism arose out of my observation of her inarticulate frustrations.

My precocious reading of women's magazine fiction convinced me that women who allowed themselves to become financially dependent on men forfeited all agency and control over their own destinies, no matter how well-intentioned those husbands might once have been, so at a young age, I realized that I would need a career that would enable me to be self-supporting. Years would pass before I was self-aware enough to identify the proposition that guided me towards ministry, as a riposte to my parents' investment in the church; something along the lines of "You think church is important? Well, watch this: I can do church like you never even thought about doing church!"

I came into seminary as part of the second wave of 20th century women demanding access to roles of prestige and attention in religious community, as well as opportunities to earn the credentials that qualified men for such positions. My facility for academic enterprise made the intellectual challenges of graduate level history and theory readily achieved, but the professional gatekeepers I encountered were neither impressed nor satisfied. Women in leadership were expected to manifest emotional fluency, and caring, neither of which was among my native gifts, nor any part of my childhood learning. I was aware that I hoped to achieve more occupational success and more financial independence than I had perceived in my mother, and more wisdom than I had observed from decades of teachers and peers. Early in the years of my first ministry I happened upon a therapy group for adult children of alcoholics, and through it, found literature on family dynamics, and thence congregational dynamics, that came as rather a revelation about my residual resentment toward my family of origin, and how I might use insights from it to function productively as a leader in church community. Feminist literature naming the work of emotional labor carried by women in most families taught me to recognize the emotional labor expected of women in ministry—functions which it seemed to me carried extra credit for my male counterparts when they fulfilled them but were seen as base level competence for me. I came to believe that I was witnessing not a cultural shift whereby the moral authority of the pulpit was being extended to women, but rather, where by the role of ministry, as it was increasingly occupied by women, came to be regarded as care giving "women's work," and to carry the same limited authority, prestige, and compensation—even for men—as the kind of care giving work traditionally assigned by the culture to women.

In the same time period, I began to develop a facility for the

intellectual badinage apparently enjoyed by my elder male colleagues with one another, and to discover that their acceptance
and respect was to be won only by the ability and confidence to
give as good as one received in these exchanges, without displaying
vulnerability, despite the ministerial culture's perpetual demands
for "authenticity." Once I understood the actual rules of this game,
I was able to play it effectively, and to perceive and participate
in—and take pleasure in—the truly affectionate respect upon
which it was based. Having learned to season my compliance
in the matter of authenticity with a grain of salt was helpful as
well in dealing with male models of leadership in the historically
Humanist congregations I was serving. I rarely felt myself to be the
recipient of actual sexist resistance to my leadership, though there
were any number of days, when shopping for birthday cakes or
flowers, to honor board members, or stuffed animals to illustrate
a particular children's story, when I went muttering through the
stores, "I KNOW A. Powell Davies never had to do THIS!"

Now in the final chapter of my own career, I contemplate
with satisfaction the flourishing ministries of many colleagues
whose field service placements and internships I have had the
honor of supervising. Perhaps the most significant contribution I
have made to the future of women in this vocation has been to
model competence, power, and continual learning both to women
proposing to enter into it, and to men for whom the pedagogical
authority of a woman supervisor was a novel experience. I have
succeeded in conducting life as a woman—as a professional and as
a wife—while maintaining my economic self-determination and
boundaries. I owe a significant debt of gratitude and affection to

the women colleagues who preceded me, not only in the history of our movement, but in the pulpits, I have occupied, as well as various roles of denominational leadership, and personal collegial support. In the same way, I am aware of a profound thankfulness for those male professional elders who welcomed me into collegial community, and who were quick to rejoice in my emergent competence and success.

I shall be fascinated to observe the ongoing evolution of the professional calling of spiritual leadership in the coming decades, and to see whether it regains any degree of culturally attributed moral authority. The feminist project as I have understood it and attempted to participate in it can only be said to have succeeded if such authority as ministry holds is vested as willingly in its women practitioners as it was for centuries in men.

Do You Know the Way to Freedom?

Carole Etzler Eagleheart

MY MOTHER WANTED TO BE A LAWYER. It never happened. For a woman born into the working class in 1904, the odds were stacked too heavily against her.

But what that meant for me, and for my two older sisters, is that she was determined we would get a good education and go on to have careers of our own.

That was a huge advantage for me. I was born in 1944, and as I was growing up I saw how the lives of other girls could be limited by the expectations of their parents.

I always wanted to be a writer. As a child I was scribbling stories in my Big Chief lined notepads. And I always sang. I made up songs and sang as I played alone in the little woods behind our house in Pennsylvania. Later, both writing and music became part of my career.

I saw my mother taking an active role in the community. She

was president of organizations like the PTA, and when she wasn't president, she was secretary. I saw her being comfortable at leading groups of people.

She wasn't afraid. So I wasn't afraid. I remember when I was 10 standing up and singing a solo without a qualm for 1,000 people at a community event. I see now that I was being raised as a little feminist, though we didn't use that word then.

Our lives as a family revolved around the church. Until I was 12, that church was a little Evangelical United Brethren congregation, a denomination that was later subsumed under the United Methodists. Both of my parents were very involved in that congregation, and I loved it. We put on plays and skits and I always had a speaking or singing role.

When I was 12, we moved from Pennsylvania to Kentucky. My father was the plant manager for a steel tubing company based in Detroit, and the company was opening a new plant in Kentucky.

This was 1957 and it was an era when there were still water fountains at the county courthouse labeled "Colored" and "White," which was appalling to me.

There was no Evangelical United Brethren church in Winchester, Kentucky, so we began looking around for a new church. We ended up with the Presbyterians.

I might have turned out to be United Methodist except that the Methodist youth group took a hike up a mountain that nearly killed me. I figured I wouldn't survive as a Methodist and lobbied heavily for the Presbyterians.

Once again, as a family we were very involved in the church. I sang in the choir, was active in the small youth group, and began to feel a call to ministry, though I didn't know what form that would take.

I went to Northwestern University because of its good journalism school. I was still determined to be a writer. I was active in its campus ministry program. But most important, I was exposed to the civil rights and anti-Vietnam-war movements. I was part of a small group that got to meet with Fannie Lou Hamer. I went to hear Martin Luther King, Jr., speak as he pushed the civil rights movement north. And I began protesting the war, standing up in sub-zero temperatures in Evanston, Illinois.

I stayed on at Northwestern to get my master's degree in journalism because they had a program where you could be a Washington correspondent for a quarter, with one of the professors as bureau chief. I covered Capitol Hill for two newspapers.

When I got my degree, I took a job that would get me back to Washington, DC. I worked at Georgetown University as editor of the Georgetown Record, a monthly publication for parents of students and people they wanted money from. I lived in an English basement apartment a couple of blocks behind the Library of Congress. The upstairs of that house was the headquarters for the Women's International League for Peace and Freedom.

This was a time of huge marches against the Vietnam war, and I was a part of them. But the most memorable moment for me was when Martin Luther King, Jr., was killed. We marched from Georgetown University down to the White House to try to get his birthday declared a national holiday. We had police escorts but on the way back they suddenly disappeared and we were left on our own to fend with traffic. When we reached the university up on the hill and looked back over the city it was like the scene from "Gone with the Wind" where Atlanta was burning: Washington, DC, was on fire. Riots had broken out, and smoke filled the air. As Dr. King had said, "A riot is the language of the unheard."

Like many women in the feminist movement I got my inspiration and early training in the civil rights and anti-war movements.

I only stayed a year at Georgetown University. It's run by the Jesuits, and the system was as oppressive as the military. I took a job as feature writer and photographer for the National 4-H Foundation. I still lived on Capitol Hill, and commuted out to the Foundation in Chevy Chase, MD—helpful because the rush hour traffic was all going in the opposite direction.

I loved being with the foreign exchange students who came to the National 4-H Foundation. And the job sent me around the country and to South America and Central America. I was doing what I loved—writing and shooting pictures.

At the same time, I got involved with the church again, which I had left after leaving Northwestern. I had a vision one night in which I was traveling up through a tunnel. I knew when I got to the top of the tunnel I would find God. But when I got there, I found only an empty, dark night sky. Then I was back in the tunnel again and this time there were people with me, and I knew that together we would make it, together we would find God.

Days after that vision I found the Church of the Pilgrims, an inner city Presbyterian Church. I became a member, helped start a coffeehouse ministry, and created slide shows for them, using my own original music.

This was the Presbyterian Church, US, known as the southern

Presbyterians, a denomination that had become separated from the northern Presbyterians during the Civil War. (It wasn't till later that the two denominations reunited.)

I got a call from the headquarters in Atlanta, from the Television, Radio and Audio-Visual Agency. When they invited me down for an interview, I thought they wanted to use my music or my slide shows. Instead, they offered me a job as Director of Media Development. I took it.

I was the only woman on staff, other than the women secretaries. There was a male mystique about the audio-visual equipment. But I found that if you twiddled this knob and turned that gizmo, the equipment worked. Why did people think only men could run it?

It was in Atlanta that I plunged into the feminist movement. With the help of my mentors Diane Tennis and Carole Goodspeed, I became part of the Presbyterian Committee on Women's Concerns. With consciousness raising, satire, and music we worked to get congregations to accept more women as ministers, elders and deacons.

It was a tough struggle. One day as the committee adjourned and we were walking down the street to a restaurant, one woman said, "Sometimes I wish my eyes hadn't been opened. It would be so much easier." About another block later she added, "But still something inside me would say 'yes' and my feet would say 'go.'"

It inspired my song "Sometimes I Wish," which became the title song for my first album and later the theme song for the Philadelphia Eleven—the first women to be ordained as Episcopal priests. Over the years the song was picked up and sung at international conferences. The last two verses go like this:

> But now that I've seen with my eyes, I can't close them,
> Because deep inside me somewhere I'd still know
> The road that my sisters and I have to travel:
> My heart would say, "Yes" and my feet would say, "Go!"
>
> Sometimes I wish my eyes hadn't been opened,
> But now that they have, I'm determined to see
> That somehow my sisters and I will be one day
> The free people we were created to be.

As I worked to get other women accepted into the ministry I enrolled in Columbia Seminary myself. I told people I was on the 14-year program because I was only able to take one course a quarter along with my more-than-full-time job.

As part of one of my seminary courses I created a radio drama about Mary Dyer, who was hanged in Boston in 1660 for being an outspoken Quaker. It became the pilot for a series of award-winning radio dramas I created called Women of Faith, funded by several denominations and broadcast not only in the United States but around the world.

I continued to perform my music, including at major marches in Washington, DC, for the Equal Rights Amendment and for Lesbian and Gay Rights.

I became part of the Committee on Women in Ministry of the National Council of Churches, where I found support from other feminist women working inside the churches. And in the summers I bonded with other women at Women in Ministry weeks at Grailville, Ohio.

But there was a hitch in my own plans for ministry. I had discovered I was a lesbian. And I couldn't imagine the Presbyterians ordaining a lesbian during my lifetime.

I was also diverging from the Presbyterians because I wanted to explore the feminine aspect of the Divine. I was reading books like Mary Daly's "Beyond God the Father," and I became increasingly distressed at religion's support of patriarchal thinking.

I treasured time I spent with feminist theologian Nelle Morton. She's the one who inspired my song "We Are Dancing Sarah's Circle," the only song of mine that is in the hymnbook "Singing the Living Tradition." She talked about how ladders—like Jacob's ladder—are symbols of patriarchy, with people climbing over each other to get to the top, and that we need to reach out our hands to each other in a circle instead. I was amused when I saw that they placed my words directly opposite "We Are Climbing Jacob's Ladder" in the hymnbook.

I was also influenced by Grandmother Twylah of the Seneca Wolf Clan. She helped me explore Native American spirituality and taught me to listen when the plants and animals speak. On a cliff above the Mississippi River a young golden eagle spoke to me and told me my name was Eagleheart.

It wasn't until 1984, after I had moved to Vermont, that I found a Unitarian Universalist congregation. I walked in on Sunday, April Fool's Day, and the creative and talented Rev. Agnes Zuniga had positioned a dummy up front to deliver the sermon—with a little help from Agnes with an easel and a pointer. I laughed in delight. I had found my spiritual home!

I had always admired the UUs for their pioneering work in eliminating sexism in language. Now I could plunge wholeheartedly into Unitarian Universalism. I found new freedom to explore the feminine image of the Divine.

I had already released a second album of my music, "Womanriver Flowing on." And in 1985, with my then-partner, cellist Bren Chambers, I released a third album, called "Thirteen Ships." And we set off across the United States on our first cross-country tour.

For me, it was the beginning of 20 years traveling the US and Canada as a UU troubadour. For the first nine years I traveled with Bren, and after she left, I continued on my own. Each year I plotted out a four-month trip from Vermont to California and back in the fall, and a three-month loop down to Florida in the spring. Each Sunday I would try to book a service at a UU congregation, with sometimes a concert and a workshop during the weekend as well.

In 1986 Bren and I wrote the theme song for the UU General Assembly, "Take Up the Song." In 1990 we did it again, with the song "Speak to the Earth." We were often invited to sing for the UU Women's Federation or for Women and Religion meetings at GA, and for other UU women's national conferences.

We continued to write music, releasing two other albums, "Rainbows in my Mind" and "You Are the One."

UU families hosted us on our tours, and sometimes we stayed with the same people year after year, watching their children grow up.

As I traveled, I could see the effects of Shirley Ranck's iconic curriculum Cakes for the Queen of Heaven. Women across Unitarian Universalism were being empowered. The impact was so striking that I thought of congregations as BC and AC—Before Cakes and After Cakes.

I became a regular part of UU Womenspirit, the delightful spring and fall Gathering and Institute at The Mountain, and traveled with some Womenspirit sisters to Greece in 2001 on Carol Christ's Goddess Pilgrimage. I funded the trip by selling the CD and songbook in advance, knowing the pilgrimage would inspire music. It did. The result was "She Calls to Us: Songs to Celebrate the Goddess."

In December, 2004, I ended my 20-year touring career and settled in New Mexico, where I took a job as a technical writer. I became active in the UU Westside Congregation, a small congregation in Rio Rancho, just outside Albuquerque, creating occasional Sunday services and also serving as their music director.

In 2013 they were without a minister. They asked me if I would step in. I told them I would serve for a year, during 2014. All those years on the road I had considered my work a ministry. The congregation ordained me, and at last my ministry became official— something I had dreamed about in the 1970s as a seminarian.

I was able to find them a consulting minister after my stint and have continued to support the congregation with Sunday service programs and with music.

During the pandemic, my background as an audio-visual producer with the Presbyterians came in handy. I was able to produce video versions of Sunday services for my UU congregations, and create in-depth video interviews, helping members get to know each other better.

The struggle for women's rights goes on, and as it does, I get letters asking permission to use my music. Because women are still pondering the question I raised in one of my songs long ago: "Do you know the way to freedom? Do you know the way to home?"

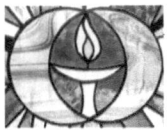

UUWF Feminist Theology Awards
FTA Selections Committee Chair 1993-1996

Anne Olson

*The following article has been edited, with the author's consent, to eliminate material mentioned elsewhere in this book.

IN 1974, THE UU WOMEN'S FEDERATION created the Ministry to Women award ceremony to draw attention to Women's issues at the annual General Assemblies of UU congregations. [Money to fund this cash award ward came from contributions by members as well as a matching grant from the Veatch Fund. Thus, the bulk of the funds came from UUWF members and laywomen.] The first awards were given to women or organizations that were not Unitarian Universalist. *Ms Maagazine* was the first recipient, but the award was not presented at that GA because the GA planning Committee would not allocate space for the ceremony. Other Ministry to Women Awards went to May Sarton, Marian Wright Edelman, Dr. Jean Baker Miller, Sarah Weddington, and Bernice

Johnson Reagan (Sweet Honey in the Rock.)

After 1980, the Ministry to Women to Award was only given to UU women. In1979 the UUWF created The Clara Barton Sisterhood to honor UU women over 80, still active in their congregations and communities.

Two books written or edited by UUWF women were *Voices of the New Feminism*, edited by Mary Lou Thompson, a joint project of UUWF and the Beacon Press and Nelle Morton's *The Journey is Home* also inspired many of us, especially since we could meet them in the UUWF booth at GA and discuss their ideas. Both books often started conversations in UUWF women's alliances and groups.

At the UUWF General Assembly in Vancouver Canada in 1983, UUWF held the 20th Anniversary Celebration of their Biennial where Carolyn McDade (Spirit of Life) was a performer and Charlotte Cowtan-Holm was the keynote speaker.

"Rise Up and Call Her Name," a curriculum developed by Elizabeth Fisher in 1994 for UUWF, also became a rich source of conversation and exploration of religious and spiritual ideas in UU congregations, as was the Women and Religion Curriculum "Cakes for the Queen of Heaven."

The next three Biennial Conferences focused on women's stories and experiences, to further explore feminist theology as experienced by UU Women. The Board moved to a programming emphasis and away from long budget discussions at biennials.

In 1985, the biennial was titled "Theology for UU Women … Search … Study … Sisterhood" held at Agnes Scott College in Decatur, GA. "Struggle is a Name for Hope: Patriarchy and Women-Church" presented by Dr. Elisabeth Schussler-Fiorenza. The UU Responders: Dr. Claire Benedicks Fischer, Dr. Betty Hoskins, and the Reverend Judith Walker Riggs. Later in the day there was an opportunity for attendees to discuss the morning program with the speakers. There were over ten workshops addressing women's spiritual and religious practices. One workshop was offered by two UU men sharing new sensitivity in male responses. Lesbian/Strait Dialogue was another workshop.

The next UUWF Biennial, "Casting New Light on Familiar Truths and Myths," was in Little Rock, AK in 1987. Beverly Wildung Harrison, led the conversation with UU women in the audience. She is the author of *Our Rights to Choose: Toward a New Ethic of Abortion* and *Making the Connections: Essays in Feminist Social Ethics*. Her main points: Women as center, women's embodiment and power of reproduction as sources of intellectual and personal strength, and fundamental relational sense of life-part of our givenness. She chooses not to use abstract ideas of justice but in experiences.

The next UUWF Biennial was in Minneapolis, MN in 1989. "Women Bringing Justice to the Work of Theology." UU women met to discuss their concerns about theology, spirituality and being women in our congregations. What did we want and what did we need? We had often not been heard and felt silenced. At this Biennial, discussion of the Feminist Theology Awards, with the first awards to be given at the Biennial in New Haven, CT in 1989, was lively.

To launch the Feminist Theology Awards, UUWF published two books of essays written by UU women. *Transforming Thought*,

Volume I in 1989 and *Volume II* several years later. The intent was to explore the status of UU feminist theology.

What happens when you get two extraordinary women, one a UUWF board member named Bernita Cogan, from Dallas, Texas, who is good at fund raising, and a feminist scholar named Betty Hoskins, from Worcester, MA, who was frequently attended UUWF board meetings. First, you get significant funding from the UUWF Southwest District, with Bernita leading the way. A $10,000 award in honor of Claire White, a former UUWF Board member, and an additional $33,000 was also raised. Later, additional funds were raised to obtain a matching grant from the Veatch fund.

Then Betty, the scholar, is appointed by the UUWF Board to be the first chair of the FTA Selections Committee in 1988. The first FTA committee was composed of James Luther Adams, PhD, the Reverend Jane Bramadot, Dr. Claire Benedicks Fischer, the Reverend Rosemary Bray McNatt and Beth Williamson. Scholars, ministers, and lay women, putting their minds together to consider what UU feminist theology might mean. Future FTA Selection Committees used that model for membership and process.

On the application for funding, it noted that feminist transformation work is difficult. Each applicant was asked in their application "What does it mean to be theological and what is specifically Unitarian and Universalist (UU) about their project?" The project was expected to be near completion the time the awards were decided.

The 1995 FTA application form "Consistent with the UUWF Mission Statement and the UUA Purposes and Principles, we seek new understandings and sensibilities as part of our search for feminist and theological truths ... Feminist and womanist authors ... use such concepts as collaborative models, pieces that are respectful and energized by difference, liberating feminist practice, collective responsibility, and the intersection of race, class, and gender. We invite such vehicles as essays, poetry, music, ritual, art, drama, and film." Shifting and learning, or leaning into the backlash with creative resistance, is work of theology and justice that must be done. The FTA's honor work by UU women who put themselves to the task of transforming thought.

Anne Olson was nominated to be the next FTA chair of the selection committee, serving from 1993-1996. Initially her committee included Dr. Cynthia Grant Tucker, Ms. Mary Lou Skinner Ross, the Reverends Jacqueline Collins and Linnea Pearson and The Rev. Dr Roberta K. Mitchell. Ms. Jacqui James, Director of the UUA Office of Worship and Diversity, joined the committee later and became the next FTA chair in 1997.

Music, dance, Goddesses, UU women's history, theater-so many ways for women to experience religion and theology. Explorations continue at UUWF.

Awards from 1989-1996 Are Listed

1989
Carolyn Nikkal, EdD
Shall You Betray Me with a Kiss?
Ethical and Religious Response to Sexual Abuse
Conference: October 5-8, 1989

Marilyn Sewell, PhD, MDiv
Female Consciousness in Worship
Supporting Workshop for Cries of the Spirit

Denise D. Tracy, MDiv
Editor, Wellsprings; Sources in Universalist Feminism

Cynthia Grant Tucker, PhD
The Church Home: A Homemaking Model for our Theology
Slide series/presentation

1990
Mary Grigolia, MDiv
Songbook of Hymns, Songs, & Chants

1991
Gail Ranadive, MFA, MA
Creative Writing: A Spiritual Quest Journal

1992

Linda Anderson, PhD

Judith Sargent Murray: A Woman of Substance

Dramatic reading play

Nancy Vedder-Schults, PhD

Chants for the Queen of Heaven:

An Audiotape of Women's Chants and Sacred Songs

1994

Irene Baros-Johnson, MDiv

Contributions of Text and Texture:

Lucretia Mott & Unitarians

Lyn Burnstine

Anita Truman Pickett: Free-Thought Preacher

Shirley Ann Ranck, PhD, MDiv

Feminist Thea/ology for the 21st Century

1995

Betty Donaldson, PhD

Images of the Goddess

Mary Anne Seibert Hamm, MDiv

Queen of the American Platform

1996
Laurie Bushbaum, MDiv
Piecework—Soulwork

Mary Ann Macklin, MDiv - Librettist
Deborah Phelps, MDiv - Composer
Universalism: Women Who Dare to
Speak the Message

*Feminism, Religion and Unitarian Universalism:
An Immodest Proposal
by the Rev. Linnea Pearson

** UU Woman-Timeline by the Rev. Elinor Artman

***UUWF History: PART II
TIMELINE: 1960s-2007

WomanSpirit

Part Three
Appendix/Resources

"*If you believe there is a direct relationship between historical religious mythology and the ways we treat women, we invite you to be a part of the implementation of the WOMEN AND RELIGION resolution.*"
--FROM THE WOMEN AND RELIGION PROGRAM
BY LESLIE ARDEN WESTBROOK

Introduction to the Women and Religion Program

UUA Minister for Women and Religion

Leslie Arden Westbrook

THE 1977 GENERAL ASSEMBLY "WOMEN AND RELIGION" Resolution asks all Unitarian Universalists to look at the ways our religious beliefs cause us to undervalue and overlook women. It asks us to look at the relationship between our religion and sexism. It asks us both to look at our interpersonal behavior in our families, friendships, and work, and to examine the prof=grams and policies of the religious institution of which we are a part, in order to determine the degree that sexist attitudes shape our lives together. It asks us, as Unitarian Universalists, to "clean house."

The WOMEN AND RELIGION Resolution is radical, in the original sense of the word for it is designed to help us 'remove the root of a disease,' i.e. sexism. It asks us simultaneously to re-member the root cause of our being together as religious liberals: "to affirm, defend and promote the supreme worth and dignity of every human personality, and the use of the democratic method in human relationships." It asks us to return to our Religious Dream.

Grassroots in its evolution, the resolution was conceived by a small group of UU women in Lexington, Massachusetts, submitted as a resolution to the 1977 General Assembly by 548 members of 57 member societies, and promoted vigorously by the Women's Federation. Now, the UAA is sponsoring a three-year effort to implement it. Because of the resolution's importance, this work is sponsored directly by the Office of the President.

The late President Paul N Carnes took an important step toward providing the leadership necessary if we are to begin to challenge sexism within our denomination when he said that the resolution "recognizes that the elimination of sexism is both an individual and institutional, a spiritual as well as socio-economic, problem ... (and that it) ... recognizes the relationship between power structures and language and mythology. Implementation of the WOMEN AND RELIGION Resolution will, therefore, require the effort of us all, lay people, churches and societies, professional religious leaders, UU affiliated organizations, UUA administration, staff, board of trustees, and districts, in 1977 recommendations for the ways the UUA can implement the resolution were developed by task forces across the continent. Since then, a continental committee has been providing continuing leadership, as the particular programs have evolved. Great numbers of men and women are working on these specific recommendations and programs.

If you believe there is a direct relationship between historical religious mythology and the ways we treat women, we invite you to be a part of the implementation of the WOMEN AND RELIGION resolution.

RECOMMENDATIONS FOR IMPLEMENTING OF THE 1977 GENERAL ASSEMBLY WOMEN AND RELIGION RESOLUTION

Ministry and Leadership

1. (A) Implementation of the Women and Religion Resolution should be promoted by the UUA President, Staff, Board of Trustees, District Leadership, and leadership in local societies. The UUA 4President should report annually to the General Assembly on the status of the implementation efforts. The President's report should be made verbally and in written form. During this report, time should be protected for an opportunity for question and input from delegates. An orderly, methodical, long-range program should be designated in order to implement the resolution at all levels of our denominational structure.

    (B) A person should be appointed at the UUA to serve as consultant and coordinator of the work of implementation. General Assembly workshops, District conferences, and local church programs should focus on the resolution. At District annual meetings the resolution should be considered and voted upon. Conferences on the topic should, at times, be interdenominational.

    (C) Commission on WOMEN AND RELIGION should be appointed and given the authority to appraise and facilitate the actual implementation of the Resolution. The Commission should be formed with the broadest representation of members by geography, affiliation, age, sex and philosophical perspective. Appropriate funds should be granted to facilitate this work.

2. An Affirmative Action Program for women ministers and women theological students should be developed by the UUA and the UU theological schools. Specific suggestions include a "circuit riding female minister" to give leadership and role exposure to lay-led fellowships; the encouragement of women speakers for local parishes and district meetings; continued participation of the UUA in the National Council of Churches Commission on Women in Ministry; a "roving program" on the Women and Religion resolution for use by societies; and the encouragement of societies by the UUA Section of Ministry to consider women candidates.

3. Conferences for settled women ministers. For women theological students, and for women lay leaders should be developed, supported and encouraged. Such conferences should address the issues of power, success and effectiveness, money management, volunteerism, and other women's issues.

4. Male ministers, members of the UUMA and LREDA, male students being interviewed by the UUA Ministerial Fellowship Committee should be educated about the relationships between religious myths and sexual stereotypes and the deleterious effects of sexist language. They should be educated on women's issues and the work in theology being done by women. Women's sermons should be distributed. A question on the record sheet of every minister

which is distrusted to churches searching for ministers to focus on the substance of the resolution.

5. The President should contact all UUA committees and affiliated UU organizations and ask them to report what their plans are to implement the resolution. Their response should be published in the UU WORLD.

   The Collegium, Beacon Press, the UUSC, and all other affiliated and assorted UU organizations should be apprised of the importance of the Resolution and asked to focus some of their work on the substance of the Resolution.

6. The UUA should appoint a staff using affirmative action guidelines. Such a program should attempt to eliminate job stereotyping and seek to avoid placing women primarily in jobs backed by "soft money." In particular, pictures of the UUA staff, UUSC staff, etc. should be included in the UU WORLD to indicate the effectiveness of each organization's affirmative action program. All UUA salaries as they appear in the UUA budget should be broken down into individual salaries.

7. UU theological schools, in their curriculum, faculty and structure, should reflect the increasing number of female students, their interests, their talents and their perspectives. Seminars for male and female students should be designed which prepare them to minister adequately to the needs and concerns of women. UUA financial aid to theological students and schools should be granted only after a "Title 9" review has occurred at the school.

8. All materials distributed through the UUA Section of the

Ministry should be revised to reflect the changing population of our ministry. In particular, the Ordination Manual should reflect the fact that women as well as men are part of liberal ministry.

Education and Program

1. Educational materials for children, youth, and adults, (including teachers and parents) should be developed. Such materials should:

   - Explore the relationships between religious myths and sexism.
   - Examine the deleterious effects of sexist language.
   - Explore the role of women in religion since pre-cultural times.
   - Tell the stories of outstanding women in our movement.
   - Promote nontraditional role models for men and women.
   - Celebrate personhood.

   These materials should be developed for men's groups, women's groups, mixed groups in our churches. Materials already developed should be revised to bring them into line with the philosophy and intent of the resolution. A Great Book discussion program should be developed which uses Beacon books on the subject of women and religion.

2. A Clearinghouse on Women and Religion should be established. The Clearinghouse should compile resources such

as sermons, discussion guides and program manuals from local societies and UUA organizations such as Beacon Press, the UUWF, etc. Other projects of the Clearinghouse should be a non-sexist liturgical resource directory; profiles of women ministers; information on courses in religion and women's affairs; a UU women's professional talent bank; and a Women and Religion Packet.

3. The UU World should carry stories and educational articles on the Women and Religion program. In particular, the World should: "carry a large article and educational questionnaire for use by UU churches, societies, families and individuals which would assess the role of women in the leadership of our societies and encourage nontraditional roles for society members.

   • Include a regular column entitled "Women's Interfaith Issues."
   • Carry the President's General Assembly report on the implementation of the resolution.
   • All stories, worship resources, etc. in the world should be edited so that sexist assumptions and language are deleted or changed.

4. A new degenderized Hymnbook should be developed. It should include non-sexist language and fresh material that is written by and for women. Local parishes should contribute work on this project by sending materials to the Commission on Common Worship, established by the President. In the meantime, the Worship Arts Clearing-

house should distribute its list of non-sexist hymns.

5. Materials previously distributed by the Worship Arts Clearinghouse should be degenderized and new materials developed should be sensitive to the issue of language and sexism. In particular, worship material for families should be developed.

6. The UUA should design educational programs on the Women and Religion Resolution which will reach individuals and groups outside our denomination. Such efforts should include:

    • Public service television spots with the target audience women

    • Letters to other denominations, institutions and coalition groups informing them of the substance of the resolution.

7. Dialogue and work with feminists of other groups in order to further examine the relationship between religious and cultural attitudes toward women. Materials on sexuality should be developed and collected, including the acceptance and celebration of women's sexuality as a part of human experience. This material should include such subjects as the reproductive cycle sexual preferences, and sexual behavior.

1977-78 Women and Religion Task Force Conveners

Drucilla Cummins, Edina, MN

Billie Drew, Lexington, MA

Mam Hogan, Hamburg, NY

Rosemary Matson, Berkeley, CA

Janet May, Willowdale, Ontario

Joan Mendelsohn, Chicago. IL

Janet Osborn, Port Washington, NY

Bea Robbins, Silver Springs, MD

Jody Schilling, Berkeley, CA

Uua Women and Religion Committee

Carol Brody, LREDA, Columbus, OH

Billie Drew, Lexington, MA

Lynn Lyle, Jacksonville, FL

Rosemary Matson, Carmel Valley, CA

Carolyn McDade, Newton, MA

Joan Mendelsohn, Bedford, MA

Jean Zoerheide, UUWF, Baltimore, MD

The Rev. Ms Denise Tracy, Ms. U.U., Lansing, MI

Uua Affirmative Action Program Advisory Committee

The Rev. Til Evans, Starr King School for Religious Leadership

The Rev. Diane Miller, San Francisco, CA

The Rev. Joanne Papanek Orlando, Hartford, CT

The Rev. Marni Politte, State College, PA

The Rev. Agnes Zuniga, Ascutney, VT

AFFIRMATIVE ACTION FOR
WOMEN IN MINISTRY: BROCHURE

- Gathered data from interviews, surveys and hearings.
- Prepared a packet of materials for search committees, ministerial settlement representatives, and women seeking settlements.
- Established a support network for UU women theological students in non-UU, often isolated schools, linking students to nearby women clergy.
- Developed a file of information on women students' experiences with clinical pastoral education. The file is available in the office of the associate director of ministry to UU students selecting CPE programs.
- Published a brochure on CPE for students.
- Trained and sent settlement consultants to visit search committees to raise awareness of facts about women in our ministry.
- Offered seminars and workshops at General Assemblies
- Communicated with UU women and men through all available channels, seeking to hear suggestions, responses and concerns.
- Consulted extensively with UUA staff to review and advise in regard to Women in Ministry

Programs for the Coming Year

- Conduct a seasonal Training Seminar to prepare women now in settled ministry to work with the Department of Ministry, serving as Settlement Consultants
- Evaluate the results at the pilot settlement program undertaken 1980-81
- Consult with the Department of Ministry on the developing ministry of religious education (MRE)
- See that committee programs and recommendations are implemented and integrated into the structure of the association and into existing ministry policies.
- Gather a circulating library of resources on Women and Ministry
- Provide UU groups with information on resources for addressing issues of Women and Ministry
- Develop and test a workshop on Women and Ministry to be used in districts and societies
- Explore and evaluate career development resources for women clergy
- Publish updated report of committee research, programs and recommendations to the UUA

How Did the Committee Begin?

In 1977 the UUA General Assembly passed the landmark Women and Religion Resolution. The Affirmative Action for Women in Ministry: UUA Advisory Committee bases its task in part on that resolution. Also shaping the charge of the committee are:

- The 1964 UU Ministry Resolution
- The 1970 Equal Opportunities and Pay Resolution
- The 1972 Equal Opportunity on Recruitment Resolution and
- The 1980 Women and Religion Resolution

In 1978 President Paul Carnes, in consultation with the Department of Ministry and the Minister for Women and Religion, appointed five Unitarian Universalist ministers to serve on the Committee. Its three-year charge was extended for 1981-82 by the UUA Board of Trustees.

Who Is on the Committee?

The Rev. Joanne Papanek Orlando

The Rev. Diane Miller

The Rev. Roberta Nelson

The Rev. Marni Politte Harmony

The Rev. Agnes Zuniga

The Rev. Leslie A. Westbrook, has staff responsibilities with the Committee

What Is the Task of the Committee?

- To survey women ministers and theological students
- To determine where needs exist for affirmative action programs.
- To examine such programs in other denominations.

- To design and recommend a program of affirmative action for women in ministry which will meet the needs of the denominations.

Did you Know?

- 109 of the 974 ministers in UUA fellowship are women.
- 73 of the ministers settled in UU churches are women.
- 11% of Unitarian Universalist ministers are female, 89% are male.
- 52% of the UU students enrolled on theological education are women.
- Women have been ordained by Universalist and Unitarian Churches for over a century.
- Since 1980, 11 women have been fellowshipped as Ministers of Religious Education.

AFFIRMATIVE ACTION FOR WOMEN: FINAL REPORT

What has the committee done?

- Gathered data from interviews, surveys, and hearings.
- Prepared a packet of materials for search committees, ministerial settlement, representatives, and women seeing settlements.
- Established a support network for UU women theological students in non-UU often isolated, schools, linking students to nearby women clergy.
- Developed a file of information on women students' experiences with clinical pastoral education. The file is available in the office of the associate director of ministry to UU students selecting CPE programs.
- Published a brochure on CPE for students.
- Trained and sent settlement consultants to visit search committees to raise awareness of facts about women in our ministry.
- Worked with UUA on transition of Minister of Religious Education settlement from section of education to ministry section.
- Offered seminars and workshops at General Assemblies
- Communicated with UU women and men through all available channels, seeking to hear suggestions, responses and concerns.
- Consulted extensively with UUA staff to review and advise in regard to Women in Ministry.

Final Report Recommendations

1. We recommend that in 1988, ten years after the inception of the AAFWIM: UUA Advisory Committee, a study be undertaken to assess the impact of women in the UU ministry and the status of programs and issues addressed by the committee.

2. In response to student requested, we recommend courses, seminars, workshops focusing on practical issues of ministry (e.g. contract negotiation, church administration).

3. Because MREs will nearly always be in multiple staff situations and because issues and concerns unique to these settings have only begun to be explored, we recommend ongoing study of the dynamics of churches with multiple staff positions.

4. We recommend continued support and funding for the Settlement Consultant Program.

5. We recommend the formation of an ongoing consulting committee for affirmative action for women in ministry. We recommend that the UUA continue to address and act upon affirmative action issues and concerns.

How did the Committee begin?

(See flyer immediately above for this information)

Who was on the Committee?
The Rev. Til Evans
The Rev. Marni Politte Harmony
The Rev. Diane Miller

The Rev. Roberta Nelson

The Rev. Papanek Orlando

The Rev. Carolyn Owen-Towle

The Rev. Agnes Zuniga

The Rev. Leslie Westbrook had staff responsibilities with the committee from 1978-1981

The Rev. Lex Crane, staff 1982

Did You Know?

- 138 of the 992 ministers in the UUA fellowship are women.
- 98 of the ministers settled in UU churches are women.
- 14% of all Unitarian Universalist ministers are female, 86% are male.
- 56% of the UU students enrolled in theological education are women, 47% studying for parish.
- Women have been ordained by Universalist and Unitarian churches for over a century.
- Since 1980, 24 women have been fellowshipped as Ministers of Religious Education

Biographies for WomanSpirit Co-Editors

The Rev. Ms. Denise D. Tracy was ordained in 1974 at the NYC General Assembly. She was the 8th woman employed in UU ministry at that time. Her Ministries: '74-'76 Campus Ministry, Hartford, Ct. Parish '76-'84 Greater Lansing, Mich. She was the first woman to hold a UUA District Executive position, '84-'92 Central Midwest. From 1992-2007 she served as a Congregational Consultant with the Alban Institute. She then became in Interim Minister serving South Bend, '07-'08, St John's Cincinnati '08-'10, San Mateo, CA 10-11. She Retired from UU Ministry in 2012. Since then, she has served as a Chaplain for the Elgin, IL Police Department ('11-'18). She received the Martin Luther King Humanitarian Award from the City of Elgin in 2014. In 2018 she founded the Chaplaincy for the Kane County Sheriff's Office

Denise D. Tracy and Emmy Lou Belcher

where she served until 2023. In 1989 she won the UUWF Feminist Theology Award to help fund her book, *Wellsprings: Sources in Unitarian Universalist Feminism.* She has written four books of stories for worship titled: *The Stream of Living Souls Series.* She also created and edited numerous curriculum materials and study guides for use in women's groups in congregations. She lives in Elgin, IL with her husband of 42 years, Bill Decker. She has three children and three grandchildren.

The Rev. Emmy Lou Belcher. After graduating from the University of Michigan. Emmy Lou began her professional life as an artist and teacher of art. While serving for six years as the Director of Religious Education at the Detroit UU Church, she became interested in becoming a minister. At that time, there were no non-residential programs offered at UU seminaries. She put together a tapestry of coursework and experiences to meet the UU Fellowship Committee's requirements for an equivalency to a seminary degree, Emmy Lou was granted Fellowship and then ordained by the Detroit church in 1989. She was the third of four women ordained by that congregation ... In 1989 she was called to the Unitarian Universalist Congregation of Grand Traverse, MI. During her fifteen-year ministry there, the congregation grew from 75 to almost 300 members and constructed their own building. In 2004, she served as the Interim minister at Morristown, NJ. She was called to the DuPage UU Church in Naperville, IL. in 2005. During that call, the congregation doubled the size of its building with a new Sancturary and basement spaces. In 2014, at age 70, she retired and was named *Minister Emerita* by the DuPage church. In 2023 she began working with Rev. Denise Tracy to put together this book. Emmy Lou now lives in Chicago near her two granddaughters, Elena and Catalina Castillo.

Biographies of Contributing Authors

The Rev. Dianne Arakawa is currently Transitional Senior Pastor at The Church of the Pilgrimage in Plymouth, MA. (It is the congregation that was gathered in Scrooby, England, in 1606, founded in Plymouth, MA, in 1620, separated from First Parish in 1801-1805, and remains affiliated with the United Church of Christ.) Dianne began serving churches in 1978 in the UUA, then after 1999 in the United Church of Christ, specializing in transitional ministry and conflict transformation. She holds degrees from the University of Chicago Divinity School, Harvard Divinity School, and Wheaton College in MA. She and her spouse, Rev. Stephen C. Washburn, reside in MA and to be close to their son.

The Rev. Joy Atkinson was ordained in 1974 after a year-long consulting ministry at the Humboldt UU Fellowship in Northern California. She went on to serve for 24 years as the parish minister in Unitarian Universalist congregations in Duluth, Minnesota, Davis, California and San Mateo, California. Upon leaving a fourteen-year ministry San Mateo in 2002, she was named their Minister Emerita. Not ready to retire at the time, she moved into interim ministry, and served ten UU congregations in California and one in Arizona as interim senior minister over the next sixteen years.

She retired in 2018. In retirement she has pursued writing, choral singing, and amateur astronomy. She is currently serving on the Board of the UU Retired Ministers and Partners Association.

The Rev. Maryell Cleary was an author and writer before and during her ministerial career. She attended Meadville Lombard and the University of Chicago for her ministry degrees. She had ministries in Ft Myers, FL. Lyons, Ohio, Greater Lansing, MI. and Toronto, On, Canada.

Peggy Collins is an eco-feminist, a mother and great grand-mother. She is a member of the Southfield (Michigan) UU Church. She worked at Ford Motor Company and attended all regional Women and Religion conferences. She served on Chapin Crane Women and Religion team. She sung in Gaia Women of Great Lakes Basin Choir which was hosted by Carolyn McDade. She attended the Goddess pilgrimage to Crete with Carol Christ.

The Rev. Nancy Wynkoop Doughty, a fifth generation Universal-ist, grew up in a small rural community in OH. She attended summer Universalist camps as a youth and later was an officer in the Liberal Religious Youth when it was formed from the Universalist and Unitarian youth organizations in 1951. She attended many youth conferences while in college at Miami University, graduat-ing in 1956. She chose to attend St. Lawrence for her theological education because Angus H. MacLean was its Dean at that time and was teaching there. She graduated in 1961 and was ordained by First Unitarian Universalist Church, Detroit, MI in 1962.

Carole Etzler Eagleheart worked as the Director of Media Development for TRAV—the television, radio and audiovisual agency of the Presbyterian Church U.S. in Atlanta Georgia before becoming UU. She is both a composer and a musician. She now lives in Rio Rancho, NM. She spends three months a year in Key Largo, FL, kayaking, snorkeling, and shooting underwater videos. She also travels internationally as a photographer and videographer. At home in New Mexico, she is active with the UU Westside Congregation, providing occasional services and music, and organizing political writing and texting campaigns through UU the Vote.

The Rev. Kendyl Gibbons served congregations in Naperville. IL and Minneapolis, MN. Kendyl then accepted the call to be Senior Minister at All soul's Church in Kansas City, MO. She has served as the President of the UU Minister's Association, Co-Dean of the Humanist Institute and in 2015 was named the Humanist of the Year.

Gordon Gibson is a retired Unitarian Universalist minister. In the course of his career, he served The Unitarian Universalist Church in Jackson Mississippi, The Unitarian Universalist Fellowship of Elkhart, Indiana, Our Home Universalist Unitarian Church in Ellisville, Mississippi and The Theodore Parker Church in West Roxbury, Massachusetts. He took part in an early phase of the Selma voting rights struggle and discovered the personal papers of Judith Sargent Murray. In retirement he and Judy, his wife, were co-founders of the Living Legacy Project, which provides experiential education about the Civil Rights Movement. He is author of the book *Southern Witness: Unitarians and Universalists in the Civil Rights Era.*

The Rev. Ellen Dohner Livingston was born in Newton, Massachusetts. Her Masters in Theology is from Southern Methodist University in Dallas, where she also worked as a chaplain at Parkland Hospital. Although she was a UU at the time, she went there because her husband had been transferred to Dallas. After passing the requirements to become a UU minister, she went on to serve her first congregation in Park Forest, Illinois. While in Illinois, she met her second husband architect Nick Livingston. During that time the congregation had to give up their old church building and were without a church home until, with the help of Nick as architect and builder, were married there in that new building thirty years ago. Ellen then served the Monte Vista UU congregation for 19 years, retiring with the title of Minister Emerita. Since retiring she has enjoyed writing a book on the subject of *Promises: Making Breaking and Keeping.*

Lucile Schuck Longview. After her husband's death in 1972, Lucile Schuck decided to spend the rest of her life working to address injustice wherever she saw it. She changed her name to Lucile Schuck Longview. She was an early member of the Grey Panthers and was part of the Boston Women's Health Collective that wrote the life changing book, Our Bodies Ourselves. In 1977 she wrote the Women and Religion Resolution urging the UUA to become a faith that recognized and worked for the equality of the sexes. The Women and Religion Resolution was passed unanimously at the

1977 General Assembly. In 1979 and 1980 she wrote and passed Resolutions against the Battering of Women and Patriarchy. She received recognition at the National Woman's Hall of Fame in Seneca Falls, NY. Her papers are now at the Schlesinger Library at Harvard University.

The Rev. Dr. Barbara Merritt graduated from the University of Texas at Austin with a major in Philosophy. After a year of travel in India, she then went on to attend Thomas Starr King School for the Ministry, where she was the Killam Fellow. She graduated and was ordained in 1975. She served the Woodstock Congregational-Universalist Church in Illinois for 8 years, and then was called as Senior minister at the First Unitarian Church of Worcester, Massachusetts, from 1983-2010. She received two honorary doctorates, one from Starr King, and another from Assumption College. She has been married to her husband Jeff since 1977. They have two adult sons and one new grandson!

Kathleen (Kay) Montgomery moved to Boston to work at the UUA in Fund Raising. In 1985 she became the Executive Vice President of the UUA, the first woman and first lay person to hold this position. The Exec VP of the UUA is the second person in charge of our Association. As the Chief of Staff, the Exec VP builds relationships with congregations and leaders to strengthen the organization. During her 30 years as VP, she excelled in outreach and advocated for greater diversity and support for racial, gender, and LGBTQ inclusion and equity. She retired in 2013.

Anne Olson joined the Unitarian Universalist Congregation of Atlanta in the late '60s. She was fortunate to be mentored by the senior minister Rev. Gene Pickett. She served on many committees, including the Board of Directors. Later she became the first Women and Religion Chair for the Mid-South District, served on the Board of UUWF, serving as program chair for three biennials. She then chaired the Feminist Theology Awards for several years. After leaving UUCA, she was a charter member of the Thurman Hamer Ellington Congregation, UU. She retired in 1999 and moved to the East Lake Commons CoHousing Community in Decatur, GA where she continues to live.

The Rev. Dr. Carolyn Owen-Towle was born in Claremont, California. She graduated from Scripps College, in 1957, having majored in Art and Art History. She was married to Rev. Dr. Tom Owen-Towle in 1973, and together they have 4 children, 7 grandchildren, and one great grandchild. The Rev. Dr. Carolyn Owen-Towle, began her ministry in 1978, and with her mate, was called to First Unitarian Church, San Diego, where they served for 24 years as co-ministers. She was president of the MsUU; the first woman President of both the UUSC and the UU Ministers Assn, each for two years. She ran as candidate for UUA Presidency, in 1993, and lost by 99 votes. She authored two books, *Step off the Sidewalk* and *Damngorgeous,* as well as numerous articles. She died in 2023.

The Rev. Dr. Tom Owen-Towle was ordained in 1967 and has continued to serve as a UU minister, preaching and conducting workshops on "Conscious Aging and Mindful Dying." He is the author of two dozen books on personal relationships, social justice challenges, and spiritual growth, his latest one being: *Making Peace with Our Own Death* (2021). Four of Owen-Towle's volumes directly explore the issues of this book on feminism within Unitarian Universalism: *New Men: Deeper Hungers; Brother-Spirit: Men Joining Together in the Quest for Intimacy and Ultimacy; Friendship Chronicles: Letters Between a Gay and a Straight Man; The Bridge Called Respect: Women and Men Joining As Allies* (co-authored with Dr. January Riddle); and *Save the Males: Changing Men ... Changing the World.*

The Rev. Dr. Linnea Pearson, Ph.D. Unitarian minister, religious scholar, and community activist, focuses on women and children and peace. She heads the National Conference for Community and Justice Task Force on Domestic Violence and serves on the Board of the Miami-Dade Victim Services Center. She has advocated for the farm worker, the environment, and is the current leader of the local branch of Women in Black. Among her publications are Separate Paths: Why People End Their Lives and Dreams on Fire: Embers of Hope, Reflections from the Pulpit following the Rodney King Uprisings in Los Angeles

The Rev. Dr. Qiyamah A. Rahman: earned bachelor's in education and a Master of Social Work from University of Michigan. She embraced UUism in 1990, and later pursued a Master of Divinity from Meadville Lombard Theological School and a doctorate from Clark Atlanta University in Africana Women's Studies. Qiyamah was ordained on October 21, 2007, at UU Church of Charlotte in Charlotte, NC. From 1999–2012 she was the District Executive in the Southern District (formerly Thomas Jefferson District), the first African-American woman to hold the position in the UUA. 2008–2012 was the Director of Contextual Ministry and Senior Lecturer at Meadville Lombard Theological School. Starting in 2005, she served the UU Fellowship of St. Croix, in US Virgin Islands. While there she was the Executive Director of Sister Source, Inc. a non-profit devoted to encouraging activity, support, and resources to heighten the awareness and presence of Black UU women and girls (womxn, LGBTQIA+, binary and inclusive). Her first book, an anthology published in 2023 is titled, The Rough Side of the Mountain: Black Women's Ministries in Unitarian Universalism. She has three children, and two grandchildren.

The Rev. Shirley Ranck attended Starr King School for the Ministry. She had ministries in Houston, TX, West Redding, Ma, Las Cruces, NM and Sacramento, CA. She then became an Interim Minster in Williamsburg, VA and Oak Park, IL. As part of the Women and Religion movement in the UUA she and Leslie Westbrook created the curriculum called Cakes for the Queen of Heaven.

The Rev. Dr. Marilyn Sewell began her career as a high school English teacher, later becoming a social worker, and finally finding her calling as a minister late in life, serving as the Senior Minister of the First Unitarian Church in Portland, OR, for 17 years before her retirement in 2009, when she was named Minister Emerita.

She holds four advanced degrees, culminating in a PhD in Theology and Literature from the Graduate Theological Union and the University of California at Berkeley. Marilyn has published many articles and books, including a ground-breaking collection of women's poetry entitled *Cries of the Spirit*, and she is the subject of an award-winning documentary, *Raw Faith*. Post-retirement, Marilyn has continued writing—she turned to fiction in her newest book, a collection of short-shorts entitled *In Time's Shadow: Stories About Impermanence*. Marilyn lives on the lovely Willamette River in Portland with her husband George Crandall and her cat Bella.

Marian L. Shatto has worked with Carolyn McDade for the past 35 years as both an archivist, editor, and friend. She attended Susquehanna University, and received a BA in English, magna cum laude, in 1967 and Lancaster Theological Seminary, MAR, magna cum laude, in 1991. She worked at Susquehanna Bank as a Loan Administration document specialist, 1970-2008. From 1979 to the present, she has been a Member of Lititz Moravian Congregation. She has sung in the choir, co-chaired the 20th Moravian Music Festival. She is the author of *Singing Our Faith: Moravian Hymns through the Seasons* and the 2012 study book commissioned by the Interprovincial Moravian Women's Board.

Misty Sheehan became a UU at East Liberty Universalist church when her children needed a reflective Sunday school. She was picked to join the Chapin-Crane Women's Team in 1978. There she was the editor of the newsletter and spoke in various churches in Michigan about the importance of women to our world. She did the first rewrite of the UU principles and worked hard to get them accepted by the General Assembly. She worked for the Central District as a member of the Women and Religion Team She continued the Continental Women and Religion Team and was President. She feels women and religion has changed UUism for the better. In her professional life she was Associate Professor of Humanities at College of DuPage in Glen Ellyn IL and Adjunct Prof of Philosophy at Northwestern Michigan College.

The Rev. Liz Strong was a third generation Universalist and earned her B.A. from Syracuse University (NY) in 1962. After she earned her M.S. degree in education, she was named the RE Director at the First Unitarian Church of Rochester (NY). She felt that children deserved a minister of their own and she was a prime mover in the development of the UUA's Minister of Religious Education program. She was named MRE of the May Memorial (UU) Society in Syracuse. She served the Parish Church (UU) of Ashbury, MA. She wrote her essay for this book, revised it and within a few weeks died. We are so glad to have her final words as a part of this volume.

The Rev. Alice Blair Wesley received her B.A. from the University of Louisville in 1960. Ordained in 1977, she received Final Fellowship for Ministry from the UUA in 1981. From 1977-1996 she served congregations in Brazos, TX ('77-'78), Silver Spring, MD (78-84), Cherry Hill, NJ ('81-'84), (Hagerstown, MD (85-88), Greater Cumberland ('85-'88), (Hartford County, MD (86-96). Besides her ministries she is a respected scholar and is known for academic strength as well as for founding the First Days Record, a

Journal for Collegial writing and sharing. Throughout her ministry she was supported by her husband Joe, who recently died.

The Rev. Leslie Arden Westbrook received her MRE from Crane Theological School and her MTh from Boston Theological School. She was the staff person at the UUA for Women's programming in the mid-1970s. The materials in the Appendix are the program documents produced by her Office. She also had ministries in Gaithersburg, Md, Evanston, IL, and Jacksonville, FL.

WomanSpirit

Endorsements for *WomanSpirit*

"*WomanSpirit: The Rise of Feminism and the Empowerment of Women in Liberal Religion* draws on archival materials and personal accounts to introduce the complex intersections of gender, spirituality, and social change. This is an engaging look at a neglected area within Unitarian Universalist historiography and an important addition to the study of progressive feminist theology. The challenges and obstacles faced by women religious leaders in the second half of the twentieth century will inspire twenty-first century UUs with their courage, compassion, and resilience."
—THE REV. MEG RICHARDSON, PH.D. (SHE/HER/HERS), ASSOCIATE DEAN OF FACULTY, ASSOCIATE PROFESSOR OF UNITARIAN UNIVERSALIST HISTORY, DIRECTOR, CERTIFICATE IN UNITARIAN UNIVERSALIST STUDIES, STARR KING SCHOOL FOR THE MINISTRY

"I was deeply moved by the generous vulnerability offered in such personal accounts, chronicling this important strand of Unitarian Universalist history. Here is a thoughtful work about hopeful realism in the face of adversity. Clearly, these twenty-first-century women ministers helped transform our denomination into the multicultural, multiracial denomination that it is today."
—The Rev. Addae A. Kraba, Minister, Unitarian Universalists of New Braunfels, Texas

"The number of women serving as ministers in North American Unitarian Universalist congregations grew from less than 1% to almost 50% between 1970 and 1990. In this important book Denise Tracy and Emmy Lou Belcher tell how this change came to be. Through the words of the women and men whose love of this religious tradition, hard work, sacrifice, and dedication to a larger vision ushered in a new age. This is a 'Must Read' book for those interested in the story of modern Unitarian Universalism."
—The Rev. Charlotte Cowtan, retired UU Minister, Winnipeg, Canada

"This is a remarkable collection! Most importantly, the very clear struggles that women experienced, the "you don't look like a minister" stuff, the groping by men at conferences, all of the roadblocks, institutionally and culturally, are unknown to most newer UU's who think that everything was fine after a few women were ordained in the 19th century. We tell our history by those few notable ministries but do not speak of the transformative ministries

within human memory for many, and the struggles they faced and pushed through."
—The Rev. Marco Belletini, Minister Emeritus First Unitarian Universalist Church of Columbus, OH

"Ordained in 1976 and fellowshipped with the UUA in 1980. My journey and work as a UU: minister, white, southern, straight male has occurred with every increasingly diverse colleague. Women were the first. I learned from them. They were great models, and a few were otherwise. I've developed friendships, deep respect, and gratitude. I'm a better person and minister because of their blessings. This work is a welcome and insightful record of a vital part of our legacy.
—The Rev. Doak Mansfield currently serves in both Newton, NJ, and Woodbury, CT. He is the author of *Kin-ship Spirituality* and *The Kin-dom Option*.

"One of the most significant contributions to the study of Unitarian Universalism, *WomanSpirit* traces the impact of second-wave feminism on the development of women's leadership and ministry in Unitarian Universalism. From the Women and Religion Resolution in 1977 to the Grailville conferences and the Principle and Purposes, this study examines a crucial part of UU history that, until now, has often been overlooked. An important volume that includes poignant, painful, and powerful voices of women who

lived and led during these tumultuous years as they transformed Unitarian Universalism."
—Dr. Nicole C. Kirk, the Frank and Alice Southworth Schulman Chair of Unitarian Universalist History, Meadville Lombard Theological School

www.ingramcontent.com/pod-product-compliance
Lightning Source LLC
Chambersburg PA
CBHW020430130626
46549CB00001B/63